A GREAT TEAMMATE

The Legend of Mickey Mantle

Randall Swearingen

SportsPublishingLLC.com

ISBN-10: 1-59670-194-3
ISBN-13: 978-1-59670-194-6

Publishers: Peter L. Bannon and Joseph J. Bannon Sr.
Senior managing editor: Susan M. Moyer
Acquisitions editor: Mike Pearson
Editors: Travis W. Moran and Suzanne Perkins
Art director: K. Jeffrey Higgerson
Cover design: Dustin Hubbart
Color insert design: Joseph T. Brumleve
Project manager: Kathryn R. Holleman and Nancy Routh
Photo editor: Erin Linden-Levy

Sports Publishing L.L.C.
804 North Neil Street
Champaign, IL 61820
Phone: 1-877-424-2665
Fax: 217-363-2073
www.SportsPublishingLLC.com

Printed in the United States of America

Library of Congress Cataloging-in-Publication Data

Swearingen, Randall, 1953-
A Great Teammate : The Legend of Mickey Mantle
p. cm.
Includes Index
ISBN-13: 978-1-59670-194-6 (softcover : alk. paper)
ISBN-10: 1-59670-194-3 (softcover : alk. paper)
1. Mantle, Mickey, 1931- 2. Baseball Players--United Staes--bigraphy. 3. New York Yankees (baseball team) I.title.

GV865.M33S94 2007
796.357092--dc22
[B]

2007000373

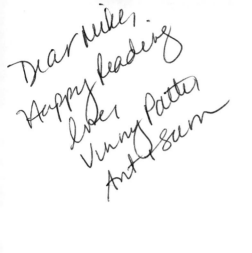

To my amazing wife Trish who gives me undying love and support and to my sons Mickey, Charles, Jason and Mark.—R.S.

CONTENTS

PREFACE

It was August of 1994 and the baseball strike, which almost killed the sport had just begun. I was 41 years old and my software company in Houston, Texas, was thriving. A year or so earlier I had seen Whitey Ford on QVC, the home shopping show. I had been fascinated as he talked about a fantasy camp that he and Mickey Mantle ran called "The Mantle and Ford Baseball Fantasy Camp." At this camp, ex-major league stars coached guys like me whose lifelong fantasy had been to play Major League Baseball. I had seriously considered attending—I had even called the number and requested a brochure, but I had never been able to convince myself to actually go. I later learned that Mickey and Whitey discontinued their camp, so I thought the opportunity had forever passed me by.

Much later, I ran into someone at a local baseball card show who told me that Mickey Mantle had started his own fantasy camp called "Mickey Mantle's Week of Dreams." Once again, I gave serious consideration to going, but I worried that that I would embarrass myself in front of my childhood idol. I was also worried about how friendly, or unfriendly, he might be. After all, who would want to spend $4,000 to meet their hero only to have that person not live up to their expectations?

As fate would have it, Mickey was coming to Houston for a book signing of his new release *All My Octobers*. My oldest son, Jason, was ten at the time and came along. He was not much of a baseball fan but, as most kids in school, was very eager to have an opportunity to skip some classes. I picked him up from school and we headed to the bookstore where Mickey was to appear. I purchased our books and we got in line to get them signed. During the two-hour wait, I coached Jason on what to say after Mickey signed his books. He was to say four simple words, "Thank you Mr. Mantle."

When we finally got up to the signing table, Mickey autographed my books first. Jason then stepped up and handed his books to Mickey, who signed them and slid them back across the table. Right on cue, Jason said the line exactly as I had told him to. Mickey looked up, looked Jason straight in the eyes, and said words that would melt my heart and set my destiny in motion. Those words still ring in my ears today. In the most sincere voice and facial expression, Mickey said, "No son, thank you." I was misty eyed and said quietly to myself, "Mickey Mantle's Week of Dreams, here I come!"

I could barely wait for Sunday, October 23 (the starting day of the fantasy camp), to arrive. On that fateful day, I embarked for Ft. Lauderdale, Florida, the home of Yankee spring training since 1962. That Sunday evening was the first get-together for the campers and the coaches, including Mickey Mantle himself. I didn't know anyone at the camp, and was very nervous to say the least. All the campers wore nametags. The first person to walk up to me was Johnny Blanchard. He addressed me as if he had known me forever. He put his arm around my shoulder and said, "Hello Randy. How you doin' buddy?" I was pretty much speechless but managed to say, "fine," and exchange the normal initial pleasantries. After a moment, Johnny said, "Let's go to the food line and see what's for dinner." He walked me to the buffet, and I joined the line assuming he was right behind me. I turned around a moment later, and Johnny had gone to welcome another camper.

Just as I was thinking that this was really cool, a hand rested on my right shoulder and a voice said, "Are these meatballs any good?" An aged but muscular arm reached around my right side to pick up one of those meatballs. "Ummmmm! They are!" said the strangely familiar voice. I had heard that voice many times before but it didn't immediately click in my head as to whose it was. Then it hit me. The voice was that of my childhood idol and the man that I came to camp to meet, Mickey Mantle! I was frozen in disbelief. I couldn't even turn my head to confirm it was him. After a few seconds that seemed like an eternity, I was finally able to turn around as Mickey was walking away. My lower jaw must have been just inches off the floor.

The rest of that magical week grew even more memorable with each passing day. I put on the Yankee Pinstripes in the same locker room where Mickey had once suited up every spring. I played on the same fields and sat on the same benches that the Yankee greats did in the 1960s. I was in the company of the very same guys whose cards I had collected years earlier, such as: Mickey Mantle, Jim "Catfish" Hunter, Enos Slaughter, and Moose Skowron. It was truly my "Field of Dreams," and now I finally understood the true meaning of the movie line, "Is this heaven?"

Undoubtedly, my most memorable moment at the camp occurred during a game that I played in at the stadium. On this particular day, I hadn't noticed Mickey around the field. During one of my at-bats, I popped out to the second baseman. I dejectedly headed for the dugout with my head down. Suddenly, there was a loud whistle from first base. I looked up, and there was Mickey Mantle standing in the first base coach's box, waving for me to come over! I casually jogged over to him. Mickey told me, "You gotta keep your weight on your back foot." He pretended to have a bat in his hands as he settled into his classic right-handed batting stance. I took the opportunity to ask Mickey for further hitting advice. "Mickey, the coaches are telling us to bat with our knuckles all lined up ... " But before I could finish my sentence, he interrupted with a boyish grin, "I never paid any attention to that sh--. I just grabbed the bat like this, and tried to knock the hell out of the ball on every swing." I courteously thanked Mickey and walked back to the dugout. All of my teammates where glued to the bench, their mouths hanging open and eyes wide with disbelief. One of them finally said, "Gee, I would pop out too if I could get personal hitting instructions from The Mick."

It turned out that I was the only one who Mickey pulled aside the entire week. I felt honored and was on cloud nine the rest of the camp.

Each day, we would play two games and eat lunch in between. During the lunch break, most of the Yankees would sign autographs. They would sign pretty much anything, but one of their habits really surprised me. If a camper gave a player a baseball to sign, he would first ask, "Do you want me to sign this on the sweet spot?" but they'd always quickly follow with, "Are you going to get Mickey to sign this ball?" If the answer was "Yes," they politely turned the ball and signed it on a side panel. If the answer was no, they would look you square in the eye and say something similar to, "Okay, but if you take this ball to Mickey to sign after I sign the sweet spot, I'll come and kick your butt!" The point is this: They had such tremendous respect for Mickey that the sweet spot was reserved for him and only him, a kind of respect that I'd never before witnessed.

That week forever changed my life in ways that I cannot explain in mere words; no other event in my life has ever affected me in that manner. For whatever reason, I came away from "Mickey Mantle's Week of Dreams" with more confidence than I had ever had before.

Sadly, Mickey passed away in August of the following year. I, like hundreds of thousands of other baby boomers, mourned the loss of our childhood hero. Mickey had meant so much to me personally because of my week at the fantasy camp, that I felt compelled to pay tribute to him in some way. I did some research and discovered that there weren't any websites dedicated to Mantle (the internet was still relatively new) so I decided to build one. I was amazed to find the domain name of www.mickey-mantle.com available. I quickly reserved it, and began a long labor of love to build an elaborate and comprehensive site that would hopefully do justice to one of the greatest baseball players the game had ever known. Since that time, I have become obsessed with collecting Mickey Mantle memorabilia and learning everything that I can about the man known simply as "The Mick."

My admiration for Mickey runs deep. I married my wonderful and beautiful wife, Trish, in year 2000. We have since been blessed with two super boys. We named our first child Mickey and the second Charles (Mantle's middle name). Interestingly enough, as I have researched this book, I have learned that there are numerous major league ballplayers who have named their sons Mickey, not to mention thousands of other baseball fans such as myself.

More than ten years after that memorable weeklong encounter with Mickey, I found myself thinking about how he always wanted to be remembered as "a great teammate." In fact, this was so important to him that the phrase is prominently engraved on his tombstone in Dallas, Texas. It is also the title line on his monument at Yankee Stadium. Numerous books, hundreds of magazine articles, and several documentaries have been written about Mickey, but none had ever addressed this claim that was so important to him. Then, an idea struck me: What if I were to write a book that explored the concept of Mickey being a great teammate? The more I thought about the idea, the more it surprised me that such a book had never been written. It would be about the essence of what it means to be a great teammate, and to honor Mickey in the way that he always wanted. The idea seemed so obvious. A few days later, and after several phone calls to some of the Mickey's teammates that I have befriended over the years at the fantasy camps, the idea was validated unanimously and the wheels set into motion.

This book has been a true labor of love. It could not have been accomplished without the help of all of Mickey's teammates who shared their treasured stories of Mickey with me. I thought that I knew a lot about Mickey as I started this book, but through my countless hours of extensive research I now know much more and have a greater respect and admiration for him. I hope that as you read this book, you too will gain a greater appreciation and admiration for Mickey Mantle, as well as a better understanding of what it means to be "A Great Teammate."

Chapter One

BORN TO PLAY BASEBALL

Mickey Charles Mantle was born and bred for one thing only—baseball. He was born October 20, 1931 in Spavinaw, Oklahoma (population 213). Mickey's father, Mutt, named him after Hall of Fame catcher Mickey Cochrane, who had just completed another excellent season for the Philadelphia Athletics by batting .349 with 89 RBIs and 17 home runs. Years later, Mickey joked that he was sure glad his father didn't know that Mickey was only Cochrane's nickname, and that Gordon was his real name.

Mutt Mantle, an old semi-pro pitcher, had one goal for his son and that was for him to play major league baseball. Mutt and his wife, Lovell, lived a meager life in a very small house in Commerce, Oklahoma. According to Merlyn Mantle, Mickey's wife, "Mickey's dad was a rabid baseball fan. Mickey's ma once told me that his dad showed Mickey a baseball when he was only 12 hours old, then got insulted because he paid more attention to the bottle. The first lullaby Mickey ever heard was a play-by-play account of a St. Louis Cardinal game."

According to Mickey's mother, his dad used to drop baseballs instead of rattles into Mickey's cradle; and that at one time, there were so many baseballs that baby Mantle was practically rolling around on ball bearings.

Mutt was completely determined to develop his young son, still in diapers, into a professional baseball player; a dream that he shared with his own father, Charlie. Between the two of them, they lost no opportunity to acclimate Baby Mickey to the game of baseball. Mickey's cousin, Helen Roberts Page, recalled how her grandparents used to love to tell stories about Mickey. Page recalled, "They told me that, when Mickey was just a baby, Uncle Mutt and Mr. Mantle, Mutt's dad, would sit Mickey up in the corner of a room to help support him, (this was before he could even walk) and roll a baseball to him slowly across the floor. Mickey would always laugh out loud when they would do this."

When Mickey was three years old, his mother made him a baseball uniform from an old pair of Mutt's baseball pants. Mutt then proudly paraded his son around town in the new attire. At the age of five, Mickey was big enough to hold a baseball bat, and his father began daily batting practice sessions next to an old leaning tin shed in their yard. When Mutt came home from working in the zinc mines—regardless of how tired he was—he would work with Mickey on his batting until it became too dark to see.

Mutt firmly believed that baseball would soon utilize the platoon system whereby right-handed hitters would be used primarily against left-handed pitchers, and left-handed hitters would be used primarily against right-handed pitchers. He further reasoned that a switch hitter would get a lot more playing time since he could hit off either type of pitcher. Thus, with Mutt's vision of the future, he insisted that Mickey be a switch hitter. So in each batting practice session, Mutt would throw right-handed to Mickey while he batted lefty; and Charlie would throw left-handed to Mickey while he batted righty. Mickey quickly grew to love those afternoons with his dad and grandfather. It wasn't long until Mickey was impressing the neighbors with his baseball skills, which were far above average for a five-year-old boy.

At the age of ten, Mickey was playing baseball in the Pee Wee League as a catcher (Mickey Cochrane's position) for a team in Douthat. His mother recalled, "Mickey only weighed 80 pounds when he was ten. He was so small they called him 'Little Mickey.'

When he had all that stuff on, you couldn't see what he looked like. With the mask, the chest protector, and the shin guards; all you could see were a couple of scared little eyes looking out at you."

At the age of 15, Mickey began playing ball in the Ban Johnson league, which was a semi-pro league for boys under the age of 21. Mickey was only five feet tall, and weighed a measly 118 pounds when he played on the Baxter Springs Whiz Kids, managed by Barney Barnett. During that same time, on weekends Mickey and his dad played on the same team for the Spavinaw, Oklahoma team. Mickey played shortstop while his dad was a pitcher. "Those games are the most cherished of my life," said Mickey. "Bigger than any World Series because we played together."

Johnny Lingo, a coach at Commerce High, recalled, "It was a hard fight to get Mickey's dad to agree to let him play anything but baseball, but finally I got him liking the other sports enough to let Mickey play them too. Mickey was a good football player, good enough to have gone to college on a scholarship. He scored ten touchdowns in seven games. He was a halfback in the T formation, a fullback in the single-wing. He had great hand movement and would have made a fine T quarterback."

According to Joe Barker, another of Mickey's high school buddies, "Mick was a great athlete. He had a lot of speed. He had a lot of power. He had pretty good size by the time he was a senior. He was also a good running back, but I think the greatest asset that he had in football was his punting ability. He could have easily been a punter in professional football. In basketball he was a point guard. He handled the ball real well and had a good set shot. But no doubt about it, baseball was where he was really an achiever. He played shortstop and pitched; and believe me, he was a good pitcher and a great shortstop."

During a football practice, in 1946, Mickey was kicked in the shin, and the bone became infected overnight, which developed into a condition known as osteomyelitis. The infection became so serious that the doctors were actually considering amputation. Upon learning this, Mickey's mother gave the doctors a piece of her mind and checked him out of the local hospital. She and Mutt drove their son approximately 200 miles to Oklahoma City. It was there that Mickey was administered a new wonder drug called penicillin that had just started to be mass produced three years earlier in 1943. He received the drug every three hours for two solid weeks before being released from the hospital on crutches. After a couple of months, Mickey happily discarded the crutches and was back to his old self, running like a jackrabbit. Later in life, Mickey looked back and actually felt that his development of osteomyelitis may have led to his swift body development. "All I know is that my brother carried me into the hospital and he couldn't carry me out," said Mickey.

Although there was no cure for osteomyelitis, Mickey's case was kept under control with periodic medication so it never really bothered him after the original episode. It did keep him out of the service, because that condition was an immediate exclusion from serving in the armed forces. Mickey was examined on more than one occasion by the military, and each time he was rejected because of his condition. During his first few years with the Yankees, the medical exclusion resulted in Mickey being scorned by fans for seeming to shun his American duty when so many other ballplayers, like Ted Williams and Bob Feller, were serving their country.

Mickey soon began receiving quite a bit of hate mail, even death threats. Bob Wiesler was Mickey's teammate on the 1949 Independence Yankees and also on the New York Yankees in 1951. According to Wiesler, "Mickey got a lot of bad mail in '51 from people saying, 'How in the hell can you be playing and running like that and my son's in the service over in Korea?' He showed me some of those letters. It looked like he could run like hell, but he had that osteomyletis."

Jerry Coleman roomed with Mickey for two years on the Yankees and said, "When I came back from Korea, I heard people in the stands yelling at him, calling him a 4-F coward, awful things. Mantle would have paid his way to go to Korea. And yet people shouted those things, things that went right to a man's masculinity. If they had said those things to me, I think I would have killed somebody. But he never said a word; Mickey never complained about anything."

Born to Play Baseball

As a senior in high school, Mickey already had a quite a strong sense regarding his destiny. He had developed into an exceptional ballplayer, and was well known for his baseball talents by all the coaches and teams in the surrounding area. Ivan Shouse was a high school schoolmate of Mickey who played baseball, football, and basketball with Mickey. Ivan's wife, Carol, recalled, "In 1949, I was a sophomore and Mickey was a senior and we had study hall together. One day, we were looking at a *Life Magazine* together and there was a picture of Joe DiMaggio out in center field. Mickey pointed to that picture and said, 'I'm gonna be there some day.'"

Mickey was a junior in high school when he was discovered by Yankees scout Tom Greenwade, who had watched Mickey hit tape-measure homers from both sides of the plate at a game in Baxter Springs. Major league rules specified that players could not be pursued for contracts until they had graduated from high school. Thus, Greenwade told Mickey and his dad that he would be back the next year.

The very day that Mickey graduated from high school—May 27, 1949—Greenwade arrived in Commerce. Mickey was handed his diploma and given special permission to be excused from the graduation ceremonies so that he could play baseball in Coffeyville that night. Greenwade attended that game and decided to stick around for Mickey's next game, which was two days later on May 29. On that day, after having seen two impressive performances by Mickey, Greenwade signed him with the New York Yankees for $140 per month plus a signing bonus of $1,150.

When asked what he thought the first time he saw Mickey play ball, Greenwade recalled, "I don't quite know how to put it. But what I'm trying to tell you is that I know now how Paul Krichell felt when he first saw Lou Gehrig. Paul told me once that the first time he saw Gehrig, he knew that as a scout he'd never have another moment like it. I felt the same way when I first saw Mickey Mantle. He's got to be one of the game's all-time greats."

Despite Mickey's outstanding talent, he was terribly insecure. Bob Mallon was a pitcher for the 1949 Independence Yankees, and was Mickey's first baseball roommate. Mallon recalled, "Mickey actually thought he was going to be released before he got his bonus money. He worried about that quite a bit, but history tells us that never happened." Seven hundred fifty dollars of the promised $1,150 was conditional on Mickey still being with the team on June 30.

When Mickey left Commerce, Oklahoma, to play for the Independence Yankees in 1949, it was the first time that he had ever been separated from his family. One thing for sure about Mickey—he loved his father.

"No boy, I think, ever loved his father more that I did," Mickey once said. "I was a good boy, really, who needed little disciplining; and I would do nearly anything to keep my father happy." So when Mickey's father turned him over to Harry Craft, the manager of the Independence Yankees, and then headed back to Commerce; it is not surprising that Mickey felt an emptiness he had never felt before. "Then my father shook hands and left me, and promptly I felt the beginnings of that dreadful uneasiness that shy people suffer when left suddenly in strange surroundings with people they do not know. I did not know where I was to sleep or take my meals, or when, and could not shame myself by asking. For a long moment, I did not want to play professional baseball at all. I just wanted to be home."

In a 1952 interview, Mrs. Mantle confirmed her son's love and respect for his dad as she explained to Mickey, "When you were a little-bitty thing, you were never satisfied. You were playing in the Pee Wee League ... you got a single and you wanted a double. You pitched in high school ... you struck out 15, and you wanted to strike out 16."

"Ma," Mickey said, "now I got to ask you something. That was the way Pa wanted it, wasn't it?"

"Yes, son," Mrs. Mantle said. "That's the way Pa wanted it." Mickey then replied, "Then that's the way I want it, too."

Mickey played his first game with the Independence team on June 14, 1949. Keith Speck, a pitcher on the team recalled the first time he ever saw Mickey, "I was pitching the night that Mick joined the ball club in Chanute. I can remember looking back from the pitching mound and seeing him on shortstop and I wondered who this kid was. But you know, he was a good kid. He could run like a deer. At that time, he wasn't very big. I have a picture of him outside the clubhouse in '49 with his undershirt and jock strap. He just does not look like a very big boy, but he developed so much after. I used to see him quite often afterwards, and he just steadily got bigger and more muscular. But at the time in '49, he wasn't a very big boy, but he could run."

It took Mickey about two weeks to adjust to his new environment, but he soon became 'one of the boys' on the Independence team. Bob Wiesler, also a pitcher for the Independence Yankees remembered this about Mickey, "He came out of high school and joined us in Independence in '49. He really didn't come into his own until the next year in Joplin where he had a hell of a year. His power was uncanny. His power right-handed was to the opposite field. He could hit the long ball left- or right-handed. He hit them for distance. He played shortstop, and he gave our first baseman fits over there the way he used to throw the ball. He threw it all over the place. He was a helluva ballplayer, and he could run."

Manager Harry Craft evaluated his newest pupil, and his report went as follows, "Can be a great hitter. Exceptional speed. Just an average shortstop. Has a fine arm and a good pair of hands. Lets the ball play him too much. Attitude excellent. Will go all the way. He has everything to make him a great ball player. I would like to see him shifted to third or the outfield."

By the middle of July, Mickey was only hitting .225 and was growing very frustrated with himself. He called his father from Independence and told him that he didn't think he was cut out to be a baseball player and that he was considering quitting baseball all together. Mutt Mantle immediately jumped in his car and drove to Independence. When he arrived there in the middle of the night, Mutt gave Mickey a major tongue-lashing.

Bob Mallon recalls, "He called Mickey gutless if he quit. Roy and Ray, Mickey's younger twin brothers, were there also. We were sitting on the front porch steps and Mr. Mantle was standing in front of us. We were both telling him how Mickey was getting better, and he had not even given it a good try yet. He told Mick, 'Get your bags and let's go back. You know you will have to work in the mines.' I think when things were going bad for Mick, he would say he wanted to quit. This was his way to get assurance from his dad—that would always pep him up. I don't think he ever had any intention to quit. He had too much guts and fight in him to really quit." Fortunately, Mickey and Bob were able to successfully talk Mutt into allowing Mickey to continue to play baseball.

In a letter from Bob Mallon to his parents dated July 26, 1949, he wrote, "I room with Mantle, the shortstop. He was hitting .230 a week ago. He went on a hitting streak and jumped up to .300 in that time. He is fast as lightning, beats out a lot of infield hits and bunts." This letter pinpoints Mutt's speech to Mickey on or around July 16. Mickey ended that season with a very respectable .313 batting average.

The Yankees got their first look at young Mickey Mantle at a special Yankee instruction camp in early spring of 1950 before he reported to Joplin to play with the Joplin Miners. Bill Dickey remembered the first time he saw Mickey hit, "I was pitching batting practice when the kid came to the plate. The boy hit the first six balls nearly 500 feet, over the lights and out of sight." Casey Stengel was also excited about the new boy wonder. "If someone asked me to list my top ten thrills in baseball, you can bet my first look at Mickey Mantle would have to be up there pretty high. When I saw him, my thoughts flashed back to many other great players I had seen breaking in, and I had to rate him up near the top with the very best of them all."

Mickey earned $225 per month in 1950 with the Joplin Miners and won the Western Association batting title with a .383 batting average. Despite his astounding baseball skills, the Yankees strongly felt that Mickey wasn't ready for the major leagues yet. On the other hand, Stengel knew that the majors were definitely in Mickey's future as he boasted to reporters, "We got a kid out in Joplin who'll singe the hair offa them pitchers' heads; he hits from both sides of the plate, whangs it into the seats either way, runs like a scared rabbit, and throws like a catapult."

Born to Play Baseball

After years of hard work and coaching from his dad, Mickey was on track to fulfill his father's dream. At the same time, Mutt was living his life through Mickey and he would accept no less than perfection from his son. He was obviously very proud of Mickey, but he rarely showed it. In fact, after Mickey won the batting title with Joplin, Mickey said to his dad, "How about that .383 average, huh?" To which Mutt replied with a slight grin, "You should have hit .400."

In the spring of 1951, Mickey was again invited to Casey Stengel's baseball school in Phoenix. This time, Mickey made a tremendous splash. Billy Martin, recalling the first time he met Mickey, said, "I remember I was standing off to one side of the batting cage talking to Gil McDougald when I heard this crashing sound from the cage. We both looked over, and there was this blonde kid getting ready to take another swing. And boy, did he ever swing! He was batting left-handed then, and the crashing sound we heard was this kid making contact with the ball. Well, he hit two or three practically out of sight left-handed, then he turned around and did the same right-handed. Gil and I just stood there. Then I turned to Gil and said, 'Did you see what I saw?' Gil sort of made a soft whistle, and said, "I'll say I saw it, but I still don't believe it!""

In Phoenix, Mickey was hitting balls well in excess of 450 feet and making it look easy. Sportswriters tried to rationalize how he could hit the ball so far. One of their theories was that the atmosphere in Phoenix was thinner, and therefore allowed the ball to travel farther. Casey Stengel had this to say about the sportswriter's claims, "All I hear from you guys, is talk about the 'stratmosphere'. All I can say is that the rest of these guys are hitting in the same air as this kid, and they ain't knockin' balls over the fences the way he is. 'Stratmosphere' my eye! Mantle just hits hard, and you'll see that when we play in other places. I been in this here league myself for a few years, and I never seen balls hit like that. This boy is the best switch hitter that ever lived. The best, I say, and I've seen 'em all for 40 years." That was quite a testimony from Stengel, considering that he had only been watching Mickey for about two months at the time.

Mickey homered and tripled in his first practice game of the spring, which was an intra-squad game between the Yankee Regulars and the Yannigans (members of the Yankee team who were not regulars). The Regulars went on to beat the Yannigans by the score of 10-8, but Mickey was definitely raising eyebrows. Mickey played center field in this game, which is noteworthy because it marked the first time in his life that he had ever played in the outfield.

In the Yankees' 16th exhibition game of the spring, they played the University of Southern California Trojans at the USC Bovard Field on March 26 in front of a crowd of 3,000 fans. Frank Gifford, former NFL great, recalled a fond memory from that day: "It was 1951, and I was participating in spring football practice on the campus of USC. Our practice facility was located just beyond the baseball field, the two separated by a high fence. We were huddling for a play when, all of a sudden, a baseball came bouncing into our huddle, ricocheting off several of my teammates' legs. There was a chorus of expletives directed towards the baseball field, then we continued practicing, and the incident was forgotten. The end of our practice coincided with the end of the baseball game. As we headed into the locker room, one of our guys asked one of the USC baseball players who the hell threw the ball over the fence. The distance was well over 500 feet, and we naturally assumed the ball was thrown. The reply was one that would only take on real meaning in the years to come. 'Oh, that was some kid from Oklahoma, a Yankee rookie named Mickey something. And he didn't throw the ball, he hit it.'"

In that game, Mickey actually hit two monstrous home runs, not to mention a triple and a single while driving in seven runs as the Yankees handily won the game by the score of 15-1. After that game, Mickey had trouble getting onto the team bus as he was besieged by USC students seeking his autograph. Someone remarked, "I've seen many a phenom in my day, but this Mantle is the phenominginest phenom I ever saw."

When the Yankees broke spring training camp that year, manager Casey Stengel was struggling with himself as to whether to promote Mickey to the big leagues or give him one more year in the minors. "That young fellow in the outfield has me terribly confused,"

Stengel said, "and he's getting me more so every day. He should have a year of Triple-A ball under his belt, but you writers have blown him up so much that I have to take him to New York. I'm not blaming you—he's everything you say he is—but it doesn't figure that he's ready. Then again, nothing he does figures."

Casey decided to take a chance on the young Mantle, and elected to keep him with the Yankees as opening day neared in April of 1951. Mickey had a huge task ahead of him and he was scared. Not only did he have the enormous pressure to follow in the footsteps of other Yankee greats, but he was also a shy country boy who had been plucked out of a small town and put in the blinding bright spotlight of New York City. The dream that Mickey and his dad shared had finally been achieved. Mickey Mantle was now a New York Yankee!

Pos	G	AB	R	H	2B	3B	HR	RB	SB	AVG
SS	89	323	54	101	15	7	7	63	20	313

Mickey Mantle's Stats—Independence Yankees

Mickey's uniform number on the Independence Yankees was No. 16.

Pos	G	AB	R	H	2B	3B	HR	RBI	SB	AVG
SS	137	519	141	199	30	12	26	136	22	.383

Mickey Mantle's Stats—Joplin Miners

Mickey's uniform number on the Joplin Miners was No. 12.

Touching All the Bases

In 1952, Casey Stengel revealed that he pushed to bring Mickey up to the major leagues sooner: "If I had my way, I woulda' brought the kid up in 1950. He was good enough to play up here then, and by this time, he woulda' had that much more experience. But the Yankees don't do things that way. 'Leave him down there,' they told me. 'Leave him down there and let him soak up more experience.' Experience my foot! With all the natural ability he has, he woulda' done all right then, too."

Mickey signed his first contract with Hillerich & Bradsby Co. (Louisville Slugger) on September 12, 1950 to use his name on baseball bats. He received $50.

Chapter Two

A GREAT TEAM

The New York Yankees were the most prestigious, intimidating, and feared team in all of baseball. They had it all: Hitting, starting pitching, relief pitching, defense, a talented bench, and great management. Al Downing, pitcher for the Yankees from 1961 to 1969, described how it felt to be part of the team, "When you walked out on the field, the other team was intimidated because they knew you could beat them. It's like Yogi said, 'It ain't over till it's over.' Because the other team always knew that as long as you had one last batter who had an opportunity to hit, there was a chance you would win the ballgame. It wasn't a case in the seventh or eighth inning you say, 'It's all done, guys. Pack up the bats.' It was always, 'Who's up this inning?' Then maybe Mickey would walk down the bench and say, 'Hey, give me one shot.' Maybe he was the fourth or fifth batter. And if he got that one shot, the opposing manager had to be sweating bullets over there, because he's saying, 'I don't want that guy coming up.'"

The Yankees were definitely an exciting team to watch; and as great teams do, they often won games in their last at-bat. After a come-from-behind victory (courtesy of a ninth-inning grand slam by Moose Skowron) against the Chicago White Sox in July of 1957, manager Casey Stengel chirped, "Maybe that'll teach those fans who leave early. Anybody who pays to get in has wasted his money if he doesn't stay to see the Yankees' last inning."

The Yankees were the consummate professionals. They went about the business of winning ballgames the way a team of highly skilled surgeons goes about performing a complex operation. Everybody had a role and knew exactly what was expected; and when it came time for them to do their jobs, more often than not, they did it. Moose Skowron described it well by saying, "We were a team. We were out to win a pennant, but we all benefited by it. We didn't care about salaries. We weren't worried about jealousy. We weren't worried about who was making more money than anybody else. We played as a team, and that's why the Yankees were successful."

Jack Reed, outfielder for the Yankees from 1961 to 1963, described how he felt as, "I have often said that if I could bottle the feeling that I had the first time that I walked into Yankee Stadium and put on a Yankee uniform, this world would be a better place to live in."

The Yankees had such a monopoly on first place in the American League, that Bob Hale, a first baseman who played for the Baltimore Orioles and the Cleveland Indians before spending half a season with the Yankees in 1961, said, "When you're on a team other than the Yankees in the '50s and '60s, you don't think you're ever gonna be in the World Series. So when I was traded to the Yankees, I became their biggest cheerleader. I wanted to get in the World Series, get the World Series ring, and be part of that great tradition."

Pitchers especially enjoyed playing for the Yankees, because it meant they would get excellent run support and be backed by great defense. They knew that if they had to call up a relief pitcher in the late innings, their lead would be protected. Art Ditmar, who pitched for the Yankees from 1957 to 1961, said, "It's quite a difference pitching for a first-division team versus a second-division team. You know that talent is behind you when you throw a pitch that should be a double-play ball, and they are played as double-play balls. But with a second-division team, they may not be double plays." Ditmar went on to comment, "If you get knocked out in the first or second inning in one start, you'd be starting four days later. At New York, you weren't sure if you would start again if you got knocked out because there were so many good pitchers waiting to take a turn."

When the Yankees made their annual pilgrimage to Florida in February for spring training, the team's two goals were: (1) Make it to the World Series, and (2) win the World Series. The Yankee players relied on the World Series bonus money the same way that employees in corporate America today rely on Christmas bonuses. Winning was serious business to the veteran Yankees.

In order to guarantee the Yankees winning tradition that had been started by such greats as Babe Ruth and Lou Gehrig, the veteran players welcomed talented new players with open arms. However, they provided the young kids with fair warning about one particularly important ground rule. Moose Skowron recalled his warning when he joined the Yankees, "I was 23 years old and I had a chance to go to spring training with the Yankees. Hank Bauer and Gene Woodling got me in a corner and I was scared. I was a young kid, I was nervous as heck, and they said, 'Moose, don't monkey around with our money. We're used to winning here. I like a new Cadillac every year, and my wife likes a new mink coat.' I never forgot that." A few seasons later, Skowron was given the responsibility of taking rookies out to dinner and giving them the "Don't mess with my money" speech.

It's safe to say that during the '50s and '60s, the Yankees were THE baseball team. From 1951 through 1959, the Yankees had a minimum of four future Hall of Famers on their team at any given time. That's basically half of the starting lineup. Becoming a star on the Yankees was not an easy thing because there was so much talent on the team. Ralph Terry hit the nail on the head when he said, "It's easy to be a big duck in a little pond, but it's hard to be a big duck in a New York pond."

In reality, Mickey was more than a big duck in the New York pond—he was *the* duck in the New York pond. The Yankee team was full of players who would have stood out on virtually any other team, so a player had to be outstanding to be noticed amongst so much talent. It could be argued that just as the Yankees stood out amongst the rest of the teams in baseball, Mickey Mantle stood out amongst the New York Yankees.

In Mickey Mantle's first 14 years with the Yankees, they won the American League pennant 12 times. Mickey summed it up when he said, "I suppose it's human nature, but the Yankees of my era looked on the World Series as kind of a birthright."

Chapter Three

LEGACY OF 'A GREAT TEAMMATE'

When Mickey Mantle walked out onto a baseball field, all eyes were immediately glued to him, watching his every move. If he were playing center field; would he make an amazing running catch, or would he gun down a runner at home? If he were running the bases; would he steal a base, or go from first to third on a single when every other player would have stopped at second base? If he were batting; would he hit one of his legendary tape-measure blasts, or get that clutch hit in the bottom of the ninth to win the game? Would he use his tremendous speed and drag bunt that would start a crucial rally? The anticipation was almost magical, and so enticing that it filled Yankee Stadium with fans for 18 excitement-filled seasons.

Mickey's burning desire to be considered a great teammate stemmed far back into his past—it wasn't something that originated in his final years with the Yankees. Bob Mallon, Mickey's first roommate on the 1949 Independence Yankees, recalled, "Being a great teammate was very important to Mickey. He always got along with everybody and was well liked by everybody."

Mickey's overwhelming desire to not disappoint his teammates caused him to become a perfectionist. Mickey felt that he needed to succeed every time up to bat, in every fielding opportunity, and in every base-running opportunity. To him, anything short of that was failure. Mickey was so talented and gifted, that he made news headlines on a regular basis. Unfortunately, success came so easily to him that he began to believe that failure was unacceptable. He was rarely satisfied with his performance on the baseball field and would get disgusted when he made a mistake or didn't get a hit. His feelings of inadequacy were reinforced by the frequent booing from the New York Yankee fans from 1951 through 1961. During those years—the best of his career—Mickey was booed regardless of how well he played. His internal anger and frustration manifested itself in his game. He would swing harder, run harder, throw harder—he would play fearlessly. Mickey took chances; but more importantly, he dared to succeed, which made him one of the best clutch hitters the game has ever known. With two outs in the bottom of the ninth inning and the Yankees down by a run, most players would have settled for a single to keep the game going. Not Mickey; he strived for the home run to win the game.

During his career, Mickey amazed fans and teammates alike by defying the odds, as well as setting new records. He did things that other players dreamed of doing—running to first base in just 3.1 seconds, hitting a ball over 565 feet, responding to a standing ovation by hitting a home run (he did this on several occasions), and playing in intense pain that would have sidelined an ordinary player. These are things that boggled the minds of baseball fans, sportswriters, Mickey's teammates, and his opponents.

When Mickey's teammate, Clete Boyer, was asked to describe Mickey, he replied, "To answer that, all you need is to look at the pictures of Mickey back then. He had everything. He had this super body beneath that boyish look. He was powerfully built and had the greatest home run trot ever. But to watch him run, really run ... well, he was gorgeous. He was what everyone wanted to be. Because of that, he was a celebrity in his own clubhouse, not just to the fans. Hank [Bauer] and Moose [Skowron] idolized him. Hell, we all did."

Mickey possessed numerous attributes that made him worthy of being called a great teammate. In interviews with several of Mickey's teammates, one attribute clearly stood out—his extraordinary ability to help the Yankees win games. Other attributes that came up were natural talent, courage, perseverance, respect, loyalty, sense of humor, generosity, competitiveness, sensitivity, and inspiration. Mickey exhibited all of these traits repeatedly during the course of his career.

Storybook moments in baseball are very rare and treasured moments, which are typically associated with championship games such as division series, league series, and especially World Series games; however, they can occur in any baseball game at virtually any time. They are moments that every American boy daydreams about and that every major league player longs to experience. These are moments like Don Larsen's World Series perfect game in 1956; and Roger Maris' 61st home run in 1961, breaking Babe Ruth's record for most home runs in a single season. These moments stand the test of time, and become permanently etched into the minds of every baseball fan.

A storybook moment can occur at any time during a baseball season; yet, a player who experiences just one of these moments during his career is very fortunate. This is one of the things that separated Mickey Mantle from other players. When the blonde-haired, Bunyonesque figure adorned in Yankee pinstripes—the number seven on his back between his broad shoulders—stepped into the batter's box and firmly squeezed the handle of his 35-inch war club made of Northern Ash, great things happened.

Considering the physical handicaps that he played with for most of his career, it is amazing to think that Mickey Mantle had so many legendary moments during his time with the New York Yankees. This is what fans, teammates, and opponents remember most about Mickey; these exciting moments are what made him special and gave him seemingly superhuman qualities.

Chapter Four

MAJOR LEAGUE DEBUT

In October 1950, the Yankees swept the Philadelphia Phillies in four games to win their second consecutive world championship, and their third title in the last four seasons. The Yankees were definitely showing signs of re-establishing their baseball dominance. Their aging legendary outfielder, Joe DiMaggio was in what would be his final year. Casey Stengel and the Yankees front office had been sweating over who would fill Joe's shoes.

The Yankees' hopes were pinned on nineteen-year-old sensation Mickey Charles Mantle. Just two years earlier, Mickey had played on a Class D team in Independence, Kansas; and he had played on a Class C team in Joplin, Missouri, the previous year. Mickey had been promoted to the Yankees Class A team in Binghamton, but before he could report to duty, he was invited to attend Casey Stengel's Rookie School in Phoenix that March. It was there that Mickey amazed fans, sportswriters, and players with his phenomenal baseball talents. He had instantly become the hands-down choice for the hottest prospect of the winter campaign. He had crushed tremendous home runs reminiscent of Babe Ruth, thrown runners out at the plate from the outfield, and ran the base paths with speed that had not been seen since that of Ty Cobb.

Manager Casey Stengel recalled, "this kid came to camp, and pretty soon word started getting back to New York that we had something out in the desert. Wow! This kid was a comer. Yessir, he hit balls right-handed and he hit balls left-handed just as far. As far as you ever want to see, right out of sight. And he ran like those jackrabbits you see on the desert, only he didn't have to run much because he was hitting the ball out of sight."

Stengel had originally planned to send Mickey back to Binghamton after the Phoenix school ended, but changed his mind after Mickey performed so well. Stengel decided to see how he played in the Yankees exhibition games. Mickey amazed everyone; compiling incredible statistics, including a .402 batting average, nine home runs, one triple, seven doubles, and 31 RBIs. Mickey performed so well that the Yankees gave him a contract with the Kansas City Blues Triple-A team. Meanwhile, Mickey continued to play the exhibition games with the Yankees and continued to excel.

Just a couple of days before the season started, Casey Stengel and the Yankees decided to give the young phenom a chance to test his skills in the big leagues so they signed him to his first Major League contract. Only three players in the history of baseball had ever gone from Class C to the Major Leagues; bypassing Single A, Double A, and Triple A levels.

April 17, opening day at Yankee Stadium, was a drab day in the city of New York. Joe DiMaggio and the Yankees took on Ted Williams and the Boston Red Sox. It was the major league debut for rookie sensation outfielder Mickey Mantle. Many of the 44,860 fans (approximately 20 times the population of Commerce, Oklahoma) had come solely to watch Mickey play.

To add to the considerable pressure that Mickey must have felt on opening day, Casey Stengel had made the decision to move him to the outfield. He later spoke of his rationalization, "I had Rizzuto at short, and you couldn't ask for anybody any better than that little guy then, could you? And besides, how did we know how much longer [Joe DiMaggio] was going to play?" Stengel continued, "The first thing I had to teach Mantle was to run in the outfield, looking back over his shoulder—which DiMaggio was so great at—and not run looking down at the ground. 'They have no plowed fields up here, boy,' I tell him, 'and you don't have to run and watch out for furrows at the same time because this is the big leagues and the fields are all level and they have groundskeepers and everything.'"

Tommy Hendrich, the Yankee outfield coach, had been handed the assignment of teaching Mantle how to play the outfield. The day before opening day, Hendrich talked about how Mickey was an unproven ball player in the big leagues, "Sure, Mickey has a lot of power and he runs like a scared rabbit, but nobody knows how good he is. Let's wait until he faces big league pitching when it counts. What everybody forgets is that he hasn't played a major league game yet. Mantle has lots to learn. He hits with amazing power, but he can be fooled by certain pitches. And he has more to learn about outfielding. He must learn how to adapt himself to different situations. When we started he knew nothing about playing the outfield. He thought all we outfielders had to do was stand out there and wait for a fly ball. He knows differently now. He learns fast."

In reality, every position in baseball has its intricacies. The ability to be a good outfielder requires great skill and has physical dangers. Outfielders must learn where to play depending on the batter. They must be able to run at full speed toward the outfield fence in order to make a catch. The trick to this is never taking your eye off the ball, while still being fully aware of the location of the fence. A good outfielder also has to know where to throw the ball under different circumstances. Great outfielders often watch their catcher to see if they can read the signal or see where the catcher sets up for the pitch so they can position themselves properly. The skill that is most difficult for an outfielder to learn is to judge the distance and direction a ball will travel merely based on (1) the batter's swing and (2) the sound of the ball hitting the bat. This is referred to as "getting a jump on the ball."

Dangers in the outfield include crashing into a wall or another outfielder at full speed. Such collisions can be catastrophic and end a player's career. It was very impressive accomplishment for Mickey, who had only ever played shortstop, to have learned the basics of playing the outfield in such a short time.

The negative side effect of Mickey's stellar performance in the spring was the fans and press had very high expectations for the 19-year-old rookie. Some writers even joked that Mickey should bypass the major leagues altogether and go straight to the Hall of Fame! It didn't help that Mickey was issued uniform No. 6. It was a strong indication that the Yankees fully expected him to be the next Babe Ruth, Lou Gehrig, and Joe DiMaggio all rolled into one. The Yankees had historically assigned the low numbers to their greatest players. Ruth had been No. 3, Gehrig No. 4 and DiMaggio No. 5.

Before the game, an awards ceremony was held. As part of the event, Casey Stengel raised the World Series pennant and Phil Rizzuto was presented the 1950 American League MVP award. After the opening ceremonies, Yankee manager Casey Stengel was talking to the reporters when he said, "I just wish I didn't have to play so many green peas today." He then added, "I like to use veterans in an opener and not a couple of untried kids like Jackie Jensen and Mickey Mantle." Jackie Jensen was now in his second season and started in left field, filling in for the injured Hank Bauer who was recovering from a charley horse.

Mickey seemed somewhat embarrassed by all the attention from the photographers and reporters who were getting their first look at the highly acclaimed sensational rookie. One of the photographers decided that it would be a good idea to get Mickey, Joe DiMaggio, and Ted Williams together for a picture. Ted and Joe greeted each other with a handshake, but Joe failed to introduce Mickey to Ted. Ted then turned to Mickey, stuck out his hand and said, "You must be Mick." According to Arthur Daley of *The New York Times*, Mantle was thus officially welcomed into the lodge.

The Yankees opening day starting lineup was as follows: Jackie Jensen leading off and playing left field. Phil Rizzuto batting second and playing shortstop. Mickey Mantle batting third and playing right field. Joe DiMaggio was batting cleanup and playing centerfield. Yogi Berra batted fifth and was behind the plate. Johnny Mize was in the sixth spot and playing first base. Bill Johnson hit seventh and played third base. Jerry Coleman hit eighth and played second base. Vic Raschi batted last and was on the mound for the Yankees.

Major League Debut

Whitey Ford, who was serving the first of two years with the Signal Corps stationed at Fort Monmouth, threw out the ceremonial first pitch and the game was under way. In the Red Sox half of the first inning, Dom DiMaggio (Joe's brother), started a rally by hitting a single to right field. Bill Goodman then followed with a blooper into short center field. It appeared to be a sure hit considering the aging Joe DiMaggio was trolling centerfield. Joe showed some of his old magic by making a sensational shoestring catch, which he then turned into an easy double play by tossing the ball to first baseman Johnny Mize. Joe's brother was so sure the ball would drop, he was practically standing on second base when Joe made the catch. Ted Williams followed with a single, but he ended up stranded on first and the Red Sox were held scoreless in the first.

In the bottom of the first inning, Mickey, in his first big league at bat, hit a curve ball on his fist, as he hit a broken bat grounder. An ordinary runner would have been out at first base by a few steps, but with his lightning speed, he was only out by half a step. Major league pitchers and infielders were put on notice that Mickey's speed made him a very difficult out.

In the third inning, Jackie Jensen belted a two-run homer into the right-field stands giving the Bronx Bombers a 2-0 lead. Mickey, in his second major league plate appearance, popped out to Vern Stephens at third base. Later, in the sixth inning, Jackie Jensen doubled for his second hit of the game. Rizzuto then attempted to lay down a sacrifice bunt, but pushed it too hard and back to the pitcher. It looked like an easy out at third base; but Vern Stephens, the Red Sox third baseman, failed to make the tag and everybody was safe.

Mickey Mantle then stepped up to the plate hitting right-handed off the lefty Bill Wight. Simultaneously earning his first major-league hit and RBI, he promptly lashed a fastball for a single into left field between shortstop and third base. DiMaggio then drove in Rizzuto with a single to left field, and Yogi Berra drove in Mickey with a single to centerfield. This put the Yankees in the lead 5-0, which was to be the final score. As Mickey returned to the dugout, he was greeted by his teammates with a multitude of handshakes and pats on the back. Mickey went one for four, with one RBI and one run scored in his major league debut. He also caught three fly balls in right field.

Later that year, Mickey recalled his feelings in his very first major league ball game.

> I don't think I will ever experience a day like opening day of 1951. Opening day was the worst day of my life. I don't think I slept a wink the night before, and I was trembling all over from the moment I reached Yankee Stadium. To tell you the truth, I don't remember much about that game. I know I did get a hit that drove in a run, but I'm just not sure when it happened. Anyway, I take no credit for it. I was so scared that I just shut my eyes and swung. I didn't see a pitch all day. Sometimes I didn't even see the pitcher. I was just too scared.

In the April 1, 1951, edition of *The New York Times*, James P. Dawson made a bold prediction. "The name is Mickey Mantle. It is worn by a husky, 19-year-old who is up from Joplin, in the Western Association, and unless all signs fail, this name eventually will ring down through the annals of baseball like some of the other greats."

Touching All the Bases

Mickey collected his first big league home run on May 1, off Chicago White Sox right-handed hurler Randy Gumpert, as the Yankees beat the White Sox 8-3. The two-run blast would travel approximately 450 feet into the right-center-field seats—one of the longest drives in the 42-year history of Comiskey Park.

Mickey hit his second home run on May 4, in the sixth inning off St. Louis Browns right-handed pitcher Duane Pillette. The 450-foot blast sailed over the right-field pavilion roof. It was also the first game that his wife, Merlyn, saw Mickey play as a New York Yankee.

Mickey's first three home runs were hit on the road, but Yankee fans would soon get the pleasure of witnessing Mickey's first home run at the Stadium on May 16 off Cleveland Indian lefty pitcher Dick Rozek. It was a two-run shot traveling 420 feet into the lower left-field grandstand bleachers. In that game, in which the Yankees soundly beat the Cleveland Indians by the score of 11-3, Mickey also drove in two more runs with a bases-loaded single, which raised his batting average to .306 and gave him a major league-leading 26 RBIs.

Chapter Five

DOWN TO KANSAS CITY

When asked how life on the Yankees compared to the minor leagues, Mickey responded, "At Joplin we only got $2.25 a day meal money. I like it up here a lot better—they've got no limit. Another thing I like is all the bats that the Yankees have. I've got a chance to experiment a little bit. Down in Joplin, you know, we only had two bats—one was a Chuck Klein model, the other a Harry Craft model, named after our manager. If one of them got broke, we had to do the best we could with the other until someone could get to a store and buy a new one."

Mickey started off his major league career slowly. By the end of April, he was hitting just .222. He picked up the pace in May when he hit an impressive .303, bringing up his average for the season to .279. At this point, Casey Stengel was like a proud father as he boasted about Mickey's unusual speed to writer, Arthur Daley, on May 15. "Take that feller out there," Stengel said nodding towards Mickey Mantle out on the field. "The other day he's on first when the feller at bat hits a line single to left. The feller in left catches the ball on one bounce, hesitates and—whoost!—my guy has gone all the way to third. My guy has run so fast that someone sez, 'He musta went through the pitcher's box.'"

Mickey may have made things look easy, but in reality they were getting pretty rough. During a doubleheader on May 30 against the Boston Red Sox, he struck out five consecutive times. It was the beginning of a 0-for-21 stretch. During that time, his batting average plummeted from .297 to .259. As of July 15, two and one-half months into the season, Mickey had played 69 games as a Yankee. He had compiled a batting average of .260; and had hit seven homers, nine double, five triples, and drove in 45 runs. Although, his stats were respectable, Casey Stengel was disappointed in the fact that he felt that Mickey had one glaring weakness: He had struck out 52 times in 246 at-bats, or once in every 4.73 at-bats. No one on the Yankees had as high a strikeout ratio as Mickey. In fact, Yankee slugger, Yogi Berra only struck out once every 27.4 times at bat, and Joe DiMaggio only once every 11.53 times at bat. The highest ratio, other than Mickey, was Gil McDougald, who had a strikeout ratio of 7.44. Stengel had little tolerance for strikeouts. Since June 26, Mickey had played in just three of 14 games and had 15 plate appearances.

How could Mickey have had such a phenomenal spring and then suddenly stop hitting? The answer may lie in the fact that under normal circumstances, Mickey would have gone from Class C to at least Triple A before advancing to the major leagues. This would not only have given Mickey more time to mature as a ballplayer, but also have given the opposing team's scouts ample time to study his hitting strengths and weaknesses. By advancing from Class C directly to the majors, the opposing teams were caught off-guard with very little information about Mickey, and opposing pitchers had to resort to trial and error. On the other hand, major league pitchers and catchers are very smart and very observant. If they are successful against you just once with a particular pitch, the odds are that they will continue to use that pitch until you prove that you can hit it. Eventually, if a hitter has a weakness, the other teams will discover it. Mel Parnell, a pitcher with the Boston Red Sox, commented some years later, "The word spread like wildfire that you could get Mantle out by throwing him on the fists."

Down To Kansas City

On July 15, one week after the All-Star game, the Yankees were in third place—just two and a half games out of first place. They had just arrived in Detroit for a three-game series with the Tigers. Casey Stengel met with Mickey before the first game of a doubleheader and painfully informed him that he was being sent down to the Yankees Triple-A team, the Kansas City Blues. Mickey sat out the first game, and then packed his gear and said his final goodbyes before the second game began. With tears in his eyes, Mickey slowly walked out of Griggs Stadium and headed for Kansas City.

In his book, *The Mick*, Mantle distinctly recalled that dreadful day in his life when Stengel called him into his office. Stengel had tears in his eyes. The conversation began:

Stengel: "This is gonna hurt me more than you, but—."

Mantle: "No, skip. It was my own fault."

Stengel: "Aww...It ain't nobody's fault. You're 19, that's all. I want you to get your confidence back, so I'm shipping you down to Kansas City. It's not the end of the world, Mickey. In a couple of weeks you'll start hitting, and then we'll bring you right back up again."

Mantle: "Uh-huh."

Stengel: "I promise. Believe it. I'm counting on you."

Mantle was sent down to Triple-A for two reasons: (1) the Yankees wanted to bring up 26-year-old left-handed pitcher Art Schallock and they had to send a player down to make room for him on the roster; and (2) since Mickey was striking out so frequently, Stengel felt he would benefit from some additional seasoning in the minors in order to learn to lay off bad pitches.

Upon closer examination, there may have been an underlying reason for Mickey's trip to Kansas City, which was purposefully kept a secret—to learn to play center field in order to be prepared to replace Joe DiMaggio. Mickey was new to the outfield and his inexperience had led to a few mistakes. Meanwhile, Joe DiMaggio had hinted in spring training that this would probably be his last season. In late May, DiMaggio was hitting .306; but by July 1, his average had dropped to .273. The day before Mickey was sent down to Kansas City, DiMaggio's average had dropped even further to .261

(just one point above Mickey's). It's very possible that Casey Stengel and the Yankees panicked and thought that DiMaggio, an extremely proud man, could call it quits right in mid-season. They might have reasoned that Mickey could have to make the move to center field much sooner than originally planned. Telling the world that Mickey was going to Kansas City to learn to play center field would have been a direct insult to Joe DiMaggio and his tremendous following of fans. Thus, the Yankees found other reasons to give for the move. Although this is merely a theory, it is interesting to note that Mickey played exclusively in centerfield for the Kansas City Blues.

As fate would have it, the day after Mickey departed for Kansas City, Art Schallock made his first mound appearance for the Yankees against the Tigers and was hit hard. Schallock gave up four runs on seven hits before being yanked after just 2 ⅔ innings. The Bombers went on to defeat the Tigers by a score of 8-6.

The July 16 edition of the *Kansas City Times* quoted Casey Stengel, "[Mickey's] still going to be a great ballplayer. He has to learn to bunt better and to pick good pitches to swing at. The habit of striking out so much must be corrected. He is a pretty good outfielder right now, but needs some polishing to be able to play center in the major leagues. He'll be back, you can be sure of that." The paper went on to report that Mantle had a hard time fighting back the tears as he said goodbye to the Yankee players.

In Mickey's mind, he felt that he had let Casey Stengel, his teammates, and the Yankees fans down. He also felt that he had let his dad down. Several years later, Mickey recalled, "Going back was the hardest thing I ever did because it meant I was a failure and that I was letting my daddy down." Mickey knew that his Dad wanted nothing more than to see his son play with the New York Yankees. For now, at least, those plans were put on indefinite hold.

Joe DiMaggio later recalled what led up to Mickey being sent to Kansas City. "He came in that spring with great fanfare. Well, the big league pitchers showed Mickey some cute stuff he hadn't seen in the minors. He started getting down on himself. He brooded. His father asked me the trouble. I told him Mickey just needed experience.

When they decided to send him to Kansas City, Mickey broke down and cried."

When the Kansas City Blues received word that the sensational and talented outfielder was coming to join them, they were obviously very excited. They were currently tied for first place, and Mickey would surely help them retain the lead. The manager of the Blues was George Selkirk, an outfielder with the Yankees for nine years from 1934 through 1942 with a lifetime batting average of .290. Selkirk also played in six World Series as a Yankee. More importantly, Selkirk had taken over outfield for Babe Ruth, so he was an ideal mentor for Mickey.

Johnny Blanchard was an 18-year-old outfielder for the Kansas City Blues when Mickey joined the team in Milwaukee. He recalled, "I was at Kansas City when Mickey came down in 1951. I had just been there for a couple of weeks when George Selkirk called me into his office. He said, 'John, the Yankees are sending me a young kid named Mickey. We're gonna have to make room for him so we're gonna have to send you down to Binghamton.'"

Binghamton, New York, was the home of the Yankees Class A minor league team. It was two levels down from Triple A. "Mickey came in the night before I left. We went shopping together. We both bought a suit. And Mick said to me, 'Make room for me down there. Binghamton is my next stop.' He wasn't kidding. He was 19 and not sure if he was good enough to make it as a ballplayer."

Blanchard then recalled the first time he saw Mickey batting as he said, "When I got my first glimpse of Mickey playing for Kansas City, he was unbelievable. The first batting practice he ever took, everybody was in awe. He was hitting balls out of sight! He hit balls further than anyone had ever hit before in that area of the country."

In his first game with the Blues, Mickey was placed third on the lineup card and played center field. He went one for four with a walk. His one hit was a bunt single. Johnny Blanchard recalled that Mickey's speed caught the other team completely by surprise. Blanchard said, "He went up and drag bunted with no play. The pitcher came off the mound, fielded the ball, and Mickey had already crossed the bag. The pitcher just stood there. He looked at Mickey and then at his infielders as if to say, 'What the hell was that?' I'll never forget that." George Selkirk then immediately chastised Mickey after his bunt, saying that he wasn't sent down to the minors to bunt, but rather to hit and get his confidence back.

The next game, Mickey went 0 for 4, but he was starting to get the hang of center field. The *Kansas City Times* recap of the game stated, "With one away in the ninth, catcher Al Unser walloped a mighty drive to center. Mickey Mantle raced to the wall and speared the ball with one hand for a sensational catch." The catch was a game-saving one, and the K.C. Blues defeated the Milwaukee Brewers 5-4.

The pressure on Mickey grew intense as he managed only five hits in his first 21 at-bats. The Blues' hopes of Mickey helping them build a lead in the pennant race soon disappeared. Since he joined the club, they had lost seven of their first nine games, and fell to five and a half games out of first place. The young Mick was obviously struggling. Keenly aware of Mickey's talents, the opposing pitchers were pitching to him very carefully, insuring that he would not get very many good pitches to swing at. Not only that, Mickey's batting weaknesses, which had been recently exposed at the major league level, were now known at the minor league level. Using that powerful knowledge, the minor league pitchers were making easy work of Mickey.

Ernest Mehl of *The Kansas City Star* wrote:

> Mickey Mantle has shown himself and it isn't difficult to read between the lines. The rather diffident youngster probably has had more advice dinned into his ears since last March than the average ball player gets during an entire career. By now Mickey possibly is so confused on certain matters it is impossible for him to do himself justice. Manager Selkirk has suggested that all he needs to do is forget everything and just play baseball. Forget about swiping at bad pitches, forget about any complex set of signals. Just play baseball. By just playing baseball Mickey was tremendous last year at Joplin, tremendous last spring. He'll need a while to adjust himself, to get the Yankee Stadium jitters out of his consciousness. Once he becomes sure of himself and isn't concerned over any mistakes he may commit, he'll make good on all the notices he has had.

Down To Kansas City

Not only was Mickey struggling with his bat, his endeavor to learn to play center field was proving to be a nightmare. He was dropping fly balls and playing halfheartedly. And if that wasn't enough, Mickey was terribly homesick. He was at his wit's end. After a rough game, one Kansas City headline read, "Mickey Mantle was a harassed and dejected young man today."

In an article in *Sport Magazine*, Mickey was quoted as saying,

> 'What did a guy have to do?' I asked myself. I knew my father would sympathize with me, for he had his own disappointments in baseball. I really longed to have him beside me, to put his arm over my shoulder and tell me that it was all right—that I had tried and failed, and that everybody was looking forward to having me home again. For a time, I had been ashamed to write him of my disgrace, but now I asked him to come meet me in Kansas City and take me home.
>
> When my father met me in Kansas City, I could not speak for crying. My throat was squeezed tight and tears ran down my cheeks, but my father's eyes were ablaze. He started in on me without preliminaries: 'If that's the way you're going to take this,' he said, 'you don't belong in baseball anyway. If you have no more guts than that, just forget about the game completely. Come back and work in the mines like me.' His tone, as much as his words, went right down through me and froze my toes. There was not a trace of sympathy in his eye. I had been looking for a comforting pat on the back, and I had not even gotten a handshake. He told me, 'Get back on the field and play ball if you've got the guts for it; and if not, then make up your mind right now you're through with the game for good.'
>
> I wanted to tell him that I had tried, that I had been up to bat 23 times with only a bunt single to show for it, but I knew better than to argue with my father when he was in this mood. I just had to bite back my shock and surprise, and tell him I wanted to stay and try to do what he wanted me to do. I did too. With his words still searing the underside of my soul, I went to bat that night and hit two home runs. I felt so damn good about it I nearly broke into tears anyway. And that night I got the handshake and the pat on the back that I longed for. And I began to suspect that I had grown into a man.

That experience in Kansas City proved to be a major turning point in Mickey's life. From that moment on, quitting was no longer in Mickey's vocabulary. Selkirk immediately noticed a change in Mickey. A few years later he would recall, "[Mickey] just seemed to be more spirited, more in command of himself after his dad visited him. It was a great thing to see that change."

Whether or not it was a result of Mutt's speech, Mickey's hitting immediately caught fire. After not hitting a home run in his first 11 games, he hit six homers between July 27 and July 31. On July 31, in Toledo against the Mud Hens; Mickey hit for the cycle with two homers, a triple, a double, and a bunt single in a 7-0 victory. The radio announcer for the Hens, Frank Gilhooley, recalled Mickey's final at-bat in that game. "Mantle got a standing ovation when he came up the last time. George Selkirk was managing Kansas City. The Toledo pitcher went 3-0, and Selkirk, who was coaching third base, gave Mantle the hit sign. Well Mantle stepped out of the box and Selkirk gave him the sign again. Mantle still looked at him, and Selkirk got frustrated. He yelled a profanity and said, 'Yeah, that's what the sign is.' So Selkirk got back into the coach's box thinking, 'I hope they lay it in for him.' And Mantle dragged a bunt! He was almost down to the bullpen by the time they got the ball over to first base."

After 40 games with the K.C. Blues, Mickey had collected 11 homers, three triples, nine doubles, 50 RBIs, and a batting average of .364. The Yankees were originally going to recall Mickey on September 1, but when outfielder Gene Woodling sustained an injury, they had to move the schedule up. On August 24, Mickey was given the call to rejoin the New York Yankees. At the time, he was in Fort Sill, Oklahoma for a physical in which six physicians examined him. For the third time, Mickey was classified as 4-F due to osteomyelitis, a bone disease, in his left leg that resulted from the high school football injury. Mickey then flew from Oklahoma City to Cleveland to meet the team as they battled the Cleveland Indians.

Going into that game, the Yankees had compiled a record of 75 wins and 46 losses, putting them in second place, three games out of first. Batting second in the lineup, Mickey played right field and was bestowed a new uniform number, which was to become his trademark: No. 7. He went 1 for 4 as the Yankees beat the Indians 2-0.

In his second game back, Mickey smashed a two-run homer and doubled, just missing another homer, to help lead the Yankees to a 7-3 win over the Indians. The homer, his eighth for the year and the first since his return from Kansas City, was a line drive directly into the teeth of a strong wind. Despite the wind, the ball still traveled 380 feet over the left-center-field fence. In addition to helping the team offensively, Mickey also spoiled a Cleveland rally. In the seventh inning, Indians second baseman Bobby Avila came to bat with one man on base and two outs. Avila singled to right field and took a big turn around first base towards second. Mickey alertly fired a strike to first baseman Johnny Mize who tagged Avila for the final out.

In his first 23 games back with the Yankees, Mickey hit six homers—including a 450-foot blast on September 8. The team won 15 games and lost eight, putting them in back first pace. Mickey Charles Mantle was definitely back after learning a very valuable lesson—never give up on yourself.

Just before the World Series, Casey Stengel reflected on his decision to send Mickey down to Triple-A, "One of my big mistakes was shipping Mickey Mantle to Kansas City for the middle third of the season. He should have been with us all through the campaign. He would have made things a bit easier for me."

Touching All the Bases

When Casey Stengel sent Mickey down to the minor leagues on July 15, his reason was that Mickey struck out too often. What Casey didn't realize was that striking out often was part of Mickey's natural style. Throughout his entire 18-year Hall of Fame career, he struck out 1,710 times out of 8,102 at bats—once every 4.74 at bats.

On July 31, Mickey hit for the cycle at Toldeo's Swayne Field in front of 8,323 fans. He had two home runs, a triple, a double, and a bunt single as the Blues defeated the Toldeo Mud Hens 7-0.

Kansas City Municipal Stadium held only 17,500. The dimensions of the minor league ballpark were 350 feet down left field, 450 feet to center field, and 350 feet to right field. Box seat tickets sold for $1.75, reserved seats for $1.50, and general admission for $1.10.

Mickey's uniform number on the Kansas City Blues was No. 20.

Chapter Six

THE KNEE INJURY

The Yankees took over first place in the American League after defeating the Cleveland Indians on Sunday, September 16, at Yankee Stadium by the score of 5-1. The game, played before a season-record crowd of 68,760, was significant because the Yankees never again relinquished possession of first place as they went on to win their fourth American League title in five years. Mickey completed his rookie season with a .267 batting average, 11 doubles, five triples, 13 home runs, 65 RBIs, and a slugging percentage of .443.

Game 1 of the 1951 World Series, which pitted the New York Yankees against their cross-town National League counterpart, the New York Giants, was played on October 5 at Yankee Stadium before a crowd of 65,673. The Giants were still walking on air after winning a best-of-three-games playoff series with the Brooklyn Dodgers in which Bobby Thomson's "Shot Heard 'Round The World" knocked off the Bums in an intensely fought series. As fate would have it, the Giants, like the Yankees, possessed a rookie phenom. The Yankees had Mickey Mantle, and the Giants had a center fielder by the name of Willie Mays. Mays had compiled a .274 batting average with 22 doubles, five triples, 20 home runs, 68 RBIs, and a slugging percentage of .472 in his rookie season. Mays played in 121 games as opposed to Mickey's 96 games.

Joe DiMaggio was nursing a sore heel during the opening of the 1951 World Series. According to Mickey in his book *The Mick*, before the first game Casey Stengel told him, "Take everything you can get over in center. The Dago's heel is hurting pretty bad." Stengel did not want to take any chances on fly balls hit into center field. In hindsight, Stengel, the Yankees, and especially Mickey, would have been a whole lot better off if DiMaggio had been told about Stengel's instructions.

Game 1 of the Series was played on October 5 at Yankee Stadium in front of a crowd of 65,673. A strong 30-mph wind was blowing in from centerfield toward home plate, favoring the Yankees' fastballer Allie Reynolds, who had thrown two impressive no-hitters during the regular season. It was predicted that the wind would hinder the Giants' curveballer, Dave Koslo. However, the Giants convincingly beat the Yankees 5-1, limiting the Bronx Bombers to just seven hits and handing them their first opening World Series game loss since 1936. The Giants' Monte Irvin was the star of the game going 4-for-5, stealing home plate, and making impressive plays in the outfield. Mickey started in right field, and had an uneventful game going 0-for-3 with two walks while batting in the leadoff spot of the lineup.

Game 2, also at Yankee Stadium, drew a paid attendance of 66,018. Mickey batted again in the leadoff position, starting in right field. The starting pitcher for the Yankees was Ed Lopat, who had compiled an impressive 21-9 record, with an equally impressive 2.91 ERA. Lopat's mound opponent was Larry Jansen, who had compiled an even better record of 23-11, with a 3.04 ERA. Jansen and Sal Maglie shared the record for most wins in the major leagues in 1951 with 23. With two different 20-game winners on the mound, the game promised to be an exciting pitchers duel.

In the bottom half of the first inning, Mickey, batting lefty against the righty Jansen, executed a perfect drag bunt between Jansen and the first baseman, Whitey Lockman. Jansen tumbled trying to field the ball, but was unsuccessful. Second baseman Eddie Stanky fielded the ball, but the lightning-fast Mantle was already safe at first. During spring training earlier this year, Mickey was clocked from the left side of the plate at an amazing 3.1 seconds from home to first. Mickey often confounded the corner infielders because they knew that he loved to drag bunt. On the other hand, nobody could hit the ball harder than Mickey. If you played him in for a bunt and he hit away, you were risking your life if his mighty swing tied into a pitch and sent the ball screaming right at you.

The second batter, Phil Rizzuto, also surprised the Giants when he executed a perfect drag bunt down the right side of the infield. First baseman Lockman fielded the ball and threw wildly to second base in an attempt to get Mickey. The throw went into the outfield, and Mickey hurried safely to third base. Now the Yankees had runners on first and third with nobody out. Gil McDougald followed with a bloop single into right field, which scored Mickey for the first Yankee run. The Bombers would score their second run in the second inning on a solo home run by Joe Collins.

The Giants were batting in the top of the fifth inning. The batter was rookie center fielder Willie Mays. Mays had gone hitless in Game 1, and once again failed to reach in Game 2. Lopat delivered a slow curve to Mays who hit the ball off the end of his bat, lofting a high fly into right center field. Mickey recounted the moment, "Mays hit a pop fly. I was in right field. DiMaggio in center. As soon as the ball came off the bat, I knew there was no way Joe could get to it, so I really moved. Just before I got there, I heard Joe say, 'I got it.' He was camped under it. I put on the brakes and the back spikes of my right foot caught on the rubber cover of a sprinkler head. This bone here," Mickey pointed to his kneecap, "was sticking out to here."

As Mickey had slammed on the breaks, a loud pop came from his right knee that even Phil Rizzuto at shortstop clearly heard. Mickey fell to the ground as if he had been shot while DiMaggio casually made the catch. Mickey was carried from the field on a stretcher and Hank Bauer took over his position in right field.

In his book *The Mick*, Mickey recalled what happened after he had fallen to the ground. "I lay there, absolutely motionless. It's been said that I went down so quickly it appeared that I had suffered a heart attack. My own recollection is at best a blurred picture of DiMaggio kneeling at my side, asking, 'Are you all right?' I tried to say, 'What happened?' I even thought I'd been shot. He leaned forward, his voice full of concern. 'Don't move. They're bringing a stretcher.'"

The Yankees' team doctor, Dr. Sidney Gaynor examined Mickey and announced that he had suffered a severe knee sprain and would not play the rest of the Series. Mantle was quoted in the *Washington Post* as saying about his knee, "I've never had any trouble with it, but it buckled when I stepped in a hole or something." Later it was discovered that indeed, Mickey's spike had become tangled in a wooden drain-head cover, which had caused his crippling injury. The Yankees went on to win the game by a score of 3-1. The victory evened the Series at one game apiece. Mickey's aggressive play in the first inning proved to be a very important run in the Yankee win.

The next day, the swelling in Mickey's leg was so bad that he went to Lenox Hill Hospital. His dad, who had flown in from Commerce to watch Mickey play in his first World Series, accompanied him to the hospital. As they were exiting the car, Mickey put his weight on his dad to support his injured knee. Mutt Mantle dropped to the ground under the pressure, which resulted in his admission to the hospital along with Mickey. Mickey would soon learn that his dad had Hodgkins disease, a form of cancer that had already taken the lives of two of his uncles and his grandfather.

Game 2 of the 1951 World Series turned out to be probably the most significant game in Mickey's entire career. He played in pain for the rest of his career. In order to keep his knee from dislocating during games, Mickey had to tightly wrap his right leg from the ankle to the hip with a rubber foam wrap. It's said that even an hour after Mickey had removed the wrap in the clubhouse, spiraling impressions running up his leg from the wrap were still clearly visible. Because of the wrap's tightness, it would begin to cut the circulation of blood in his leg. During doubleheaders, Mickey had to carefully time when he wrapped his leg. He would skip batting practice, wrap the leg just before the first game began, and he would not remove the wrap until approximately seven hours later when the second game had ended. By that time his leg would be almost numb.

The Knee Injury

Keith Speck, a teammate of Mickey's on the 1949 Independence Yankees, visited with him in the locker room after a game during the '50s and recalled, "Mickey showed me how his legs were all wrapped up, and how that bone in his one leg would move. He showed me when he took that wrap off his leg, and he pushed in right behind his leg and he pushed that bone and it come right out. It came right out frontward. That was kind of a gory looking thing, but that is why he was all taped up."

Even after his World Series injury of 1951 had healed, his knee never regained full strength. Accordingly, Mickey's muscular body tried to compensate for the weakness, but in doing so, it caused an ongoing chain reaction of injuries to both of his legs that would plague him for the rest of his playing days. Mickey's teammates often wondered how much better his career may have been if he had not injured his knee so badly in his rookie season.

Touching All the Bases

The Yankees won the 1951 World Series in six games against the New York Giants.

Mickey's salary in 1951 was $7,500. Joe DiMaggio's salary was $100,000.

Mickey was voted a full share of the World Series money ($6,446), which he used to pay the final mortgage on a home for his mother.

The Louisville Slugger baseball bat, model T41, that Mickey used for his at bats during the 1951 World Series sold in a 2004 Lelands auction for $111,551.

On December 23, 1951, Mickey married his high school sweetheart, Merlyn Louise Johnson.

Mickey's father, Mutt, died of Hodgkin's disease on May 6, 1952.

Mickey became the Yankees' regular center fielder on May 20, 1952.

Chapter Seven

BIRTH OF TAPE-MEASURE HOMERS

The 1952 season had been very good to Mickey Mantle: He had compiled a .311 batting average, 37 doubles, seven triples, 23 home runs, 87 RBIs, and a slugging percentage of .530. In the 1952 World Series, where the Bronx Bombers edged out the Brooklyn Dodgers in seven games, he had also excelled, hitting .345 in 29 at-bats with one double, one triple, two home runs and three RBIs. In the seventh and decisive game, he hit a solo home run to break up a 2-2 tie; and later singled in another run to lead the Yankees to a 4-2 win over the Dodgers. Mickey had impressed the Dodgers, especially Jackie Robinson. In a *Chicago Daily Tribune* article, Robinson was quoted as saying, "It was that Mantle, that Mickey Mantle killed us. If it hadn't been for him I think this would have been a very different Series. We came so close. We had so many opportunities. But Mantle was the difference."

On October 26, 1952, the town of Commerce, Oklahoma, gave Mickey a hero's welcome when he returned home. Merlyn Mantle recalled the reception: "Commerce had a Mickey Mantle Day after the World Series last year. It was the town's first parade since World War I, and they had a two-dollar-a-plate dinner at the Spartan Cafeteria. They even let the kids out of school."

Despite Mickey's great performance in 1952, he was not satisfied. While talking to *New York Times* writer Arthur Daley, he lamented, "Gee, but I have so much to learn. I know that I hit .311 last year, but I struck out too much. I can't get it through my thick head that I should let certain pitches alone. I swing at them and it gets me into trouble."

By the spring of 1953, the new season was arguably just as eventful for Mickey as the previous one had been. In March, he had developed a skin rash along with swollen glands under his arms, which kept him sidelined for about ten days. On April 9, batting left-handed at Pittsburgh's Forbes Field in an exhibition game with the Pirates, Mickey clobbered a seventh-inning pitch from right-handed Bill MacDonald, which sailed completely over the stadium roof in right field. Only Babe Ruth (1935) and Ted Beard (1950) had previously accomplished this feat. On April 12, Mickey became a father for the first time. Merlyn and he named the eight-pound, nine-ounce baby boy "Elvin 'Mutt' Mantle." Just five days later, Mickey would make baseball history.

On April 17, there were only 4,206 witnesses in the stands at Griffith Stadium as a stiff wind gusted out towards left center field. The Yankees had sent Ed Lopat to the mound, while the Senators called upon left-hander Chuck Stobbs. The 21-year-old Mickey Mantle was suffering from a charley horse in his left leg, but he did not let it bother him as he began batting practice prior to the game.

In the third inning, Billy Martin hit a solo home run, which gave the Yankees an early lead. The Washington Senators came back in the bottom of the frame with a run to tie the game at 1-1. In the fourth inning, Hank Bauer doubled, and then scored on a single by Joe Collins to put the Bombers ahead 2-1.

In the top of the fifth inning, there were two outs, and Yogi Berra was on first base by virtue of a two-out walk. Mickey Mantle stepped to the plate hitting right-handed off the lefty Stobbs. On this particular at-bat, Mickey had decided not to use his signature Louisville Slugger bat. Instead, he had borrowed a 33-ounce bat from teammate Loren Babe in hopes that it had a few hits in it.

Yankee announcer Mel Allen called the play like this:

Birth of Tape-Measure Homers

> Yogi Berra on first. Mickey at bat with the count of no strikes. Left-handed pitcher Chuck Stobbs on the mound. Mantle, a switch-hitter batting right-handed, digs in at the plate. Here's the pitch ... Mantle swings. ... There's a tremendous drive going into deep left field! It's going, going, it's over the bleachers and over the sign atop of the bleachers into the yards of houses across the street! It's got to be one of the longest home runs I've ever seen hit. How about that!

Mickey had belted the chest-high fastball with such incredible force that the Washington outfielders stood frozen as they watched the ball heading out of the stadium. On its way out of the ballpark, the ball glanced off the National Bohemian Beer sign, which was 460 feet from home plate. Despite nicking the sign, the ball continued to soar yet another 105 feet.

Arthur (Red) Patterson, Yankee press attaché, immediately ran out of the ballpark to recover the historic ball and to determine an exact measurement of the amazing distance that it had traveled. The ball had landed in the backyard of Perry L. Cool at 434 Oakdale. Ten-year-old Donald Dunaway was in possession of it when Patterson arrived on the scene. Patterson paid the boy $1 for the ball, and later sent him five more dollars plus two autographed baseballs. The ball was measured to have traveled 565 feet from home plate, and thus gave birth to the phrase "tape-measure home run."

In the ninth inning, Mickey batted against righty reliever Julio Moreno. He surprised everyone by pushing a bunt that went all the way into center field for a single. In one game, Mickey went on record as hitting the longest home run and the longest bunt!

After the game, Chuck Stobbs discussed Mickey's record homer. "The kid's a good hitter. What the hell's the difference? It's just a home run. It only counts for one run." Bill Dickey exclaimed, "I never thought I would live to see a man who could hit a baseball as far as Ruth. But now I've seen a man who could hit 'em further."

Reporters stormed the locker room to get an interview with Mickey. He recalled the reception that he received from his teammates when he returned to the dugout. "My teammates beat my back black and blue, and 'atta boyed' me all over the place."

Mickey's Herculean blast had the whole nation talking. A few days later, his monumental home run was still the main topic of conversation, but now it had become a controversy. Some people were claiming that the ball was livelier this year, to which A. G. Spalding (president of the company that manufactured the baseballs for Major League Baseball) responded: "There has been no change in the ball from last year, and no change for many years before that." Others claimed that the bats were livelier this year to which a representative from Louisville Slugger responded: "The bat that Mantle used was essentially no different than the Sluggers with which Ruth, Foxx, and the others made their longest hits."

Others attempted to explain the home run by recalling the brisk tail wind. One source reported that there was a 43-knot (50-mph) wind. U.S. District Judge James R. Kirkland was at the game and witnessed the famous homer. He publicly stated that there wasn't any wind blowing. He further stated that he had been attending baseball games for 30 years, and Mantle's swat was the greatest of them all—that went for homers by Ted Williams, Babe Ruth, and other power hitters. Clark Griffith, a Yankee hater from far back and the namesake of the Senators' stadium, said, "Maybe the wind did help him but that wind has been blowing off and on for 51 years out here, and nobody else has ever put one over that fence."

Shirley Povich of *The Washington Post* revealed an interesting side effect of Mantle's homer. The blast had apparently lifted a burden off the back of pitcher Sid Hudson. Povich wrote, "Mantle made a happy man, however, of another baseball figure. He is Sid Hudson, now with the Red Sox, but remembered best perhaps for the tremendous home runs hit against him in Griffith Stadium by Larry Doby of Cleveland. Yesterday, Hudson was beaming broadly when they pointed out to him where Mantle had banged his long swat. 'Good,' said Hudson. 'That takes me out of the Hall of Fame. In my time, I pitched some pretty good ball games for the Senators, but somehow they always remembered me best for those two homers Doby hit against me four or five years ago. Chuck Stobbs can have the honor of pitching the longest homer in the biggest park in the league. I don't want it.'"

The Washington Senators honored Mickey's blast by painting a baseball on the beer sign where the ball nicked the sign on its way to history. Unfortunately, the tribute to Mickey was short lived as the Senators manager, Bucky Harris did not want a constant reminder of the event; he ordered the painting of the ball removed. However, the whole world already knew of the tape measure homer.

Sid Keener, curator of the Baseball Hall of Fame in Cooperstown, New York, soon contacted Arthur Patterson of the Yankees requesting the bat and ball that Mickey had used to hit the historic home run because he wanted to put them run on display in the Hall of Fame. The Yankees agreed to send the items to the Hall of Fame, but first wanted to display them at Yankee Stadium for the Yankee fans to enjoy for the duration of the season. Unfortunately, on Memorial Day, the bat and ball were stolen from the display case in the lobby of Yankee Stadium while the Yankees were out of town playing in Philadelphia. Three small boys, all approximately ten years old, returned the items around June 7. The Yankees then decided not to take any more chances with the historic items and immediately shipped them off to Cooperstown for safe keeping.

Touching All the Bases

On April 28, just 11 days after Mickey's Griffith Stadium blast, he hit another tape-measure blast out of St. Louis' Sportsmans Park. This home run, which Mickey also hit right-handed, is measured at 512 feet. It left the stadium, cleared the street, landed against a second-floor porch, and bounced into a yard on Sullivan Avenue before finally coming to a rest.

On July 6 at Connie Mack Stadium in Philadelphia, Mickey hit a right-handed home run that soared over the double-deck stands in left center field, clearing the roof by at least 25 feet. The tape-measure blast traveled over 500 feet.

On September 7 at Fenway Park in Boston, Mickey received a death threat letter from a Red Sox fan who wrote, "Don't show your face in Boston again or your baseball career will come to an end with a 32 [rifle]." Authorities were notified, and Mickey was provided two bodyguards who urged him not to play. Mickey refused to give in to the threat and played the entire game.

On September 12 at Yankee Stadium, Mickey crushed a home run into the left-field upper deck. The ball hit a seat with such incredible force that it bounced back into the playing field. If the seat had not obstructed the ball's flight, it was estimated that the ball would have traveled in excess of 600 feet.

On May 17, 1953, Mickey appeared on the popular TV show, *What's My Line?*

Chapter Eight

THE ORIGINAL M&M BOYS

The 1953 World Series pitted Mickey Mantle and the four-time consecutive champion New York Yankees against Duke Snider and the Brooklyn Dodgers. The Yankees had won 99 games and lost 52. Overall, they finished eight and a half games over the second-place Cleveland Indians in the American League. Brooklyn, on the other hand, won an impressive 105 games and only lost 49. They finished 13 games over the Milwaukee Braves.

The Dodgers were a fast offensive team. They led the National League in batting average (.285), slugging percentage (.474), home runs (208), triples (59), walks (655), and stolen bases (90). Their pitching was third best in the NL, with a team ERA of 4.10. The Dodgers had also committed the fewest errors in the NL with 118. On the other hand, the Yankees were a strong defensive team. They led the American League in ERA (3.20), shutouts (18) and saves (39). Offensively, the Yankees led the AL in batting average (.273) and walks (656). Yankee manager Casey Stengel said this about the pending Series, "We've got a nice team and they have a splendid team over there, so it should be a splendid World Series."

Mickey Mantle finished the season with a .295 batting average, 21 home runs, 92 RBIs, and a team-leading eight stolen bases. As a team, the Yankees had only stolen 34 bases all season. Mickey had also walked 79 times, and struck out 90 times in 461 at-bats.

Game 1 of the highly anticipated 1953 World Series occurred on Wednesday, September 30 at Yankee Stadium. In addition, it was the 50th anniversary of the Fall Classic. In honor of this, 86-year-old Hall of Fame pitcher Cy Young was to throw the ceremonial first pitch. Young had won two games for the Boston Braves in the first ever World Series in 1903. With over 25 million television sets and 70 million radios in the U.S., this Series promised to be seen or heard by almost every American. This year, the 69,734 fans in attendance had paid significantly higher prices for tickets to the Series as compared to last year's prices. The price for a box seat ticket had climbed from $8 to $10. Reserve seats were $7 compared to $6 last year, and bleacher seat prices doubled from $1 to $2.

Billy Martin, Mickey's best friend, turned out to be the hero of Game 1. He had led a first-inning attack by the Bronx Bombers as he tripled with the bases loaded, driving in three runs. Mantle had just walked on four straight pitches so he was one of the three Yankees who scored on Martin's triple. After a fifth-inning homer by Yogi Berra, Stengel's team had built a commanding 5-1 lead. The Dodgers fought back in the sixth inning, with homers by Gil Hodges and pinch hitter George Shuba, which put them one run behind at 5-4.

The pivotal point came in the seventh inning. The Dodgers had just tied the game on three straight singles by Campanella, Hodges, and Furillo. They had no outs when they failed to execute two consecutive sacrifice bunts. This took the team out of a possible big inning. A home run in the bottom of the seventh inning by Joe Collins put the Yankees ahead again as they went on to defeat the Dodgers in Game 1 by the score of 9-5. Mantle was 1-for-3, and had drawn a walk.

Game 2 showcased a pitching matchup between two 35-year-old lefties; Preacher Roe for the Dodgers, and Eddie Lopat for the Yankees. The Yankees jumped out to a 1-0 lead in the first inning without the benefit of a hit. Gene Woodling and Joe Collins walked. Hank Bauer's fly out advanced Woodling to third base. Yogi Berra followed with a sacrifice fly to drive in Woodling before the inning ended.

The Dodgers began a two-out rally in the fourth inning with singles by Gil Hodges and Carl Furillo, followed by a two-run double by Billy Cox to give them a 2-1 lead. The scored remained unchanged until the bottom of the seventh when Billy Martin hit a solo homer that barely cleared the lower left-field fence, and just missed being caught by Jackie Robinson. Martin's blow tied the game 2-2.

In the eighth inning, with one out, Hank Bauer singled off Preacher Roe for what was only the Yankees' fourth hit of the game. Berra then flew out for the second out. Mickey Mantle stepped to the plate hitting right-handed off the tall, lanky, lefty Roe. So far in the game, Mantle was 0-for-2 with a walk, ground out, and fly out. Mickey slowly waved his bat back and forth as he awaited Roe's first pitch. Roe went into his stretch, checked Bauer at first base, and delivered the first pitch.

"Ball!" yelled home plate umpire Bill Stewart.

Roe gripped the ball, took his sign from Roy Campanella and delivered the next pitch.

"Ball!"

The count was now two balls and no strikes. Mickey stepped out of the batter's box and looked down to the third-base coach for a sign. Roe had already walked four batters and hit another already in the game. Manager Casey Stengel said later that he was tempted to give Mickey the take sign. Instead, Stengel gambled and flashed the hit sign.

Roe delivered the next pitch—a screwball on the outside corner of the plate at the knees. Mickey swung at the pitch. As the bat made solid contact with the ball, Preacher Roe turned toward left field to watch the flight of the ball. It sailed into the lower left-field stands—about ten rows deep—for a two-run home run. Roe bent over in disgust and put his hands on his knees.

The homer put the Bronx Bombers ahead 4-2. The 66,786 fans in attendance celebrated wildly as Mickey jogged around the bases in his typical fashion with his head down. When he arrived at home plate, Mickey was mauled by his elated teammates. In addition to his game-winning homer, Mickey made a fine running catch in the third inning on a fly ball off the bat of Duke Snider. He had caught the ball in front of the auxiliary scoreboard 380 feet from home plate. But it was the 400-foot home run that was the topic of conversation in the clubhouse.

The Yankees won the game and went ahead in the Series two games to none. After the game, Mickey received royal treatment from newspapermen, photographers, and policemen in the Yankee clubhouse as he posed for pictures with Eddie Lopat and Billy Martin (the other two heroes of the day). Mantle described his homer, "I never did think it would be a home run. It wasn't particularly well hit." Red Patterson, the Yankee publicity director, asked Mickey if he wanted to be interviewed on TV. Mickey blushed and replied, "Put Eddie Lopat on, can't you?"

In the Dodger clubhouse, Preacher Roe said in disbelief, "I thought it was a heck of a pitch. I don't see how he hit it. It was way below his knees. It was a change-up screwball. I had never pitched him one like it before. But I thought it was a good pitch and it went just where I wanted it to go. He just got hold of it and slammed it out of the park, that's all. It was some hit."

Dodger manager, Chuck Dressen, added, "You can't second guess home runs. We're in bad shape, that's for sure, but if Erskine can win tomorrow maybe we'll be all right."

The Series now moved across town to Ebbets Field in Brooklyn for Game 3. Starting pitchers were Vic Raschi for the Yankees and Carl Erskine for the Dodgers in front of a crowd of 35,270. Erskine had won 20 games during the regular season and had struck out 187 batters. He pitched a masterful game and set a new World Series record striking out 14 batters; Mickey was a strikeout victim four times. The Dodgers won the game by the score of 3-2 on an eighth-inning home run by Roy Campanella. Erskine was near flawless as he carried a no-hitter into the fifth inning and allowed only six hits (all singles) over the nine innings.

In Game 4, the Dodgers continued to show their resilience. Bill Loes started for the Dodgers versus Whitey Ford for the Yankees. The Dodgers got three runs off Ford in the first inning, which forced Casey Stengel to bring in reliever Tom Gorman. The Dodgers added one more run in the fourth inning, two in the sixth, and another one in the seventh for a total of seven runs. The Yankees managed only three runs on nine hits. Mickey was 1-for-5 with a two-out, RBI single in the ninth inning.

On October 5, it was another beautiful, sunny day at Ebbets Field as 36,775 fans crammed into the stadium for Game 5. Twenty-six-year-old Jim McDonald took the mound for the Bronx Bombers. He had won nine games and lost seven during the regular season for the Yankees. The Dodgers called on 21-year-old rookie pitcher Johnny Podres, the second youngest pitcher ever to start a World Series game.

Tragedy almost struck the Yankees during the pregame batting practice session. Mickey had struck out six times in the past two games so he was taking extra batting practice. In his eagerness to hit, he entered the cage prematurely and caught a line drive off the bat of Irv Noren. The ball glanced of Mickey's hand and smashed into his left thigh. The result was a badly bruised left thigh and bruised knuckles on his left hand. Casey Stengel came close to scratching Mantle from the lineup, but with treatment of a chloride compound to "freeze" the pain, Mickey insisted on playing.

The Yankees jumped out to a quick 1-0 lead on a leadoff homer by Gene Woodling. The Dodgers countered with a run in the second inning, tying the game at 1-1. In the top of the third, a couple of strange events occurred. First, a rare error by Gil Hodges opened up the game for the Yankees. Rizzuto had walked, and then was bunted to second by McDonald. Woodling then grounded for the second out while Rizzuto moved to third base. The next batter, Joe Collins, hit a ground ball to Dodger first baseman Gil Hodges, who muffed what should have been an easy third out. Rizzuto scored, giving the Yankees a 2-1 lead. After the game, Hodges confessed, "I just missed it, that's all. It was an easy play. I should have had it. The ball hit the heel of my glove and bounced out."

With one run in and Collins on first base, Podres then hit Hank Bauer. As Yogi Berra stepped into the batter's box, the next strange occurrence happened. At that moment, Berra called time out to complain about a strong reflection from center field blinding him.

The umpires gathered around home plate, but could not see the object, so play continued. Podres proceeded to walk Yogi Berra, which loaded the bases.

With Mickey Mantle now stepping to the plate, Chuck Dressen had to make a tough decision. He could leave the young, inexperienced, left-handed rookie Podres in to pitch to Mantle, who would be batting right-handed. Or, he could bring in the veteran right-handed Russ Meyer to pitch to Mickey batting left-handed—the right-field wall was only 297 feet away, but was 40 feet tall. Dressen decided that he needed to go to his veteran Meyer.

As Meyer made his warm-up tosses, Mickey quietly studied him from the on-deck circle. With two outs, Meyer was potentially one pitch away from getting the Dodgers out of a big jam. Unfortunately for the Dodgers, Mickey hit the first pitch. It was a belt-high curveball on the outside corner of the plate, some 400 feet to the opposite field into the upper deck of the left-field stands for a grand-slam home run. In one mighty swing of his bat, Mickey had changed the score from 2-1 to 6-1. As he jogged out to his position in center field in the bottom of the inning, the Brooklyn fans actually applauded Mickey for his clutch performance.

The Yankees won the game 11-7, with the help of four home runs. Combined with the Dodgers' two homers in the game, there were a total of six long balls, which set a new World Series record. Mantle only had one hit in the game, but it was an important one. After the game, Mickey confessed that due to his batting practice injury, "I couldn't squeeze the bat hard. It was a belt-high curve—the same kind of ball they were throwing me the other day."

Russ Meyer recalled the pitch that he threw to Mickey saying, "When you throw your best pitch and a guy hits it like that Mantle did, then there's just nothing you can do about it. Carl Erskine had been telling me—and we had been noticing it—Mantle had been running away from the pitches. So I fed him a slow overhand curve—a beauty. Just the kind Erskine was giving him Friday when he whiffed him four times. It was a low one and a good breaker, but this time Mantle didn't fall away from it. He stepped into it like he was mad at somebody and murdered it. It was as if somebody had told him where the pitch was going to be, for he stepped in almost before I let the ball go."

The issue of the blinding reflection in hitters' eyes remained a mystery after the game. The glare that overwhelmed hitters appeared to be coming from the third floor of an apartment building on Bedford Avenue some 500 feet from home plate. The umpires paused the game on several occasions as police tried to identify the source. Casey Stengel said, "Somebody had it in a window about on the third floor. He always came up with it when a guy was swinging. It looked like a big mirror. He was doing it to both teams. It bothered the umpires, too." During a televised interview, umpire Ed Hurley said a man in the apartment complex was shining a mirror in the eyes of Yankee hitters. The problem was resolved when workmen deployed a tarpaulin over the stadium railing, directly in line with the batter's box.

The Series moved back to New York and Yankee Stadium where the stage was set for Game 6. Whitey Ford, who was knocked out after one inning in Game 4, was Stengel's choice for starting pitcher for the Yankees. Chuck Dressen, with his back against the wall, decided to call on Carl Erskine. Erskine had pitched brilliantly in Game 3, striking out 14 Yankee hitters, but he would be pitching on only two days of rest.

The Yankees drew first blood in the contest, just as they had in four of the five Series games thus far. In the first inning, a walk, a single, a double, and an error gave the Bronx Bombers an early 2-0 lead. Mantle was intentionally walked in that inning, and was left stranded on second base. The Yankees tallied again in the second inning on singles by Phil Rizzuto, Whitey Ford, and Joe Collins. As the game progressed to the sixth inning, the Yankees were enjoying a 3-0 lead over Brooklyn. The Dodger countered with one run in the sixth, which made the score 3-1.

As the game entered the ninth inning, it was looking as if the Yankees would surely win their record-breaking fifth straight world championship. That situation changed quickly. With one out, Duke Snider drew a walk, and the National League batting champion, Carl

Furillo, hit a dramatic two-run home run to tie the game at 3-3; stunning the crowd of 62,370 at Yankee Stadium. Allie Reynolds, who replaced Whitey Ford in the eighth inning, responded by striking out the next two Dodger hitters to stop the bleeding. The game was now heading into the bottom of the ninth.

Hank Bauer worked a leadoff walk. After Yogi Berra lined out to right field for the first out, Mickey Mantle, who had remained hitless in three at-bats, stepped up to the plate. He chopped a slow bouncer to Dodger third baseman Billy Cox, who didn't even bother to attempt a throw when he saw how fast Mickey was moving to first base. It was an infield single for Mantle, which moved Bauer to second base and thereby set the table for his good friend and fellow World Series hero, Billy Martin. Martin, with a one-strike count, promptly hit a single to drive in Bauer for the game-winning run. The Yankees took the game 4-3, and the Series 4-2.

The 1953 World Series proved to be won by the M&M boys—Mickey Mantle and Billy Martin. Between them, they accounted for 15 of the Yankees' 32 RBIs and four of the nine home runs in the six-game Series. Mickey was only 5-for-24 (.208) in the Series, but he had seven important clutch RBIs that were instrumental in two of the Yankees' four Series wins.

Touching All the Bases

Mickey's salary was $17,500 in 1953. Yogi Berra made $36,000. Mickey and each of his teammates received a bonus of $8,281 for winning the World Series. The Dodgers each received $6,178.

The book *The Mickey Mantle Story*, by Ben Epstein, was released in 1953.

Chapter Nine

TWO-SIDED BLASTS

Entering the game against the Detroit Tigers on May 13, 1955, the Yankees were in third place in the American League with a 14-10 record. They were four games out of first place, behind the Cleveland Indians who had compiled a 19-8 record over the same period. The Yankees also trailed the Chicago White Sox, who were in second place with a 16-9 record.

Mantle started the day with a .256 batting average, collecting just 22 hits in 86 at-bats. Among his 22 hits were three doubles and seven home runs, which accounted for 23 runs and 16 RBIs. Concerned about Mickey's low batting average, manager Casey Stengel had been urging Mickey to cut down on his swing and concentrate on meeting the ball with extra wrist action.

About an hour before the game, Casey proclaimed, knowing that Mickey was in earshot, "I've got a feller on my team who thinks he should hit a homer every time, and gets mad when the other pitcher won't let him. If he'd just fling his bat at the ball, like this," Stengel would add, with appropriate wrist-snapping gestures, "he'd hit it just as far and maybe wouldn't strike out so much and get so mad."

Thus, this day, as in the two previous days, Mickey arrived extra early to Yankee Stadium for special batting practice with coach Bill Dickey. Paid attendance for the game had been 7,177, which ironically echoed Mickey's famous uniform number. The day also happened to be Friday the 13th. The Yankees sent their lefty-pitching ace, Whitey Ford, against the Tigers' right-handed hurler Steve Gromek. Ford entered the game with a 3-1 record, while Gromek garnished a more impressive 5-1 record.

In the first inning, with one out, Andy Carey bunted for a single. Twenty-five-year-old Mickey Mantle stepped to the plate. Using a bat that Enos Slaughter had left behind after being traded to the Kansas City Athletics, Mickey worked the count to two balls and two strikes before smashing a screaming line drive that cleared the bleacher wall above the auxiliary scoreboard to the left of the Yankees bullpen. The clout gave the Yankees an early 2-0 lead. Mickey's next at-bat came in the third inning. Gromek was still on the mound for the Tigers, and Hank Bauer was on second base. Mickey singled to center field driving in Bauer, giving the Yankees a 3-0 lead. Thus far, Mickey had all three of the Yankee RBIs.

In the fifth inning, Mantle stepped to the plate for his third at-bat of the game. Once again he was brandishing the Enos Slaughter bat that he had homered with in the first inning. With nobody on base and a two-ball, no-strike count; Gromek delivered a belt-high pitch, which Mickey lofted for a towering fly ball. The ball carried well into the seats just to the right of the 407-foot sign in right center field for his second homer of the game. The Yankees now led the Tigers by the score of 4-0.

In the seventh inning, Tiger hitter Ray Boone hit his sixth homer of the season with J.W. Porter on base. This was one of only three hits allowed by Whitey Ford before Casey Stengel removed him from the game in the eighth inning, and brought in Tom Morgan in relief.

Mantle had his last at-bat of the game in the bottom of the eight inning. The bases were empty as Mickey faced Tigers southpaw relief pitcher Bob Miller. This time, batting right-handed, Mickey used a bat that he had borrowed from his teammate Moose Skowron. Miller delivered his first pitch on the outside corner, and Mickey unleashed another swing that drove the ball farther than his first two titanic homers. This ball basically traveled the same path as the first ball but was hit even deeper, landing 18 rows deep into the right-field bleachers.

This landmark effort by Mickey set a few records. The combined distance of the three home runs was well over 1,300 feet. It was the first time in Mickey's career that he had hit three homers in one game, and the first time that an American League hitter had hit home runs from both sides of the plate in one game. Two players had previously accomplished this feat in the National League, Jim Russell of the Dodgers and Red Schoendienst of the Cardinals. Mickey would go on to accomplish the feat of hitting homers from both sides of the plate for a total of ten times during his career. Nobody had ever hit two homers into the cavernous center-field bleachers of Yankee Stadium before. The three home runs increased Mantle's total homers for the year to ten, moving him into a tie with Kansas City's Gus Zernial for the major league lead.

Mickey ended the day going 4-for-4, and raising his average by 33 points to .289 as he drove in all five runs in the Yankees' 5-2 victory over the Tigers. The win moved the Yankees up one game in the standings to just three games behind the league-leading Cleveland Indians. This game was a prime example of Mickey's ability to help his team win, not to mention his great natural abilities.

After the game, Mickey said this about his extra batting practice, "Yes, I'm trying to shorten my swing. And I think I'm getting the idea. At least it worked today. Now if only I don't go 0-for-5 tomorrow. That's usually what happens after you have a big day."

When asked what pitches he had hit for his homers, he stated they were all fastballs and added, "You never know. I generally don't have much luck against Gromek. He got me out with the same pitches in Detroit a couple of weeks ago."

Obviously, Casey Stengel's prodding and Bill Dickey's coaching taught Mickey a valuable hitting lesson. As the season progressed, his batting average continued to climb. By the end of the 1955 season, he had compiled a very respectable .306 batting average, 27 home runs, and 99 RBIs. His slugging percentage was the highest of his career thus far at .611.

Touching All the Bases

This was the first of ten times during Mickey's career that he would hit home runs from both sides of the plate in the same game. Mickey would accomplish the feat again this year on August 15 against the Baltimore Orioles.

On June 21, Mickey hit a monumental home run off a changeup from Alex Kellner of the Kansas City Athletics at Yankee Stadium. The ball was the first ball ever hit over the hitters' backdrop in center field. It landed nine rows up for a total distance from home plate of 486 feet.

Mickey led the American League in triples (11) and home runs (37) in 1955.

In 1955, Mickey's salary was $25,000. Yogi Berra earned $48,000.

The Yankees went on to win their sixth American League championship in the past seven years. Mickey tore a hamstring in his right leg on September 16 against the Boston Red Sox while beating out a bunt. He was still nursing the injury during the World Series against the Brooklyn Dodgers, and only appeared in three of the seven games. He still managed two hits in ten at-bats, including one home run as the Yankees lost the Series in seven games.

David Mantle, Mickey and Merlyn Mantle's second son, was born on December 26, 1955.

Chapter Ten

OPENING-DAY EXPLOSIONS

The time between the 1955 World Series and Opening Day in 1956 was very busy for Mickey Mantle. After the World Series, the Yankees headed to Japan to play a series of games against some Japanese teams. As they boarded the plane for Japan after losing the World Series to the Brooklyn Dodgers, the flight captain welcomed them aboard over the intercom and then announced, "You know, you guys cost me $50 in that Series."

From somewhere in the back of the plane, Mantle shouted back, "Yeah, we cost ourselves $3,000!"—the difference between the winners' and losers' shares.

After arriving in Japan, Mickey was very impressed with the local fans, as he told the *New York Times*:

"Japan has the best baseball fans in the world. They don't come out to holler at the player—they come out to watch a baseball game." Mickey had to leave the tour early to return to the states because his wife, Merlyn, was pregnant with Danny and expecting to deliver any day.

During Spring Training of 1956, Mickey started an astonishing trend, which he would repeat time after time during his baseball career: He would have an injury, miss a couple of games, and then come back with a vengeance and have a banner day. On Sunday,

March 10, the Yankees played the St. Louis Cardinals in St. Petersburg, Florida, in the first exhibition game of the spring. In the ninth inning of a scoreless game, Wally Moon was on second base when Pete Whisenant singled to center field. Moon rounded third and was waved home, but Mickey made a great throw, nailing Moon at the plate.

Later, in the 11th inning, the same scenario happened—Moon doubled and Whisenant singled to center field. Mickey once again heaved a strong throw to the plate but missed. The Cardinals edged out a victory by the score of 1-0. This type of action so early in the spring usually took a toll on Mickey. It took a couple of weeks of regular throwing before his arm was in shape for hard throwing. On Monday, March 12, Mickey complained of a sore arm and leg and was sidelined until Friday, March 16, when the Yankees hosted the Detroit Tigers at St. Petersburg. Mickey went on a hitting binge in that game with two singles, a triple, and a 420-foot home run accounting for four RBIs to lead the Yankees to a 7-5 victory.

In 1956, hitters began wearing batting helmets; however, they were not required to do so. Mickey opted not to wear one, claiming it made him feel "like a sissy." The New York Yankees opened the season on April 17 in Washington, D.C. squaring off against the Washington Senators. Last year, the Senators had finished in eighth place with a 43-101 record—43 games out of first place.

The day of the game was cold and rainy. President Eisenhower threw out the ceremonial first pitch before a crowd of 27,837 fans. Gil McDougald was the lucky recipient of the first toss. The lopsided pitching matchup for the day was the Yankees' Don Larsen against Cuban hurler Camilo Pascual. The previous year, Pascual suffered through a 2-12 season with a 6.14 ERA. Larsen enjoyed a 9-2 record with a 3.06 ERA.

Griffith Stadium is a very large ballpark where historically it has been proven difficult to hit home runs. If fact, only 45 round-trippers were hit in that ballpark in 1955 when the dimensions were 388 feet down the left-field line, 421 feet to center, and 320 feet down the right-field line. During the off-season, the Senators had brought in the left-field fence by two feet and by as much as six feet in left center. Center-field and right-field distances remained unchanged.

In the first inning, Hank Bauer fouled out, and then Jerry Lumpe struck out. It was then Mantle's turn to bat. Batting lefty against the right-handed Pascual, Mickey took the first two pitches for balls, but took a vicious cut at the third offering. The ball struck the bat directly on the sweet spot, and rocketed toward centerfield with tremendous thrust. The Senators' center fielder, Karl Olson, who had been acquired from the Boston Red Sox in the off-season, took one step toward the 31-foot-tall center-field wall and then stopped to watch the ball sail over the fence and completely out of the stadium. The ball landed on the roof of a house at 2014 Fifth St. NW. It was later estimated that the ball had traveled well in excess of 500 feet. Pascual finished the first inning having only given up that one run, but the fans were still buzzing about Mickey's blast as the Nats came to bat in the bottom half of the inning.

Senators left fielder Dick Tettelbach quickly evened the score at 1-1 with a line-drive homer that fell between the old and new fences. The Yankees renewed their scoring attack in the third inning. Jerry Lumpe reached base on an error, but when Pascual struck Mickey out on three straight pitches, the crowd roared with approval. Yogi Berra then lined a homer over the left-field fence to give the Bombers a 3-1 lead. Pascual got into trouble again in the fifth inning after walking both Bauer and Mickey. Berra picked up his third RBI of the game with a single, which increased the Yankees' lead to 4-1. In the bottom of the fifth, Olson hit a solo homer to center field to bring the Senators to within two runs of the Yankees, but that would quickly change in the sixth inning.

In the Yankees' sixth, Elston Howard and Andy Carey opened with singles. Pitcher Don Larsen struck out while attempting to lay down a sacrifice bunt. Hank Bauer fanned, which led to a thunderous ovation from the fans for Pascual. Jerry Lumpe then singled to score Howard, which put the score at 5-2. Mickey then stepped to the plate and accomplished a feat that nobody had ever done at Griffith Stadium: He hit his second home run of the game, over the center-field fence at the 438-foot mark. Not even Babe

Ruth had breeched the center-field wall twice in one game before. The three-run blast went over the center-field bullpen wall and increased the Yankee lead to 8-2. The ball was later estimated to have traveled in excess of 500 feet. Even President Eisenhower, in appreciation Mickey's performance, rose and cheered as Mickey quietly rounded the bases.

The Yankees went on to win by a score of 10-4, the major offensive heroes being Yogi Berra, who went 4-for-4 with five RBIs, and Mickey Mantle, who went 2-for-3 with four RBIs and two homers. Don Larsen pitched seven innings, yielded four runs on six hits, and picked up his first win of the season.

The next day, Bob Addie wrote in *The Washington Post*, "It's been a long time since anybody made a miniature golf course out of Griffith Stadium, but that's what happened yesterday when the Yankees' 'Mr. Wonderful,' Mickey Mantle, made those formerly faraway fences shrink like a $10 suit caught in the rain. The barrage of home runs sounded like an artillery duel, but Mr. Mantle's booming shots made the other four-baggers look embarrassingly puny by comparison."

Shirley Povich of *The Washington Post* and *Times Herald* wrote, "Russia can boast about its other weapons, but they have nothing to compare with the Mantle missiles. It was nice of President Eisenhower to come out for Mickey Mantle Day. Mickey had just hit home run No. 2 into Fifth Street, which has been reduced to a four-lane receptacle for Mantle homers. If you're asking where Mantle gets that enormous power, his teammates who see him in the locker-room attire could enlighten you. Ben Epstein, of the *N.Y. Mirror*, who wrote the still hot-selling *Mickey Mantle Story*, describes the fellow's physique best, perhaps, when he comments on Mantle's muscles of the neck, shoulders, back and arms, and says, 'A symphony, that's what.' Baseball players all over the league talk of the Mantle home runs like they used to talk of Ruth's, and point out the spots where they hit into the stands or went out of the park."

A week later, Mantle discussed his Opening-Day homers with *New York Times* reporter Arthur Daley. In the interview, Mickey told Daley, "I'm beginning to learn that easy does it. Take those two homers I hit in Washington the other day, the ones they made all the fuss about. I didn't swing hard at either of them. I did what I've been trying to do all along—just meet the ball. If I can cut down my strikeouts and keep getting wood on the ball, enough of them will go out of the park. I can get more homers that way than I can by deliberately going for the long ball. I've found that out already."

Ted Williams, who was in New York with the Red Sox to take on the Yankees, told Daley, "Don't worry about Mantle. In another 15 or 20 years, you'll be voting for him for the Hall of Fame."

Roughly a month later, the *New York Times* interviewed Jerry Coleman. He said, "I'd say that Mickey attained maturity on Opening Day this season. It was—Boom! Boom!—and he had two tremendous homers without even trying. It gave him confidence. I've noticed since that he's giving in to the pitchers. If they pitch him outside, he'll slice to the opposite field. Last year, he'd have tried to overpower by pulling the ball anyway. The boy has come of age."

In Don Larsen's book *The Perfect Yankee*, he recalls, "On Opening Day, with me pitching against Washington Senators hurler Camilo Pascual, Mantle served notice of the great things that were to come that season. In front of President Dwight Eisenhower, the great outfielder hammered two home runs, one a tremendous clout over the center-field fence that Senators announcer Bob Wolff called one of the longest balls he ever saw sail out of the stadium."

Touching All the Bases

Mickey hit home runs from both sides of the plate, in the same game, on May 18 versus the White Sox; and again on July 1 against the Senators.

Chapter Eleven

18" FROM HISTORY

Nineteen fifty-six proved to be a great year for the Yankees—especially Mickey Mantle. As of May 30, they had been in first place all month except for one day.

The Yankees hosted the Washington Senators at Yankee Stadium for a Memorial Day doubleheader with 29,825 fans on hand. The overcast sky spat light rain, but the temperature was 83 degrees just prior to the first game. A pregame Memorial Day ceremony was held that had the Washington Senators line up on the third-base line and the Yankees on the first-base line. A Marine color guard raised the flag and played "Taps" before a moment of silence was observed.

The pitchers for the first game were Johnny Kucks (5W-2L) for the Yankees and Pedro Ramos (3-1) for the Senators. The Senators jumped out to an early 1-0 lead in the second inning. Ramos successfully held the Bronx Bombers hitless until the fourth inning when Mickey Mantle reached base on a bold drag bunt with two strikes already against him. The Yankee rally was short lived, but Mickey had played an important role by demonstrating his leadership skill and breaking the Yankees' hitless streak.

In the Yankee fifth inning, with one out, Johnny Kucks drew a walk, and Hank Bauer grounded into a fielder's choice as he reached first base. Gil McDougald then singled after a controversial call on a pitch that the Senators claimed should have been strike three, which would have ended the inning. Mickey came to bat, hitting left-handed against the righty Ramos, and worked a 2-2 count. He then launched a monstrous line drive to right field that just kept going up. It sailed high over the right-field fence that was 345 feet away. For a moment, it looked like the ball would become the first fair ball ever hit out of the friendly confines of Yankee Stadium. It then abruptly struck the façade just 18 inches from the stadium roof and 117 feet above the playing field, and bounced back onto the playing field. Mickey's teammate Johnny Blanchard recalled that at the moment the ball left Mickey's bat, "Everybody got up and jumped out of the dugout to look. And before it hit, everybody thought it was gone out of the stadium. And then it hit right 18 inches below the façade and fell back into the park."

In the 33 years since the construction of The House that Ruth Built in 1923, nobody had ever come that close to hitting a fair ball out of the Stadium. The monumental blast was Mickey's 19th homer of the season and his 15th in the month of May. The mammoth smash, estimated to have potentially traveled 550 to 600 feet, gave the Yankees a 3-1 lead. Each time that Mickey came to bat the rest of the way through the twin bill, he received a thunderous ovation from the appreciative fans at Yankee Stadium.

The Yankees added an additional run in the sixth inning, which put them ahead by the score of 4-1. During that inning, Yankees first-base coach Bill Dickey was struck on the right shin by a sharp foul ball off the bat of Joe Collins. He had to come out of the game and was replaced by Jim Turner. Dickey later said, "I was still thinking about that ball Mickey hit and didn't react fast enough." Bill Dickey and Frank Crosetti, teammates of Babe Ruth and Lou Gehrig, later agreed they had never seen a ball travel farther. The fact that Dickey was still daydreaming about Mickey's blast during the next inning says a lot about the magnitude of the feat that Mickey had accomplished. It was reported in the papers that even in the inning after the blast, many fans were still pointing to the spot where the ball struck the façade.

The Senators bounced back with two runs in the seventh inning, but it was not enough. The Yankees won, 4-3. Mickey had gone 3-for-4 (two singles and a homer), and drove in three of the Yankees' four runs. As far as the fans were concerned, they probably didn't remember much that happened after Mickey hit the Bunyonesque shot off the façade.

After the game, Mickey described his historic homer by saying, "It was the best I ever hit a ball left-handed." Johnny Blanchard was awestruck when he said, "We couldn't believe it; and after the game, a couple of us went out to home plate and looked up. You stand at home plate and you look and see where he hit it, you can't believe it. You just can't believe it. You can't fungo a ball that far!"

The Yankees won the second game of the doubleheader by the score of 12-5. Mickey went 1-for-4 and hit his 20th homer of the season to break a 3-3 tie in the fifth inning off Camilo Pascual. Mickey's 450-foot homer carried halfway up into the right-field bleachers just to the right of the bullpen. Mickey was excused from the game after the seventh inning since the Yankees had the game well in hand, and it was a great opportunity to give Mickey a well-deserved rest. At the end of the day, Mickey led the major leagues in six offensive categories including runs (45), hits (65), total bases (135), home runs (20), RBIs (50), and batting average (.425). As for the Yankees, they were now six games ahead of the second-place Chicago White Sox.

After his two homers on the day, a hot topic was the fact that Mickey's 20 homers put him well ahead of Babe Ruth's home-run pace in 1927 in which Ruth hit 60 homers. That year, Ruth did not have 20 homers until June 11.

A few days after Mickey hit his tape-measure home run in Yankee Stadium, the Detroit Tigers came into town to play the Yankees. Howard Cosell, eyewitness to the amazing blast, described it to Harvey Kuenn, shortstop for the Tigers. Kuenn asked, "Did he really hit it up there? Really? His strength isn't human. How can a man hit a ball that hard?"

American League president Will Harridge acknowledged Mickey's impact on the game of baseball and attendance. He said,

"The reaction our office has received to Mantle's homers—distance homers—is positively stunning. I can't ever recall anything like it. Everywhere I go—in the restaurant, in the elevator, and in the barbershop—it was Mantle, Mantle, Mantle. They exclaim, 'Mantle's in town,' just like they did for Ruth and Feller. Mind you, they said Mantle first and the Yankees second."

Many fans came to the ballpark just to see Mickey Mantle—especially when the Yankees went on the road. Certain baseball teams didn't draw big crowds throughout most of the season, but the stadium would be filled to capacity when Mickey Mantle and the Yankees came to that town. Ralph Houk described this phenomenon, saying, "In every city on the road, it's almost a sure thing that I will get a phone call early in the morning from a fan. They'll have a single question: 'Is Mantle playing?' I never know what to tell them. Often I can't tell about Mickey until I get to the ballpark. Even at the park when I leave Mantle out of the lineup, the kids lean over the dugout and yell, 'Where is he? Where's Mickey, why isn't he playing?' He's the Yankee a lot of them come out to see."

A couple of weeks after Mickey's mammoth blast, Bob Sheppard, the Yankees public address announcer at the Stadium penned this poem about Mickey.

MICKEY MANTLE
No Ruthian legends shade this lad,
No feats of Foxx or Greenberg awe him.
His home run progress marches
On prodigious parabolic arches.
No puny efforts here—
Each jet-propelled beyond the normal reaches.
In time each park
Contains a landmark
Where a Mantle blow was struck …
Here a towering facade was dented …
Here a distant scoreboard smashed …
Here a roof was cleared …
Here an apartment window shattered.

18" From History

We mortals should exult
To a legend in the making:
The era of atomic power and Mickey Mantle.
Paul Bunyon in baseball togs!

Late in the 1956 (Triple Crown) season, Paul Richards, manager of the Baltimore Orioles paid Mickey the ultimate compliment after he went 7-for-12 against Baltimore pitching.

"Baseball has been looking for a long time for the super player," Richards said. "Now it can stop looking because Mantle is that player. He can hit better than anyone else; he can field better than anyone else; he can throw better; and he can run better. What else is there?"

Also in 1956, in a game against the Chicago White Sox, Mickey went 4-for-4 with home runs from both sides of the plate. His second homer came in the ninth inning with two outs and the Yankees trialing by the score of 7-6. The Yankees won the game in 10 innings. After the game, White Sox manager Marty Marion was in awe, saying, "Mantle should be in a league by himself."

Touching All the Bases

Nine-year-old Billy Crystal went to his first major league baseball game on May 30 at Yankee Stadium and instantly became a lifelong fan of Mickey Mantle. Crystal said that he began limping so that he could be just like Mickey Mantle, and even gave his bar mitzvah speech in an Oklahoma drawl.

Mickey's home run that hit the façade on May 30 may not have been his first assault on the distant target. According to eyewitnesses, he also hit the façade approximately three weeks earlier on May 5 in a game against the Kansas City Athletics. A's broadcaster Merle Harmon said, "I thought it was going completely out of the park. If not for the roof, it would have hit the subway across the street."

Mickey hit 16 home runs in May of 1956.

On June 5, Lou Boudreau, manager of the Kansas City Athletics and creator of the Ted Williams Shift back in 1946, devised and implemented the first Mickey Mantle Shift to use when Mickey batted left-handed. In the shift, the shortstop moved to the right of second base, the second baseman played a very shallow right field, the third baseman moved to shallow center field, the left fielder moved to deep third base, the center fielder moved to deep left-center, and the right fielder moved to deep right center field. In the eighth inning, Mickey hammered his 21st homer of the season into the right-field stands, but the shift wasn't on at the time.

Mickey's 50th home run of the season came in the 11th inning on September 18 against the Chicago White Sox. The home run gave the Yankees a 3-2 win, but more importantly it clinched the American League pennant for the Bronx Bombers.

Chapter Twelve

A PERFECT DAY

The 1956 baseball season featured a very magical Mickey Mantle. Entering September, he was already on his way to beating Babe Ruth's cherished single-season home run record. In 1927 Babe Ruth's 60 homers bested the previous record of 59 homers, which he had set in 1921. His new record of 60 had gone virtually unchallenged for 29 years. Mickey ended the season with only 52 homers. This may have been the best record in the American League and major leagues, but it wasn't good enough to beat the "Ghost of Babe Ruth" for the home run record. However, this may have been for the best because, in the final week of the season, Mickey was able to focus all of his concentration on his amazing assault on the Triple Crown.

In his quest for the Triple Crown, Mickey was in a tight race for the batting title with Red Sox hitter Ted Williams, and for the RBI title with the Tigers' Al Kaline. On September 18, the Yankees clinched the American League pennant when Mickey hit a clutch home run—his 50th of the season—in the 11th inning of a 2-2 game against the Chicago White Sox. The home run sailed over Comiskey Park's left center-field roof, and was measured at an impressive 550 feet, making it the longest ball ever hit at that stadium.

With eight games left to play, Mickey was trailing Ted Williams in batting average, .355 to .350. In the next two games, Mantle went 5-for-8, boosting his average to .354 while Williams only went 2-for-8, lowering his average to .353. Mickey then pulled a muscle in his right thigh and was confined to pinch-hitting duty for the next four games. The injury put Mickey's RBI lead in jeopardy because Al Kaline continued to get his normal number of at-bats per game. However, Mickey's handicap didn't affect his statistics too much: He beat Kaline for RBIs with 130 to 128, and Williams for batting average with .353 to .345. Mickey Mantle was the 12th player in baseball history to win the Triple Crown. What made this feat even more incredible was that Mickey led the *entire* major leagues in those categories. He was only the fourth person in baseball history to accomplish this.

Ted Williams, after losing the batting crown to Mickey, was quoted as saying, "If I could run like that son of a bitch, I'd hit .400 every year."

Casey Stengel marveled over Mickey's accomplishments. "The thing too many people overlook about him is that he's been doing all he has been doing this year as a cripple. He still hasta have his right leg bandaged before every game, and then he pulled a muscle on the back of the same leg under his knee, which was so sore you couldn't touch it. And that knee he had operated on a few years ago after he fell over like he was dead in the World Series still bothers him. So he's doing a great job for the Yankees without really being in the shape to do it; but he is, so you can't take anything away from him."

The Yankees, who clinched first place on September 18, finished the season with 97 wins and 57 losses. They met with the Brooklyn Dodgers at Ebbets Field on October 3 to battle in the World Series.

The Yankees lost Game 1, 6-3, despite a home run and two RBIs by Mickey Mantle. Don Larsen started Game 2 for the Bronx Bombers but was removed in the second inning after being touched up for six Dodger runs. The Dodgers went on to a 13-8 win with Don Bessent as their winning pitcher. As the Series headed to Yankee

Stadium, the Bronx Bombers found themselves quickly down two games to none.

In Game 3, Whitey Ford pitched the Yankees to their first win of the Series as the Yankees edged out the Dodgers 5-3. Tom Sturdivant got the win in Game 4 by the score of 6-2 as Mantle hit his second homer of the Series. The Series was now tied at 2-2 as it entered Game 5 at Yankee Stadium. The starting pitchers were announced as 27-year-old Don Larsen for the Yankees and veteran 39-year-old Sal Maglie for the Brooklyn Dodgers. The Dodgers had picked up Maglie in the middle of the season for the sum of $1,000. He had pitched magnificently down the stretch with a record of 13 wins—including a no-hitter on September 25—and only five losses. Maglie was also the winning pitcher in Game 1 of this Series. On the other hand, The Dodgers' hitters had thrashed Larsen in Game 2, so he was hoping to redeem himself. During the regular season, Larsen's record was 11-5 with a 3.26 ERA.

Mickey said it best in his book *My Favorite Summer 1956*, "Monday, October 8, was a beautiful autumn day in New York. The sun was shining brightly, the temperature was in the sixties and there were 64,519 fans in the big ballpark. A perfect day for baseball, and that's what it turned out to be for Larsen—a perfect day."

During batting practice, Hank Bauer was talking to *New York Times* writer Arthur Daley about how Mickey used to borrow his bats. Hank said, "He's quit on me. Now he's using Joe Collins' bat, ain'tcha, Mick?" Mickey replied with, "Nope. I'm using Jerry Lumpe's bat today." Bauer retorted with, "You're nuts. All a guy on this team has to say is, 'Hey, Mickey, I got a good bat,' and Mickey will say, 'Let me try it.'"

The fact that Mickey regularly borrowed bats from his teammates says a lot about the relationships he shared with his fellow Yankees. Mickey certainly had his own supply of his personal model bats from the Louisville Slugger bat factory. In fact, the accounting records at Louisville Slugger reveal that Mickey had received 25 bats during the 1956 season. In late August he had gotten a half-dozen model W148 bats, each 34.5 inches and 32 ounces. In addition, he had ordered two more W148 bats with the exact same specifications specifically for the World Series.

Baseball players, like all athletes, are very protective of their personal equipment for obvious reasons, since they are the tools of their trade. If a player is not completely comfortable with his tools, he is unlikely to perform to his maximum potential. Baseball players are especially protective of their game gloves and their game bats. Most hitters have their favorite bats and keep a very close eye on them. Furthermore, in an effort to avoid the possibility of breaking his favorite bat unnecessarily, a hitter will never use his game bat during batting practice.

Why then would Mickey's teammates continually offer their best bats to him? The answer is that a player might receive a dozen bats, but maybe only two or three would have just the right grain spacing and density. To most hitters, every bat they receive is an acceptable bat, but Mickey needed the absolute strongest bats to support his mighty Herculean swing. It is an incredible sign of respect that the Yankee hitters offered their most powerful bats to Mickey.

In the bottom of the fourth inning of Game 5, with two outs, Mickey Mantle stepped to the plate for the second time that day. Incredibly, both Larsen and Maglie were pitching perfect games. Stepping up to the left side of home plate, Mickey took a few practice swings, dug in, and looked intensely toward the mound. The Brooklyn Dodgers used a modified Ted Williams Shift when Mickey batted left-handed. This particular shift left a big hole open in left center field, which Mickey rarely touched as a left-handed hitter.

Maglie was nicknamed "The Barber" because he was notorious for throwing high and inside, right under their chins—'a close shave.' He once said, "When I'm pitching, I own the plate." The first pitch was a 'back-door' curve ball, which hit the outside corner for a called strike. Mickey was obviously looking for a better offering before unleashing one of his mighty swings. Maglie looked in for his next sign and delivered a fastball, which Mickey took for a ball. The count was now even at one ball and one strike. The following pitch was another 'back-door' curve. Just as before, Mickey didn't swing, and just as before, it was called a strike. With the count now at one ball and two strikes, Mickey had to 'protect the plate,' which means that he had to swing at borderline pitches, like the first two called strikes. On the other hand, Maglie could afford to waste a pitch or two. Perhaps he would try to tease Mickey into swinging at a pitch that started in the strike zone, but then darted out, or maybe he would give Mickey a close shave to back him away from the plate.

The capacity crowd at Yankee Stadium of 64,519 grew nervous with anticipation as the pitch was hurled. Mickey took a vicious cut and fouled the ball over the roof behind home plate. Maglie threw another curve ball, but this time it was too low, evening the count at two balls and two strikes. Mickey fought off the next pitch, lashing it foul into the stands on the left side. Mickey took this opportunity to step out of the batter's box to collect his thoughts and try to relax his body. His goal was clear: Get a base hit to break up the no-hitter.

Mickey was no stranger to breaking up a no-hitter. On July 12, 1951, Bob Feller of the Cleveland Indians and Allie Reynolds were both pitching no-hitters in the sixth inning of the game. With one out in the top of the sixth, Mickey doubled, breaking up Feller's no-hit quest. His teammate, Reynolds, went on to record a no-hitter with a 1-0 victory. Maybe Mickey was thinking about this as he took a deep breath, stepped back into the batter's box, dug his left cleat into the dirt, anchored his left leg, and waved his bat back and forth in a rhythmic motion.

Most major league hitters confess to being "guess hitters," which means they can't tell what pitch is coming until it's too late to swing, so they guess what each pitch will be before the pitcher delivers. On the other hand, some hitters, such as Ted Williams, can actually see the rotation of the red seams on the white ball, allowing them to determine what pitch is coming at them. Mickey was a guess hitter, but luckily for him, Bob Turley, one of the Yankee ace pitchers, had an extraordinary knack for being able to tell whether the opposing pitcher was about to throw a curveball or a fastball. He had worked a system out with Yankee hitters and especially Mickey, that if he whistled his unique, shrill whistle, then the next pitch was going to be a curveball. Maybe Mickey heard a whistle from Turley, or maybe Mickey guessed the next pitch to be a curveball; but Mickey described what happened next in his book *My Favorite Summer 1956*:

> Maglie threw me a curveball that got up a little more than he wanted, and I hit it good. You always know when you've hit one. There's a special feeling when the bat makes contact with the ball. I knew I hit that one good and I knew I hit it far enough. It was just a question of staying fair. The ball just made it inside the right-field foul pole and into the seats. But anyway, with my home run we had our first hit off Maglie and we led, 1-0.

Mickey's homer was his third of the Series and the only hit the Yankees had in the first five innings of the game.

The next hitter, Yogi Berra, lashed a line drive to left center field. Dodger center fielder Duke Snider made a remarkable diving catch for the third out and held the Bronx Bombers to one run. As the Dodgers came to bat in the top of the fifth inning, a warm breeze was blowing out to left field. Dodger first baseman Gil Hodges had struck out in the first inning and he now stepped to the plate. As Hodges dug in at the plate, Yankee manager Casey Stengel caught Mickey's attention in center field, and instructed him to move a few steps toward left field. Hodges worked Larsen to a two-ball, two-strike count.

Hodges then called time and stepped out of the batter's box. During the regular season, Hodges had hit .265 with 32 home runs and 87 RBIs—Larsen knew he was not an easy out. Hodges stepped back into the batter's box and awaited the next pitch. Larsen delivered, and Hodges hit a scorching line drive to deep left center field. Mickey took off at top speed running back and to his right toward left center field. In the middle of his gait, just as the ball was about to sail past, he reached up across his body and speared the ball backhanded for a tremendous running catch, which robbed Hodges of an extra-base hit. At approximately 450 feet, it turned out to be the Dodgers' longest ball of the day. In *My Favorite Summer 1956*, Mickey wrote:

A Perfect Day

> Now [Gil Hodges] was batting with one out in the top of the fifth and the Dodgers were still without a hit. Because Hodges was so strong and such a pull hitter, I backed up a few steps and moved over a bit toward left field. It was a good thing I did. The count went 2-2, and Hodges grabbed hold of a fastball and drove it on a line into left center. It would have been in the seats in Ebbets Field, but there was plenty of room to run in Yankee Stadium, and I ran like hell. I just put my head down and took off as fast as I could. I caught up with the ball as it was dropping, more than 400 feet from home plate. I had to reach across my body to make the catch and luckily the ball just plopped into my glove. If I'd started a split second later, or been a step slower, or if I hadn't shaded over on Hodges, the ball would have dropped for at least a double. It was the best catch I ever made. Some people might question that, but there's certainly no question that it was the most *important catch I ever made.*

The game went into the ninth inning, and Larsen had not allowed a single base runner. Carl Furillo, Roy Campanella, and pinch hitter Dale Mitchell were all that stood between Larsen and the history books. Every Yankee—fans and players—nervously awaited every pitch. The stress was greatest for the Yankees on the field. Mickey recalled his feelings in *My Favorite Summer 1956*:

> The crowd was on its feet and I was so nervous I could feel my knees shaking. I played in more than 2,400 games in the major leagues, but I never was as nervous as I was in the ninth inning of that game, afraid I would do something to mess up Larsen's perfect game. If I dropped a fly ball, it wouldn't stop his no-hitter, but it would end his perfect game, and that added to my nervousness. 'Should I come in a few steps? Go back? Should I move to my left a few steps? To my right?' I looked to the bench for help, as an outfielder usually does in this kind of situation, but nobody was looking at me. They were leaving it up to me. They didn't want to be responsible if I should mess up. So I just stayed right where I was.

In the ninth inning, with the crowd on the edge of its seats, Larsen got Carl Furillo to fly out to right field, and then Roy Campanella grounded out to Billy Martin. Pinch hitter Dale Mitchell then took a call third strike from home plate umpire Babe

Pinelli to end the game. Larsen was the first person to pitch a perfect game in World Series history. He had retired 27 consecutive Dodgers—seven on strike-outs, seven on ground balls, nine on flies to the outfield, three pop-ups to the infield, and one live drive in the infield. He had thrown 97 pitches, of which 71 were strikes in a short two-hour, four-minute game. Larsen's control was so accurate that he only had three balls on one hitter, Pee Wee Reese in the first inning.

After the game, several players made interesting statements about Mickey's role in the perfect game. Don Larsen told the *The Los Angeles Times*, "I had plenty of fielding help. That catch Mickey Mantle made on Gil Hodges' long liner in the fifth saved my bacon." Yogi Berra, also quoted by *The Los Angeles Times*, said, "Larsen made only one bad pitch. That was the pitch to Gil Hodges in the fifth inning. It took a great running catch by Mickey Mantle to grab Hodges' hit to deep left center." Gil Hodges, in the *New York Times*, referring to the much shallower fence at Ebbets Field, said, "Anyway, Mickey would have had to climb mighty high if he'd caught that one in Brooklyn." In regard to the pitch that Mickey hit for his home run, Sal Maglie told the *New York Times*, "The pitch to Mantle was a curve that broke, I'd say right over the middle of the plate." Mickey probably had the best quote of the day, which was printed in the *New York Times*, with, "This will be the first time a home run by me will not make the headlines."

The Yankees lost Game 6 in Brooklyn by the score of 1-0, thereby forcing a decisive Game 7 to be played at Ebbets Field. The Yankees would win the game convincingly by the score of 9-0. The victory made the Yankees the world champions for the fourth time in the six years Mickey had spent with the club.

Don Larsen summed it up perfectly in his book *The Perfect Yankee*:

> What a sight it was for me to see Mickey bat over my years with the Yankees. I always felt a sense of excitement like none I had ever known. To me, he was flat out the greatest switch-hitter I ever saw in the game. Mickey was a fierce competitor who could not bear to make an out. He just hated to make an out, and sometimes in the next at-bat he seemed determined to hit

the ball 5,000 feet just to make it up. The facts about Mickey are pure and simple. The good Lord never put a better ballplayer on the face of the earth. He had it all—speed, power, athletic ability, a great instinct for the game, and a way to rise to the occasion when our team needed a superhuman play to save us from defeat. To me, Mickey was the Yankees, just like the great players of the past like Gehrig, Ruth, and DiMaggio had been in their time. He used every ounce of talent God gave him, and when the pressure was on, we could always count on him.

Touching All the Bases

Mickey's salary for 1956 was $32,000. Yogi Berra earned $50,000, and Whitey Ford earned $30,000.

Despite Mickey's heavily taped right leg, he beat out 47 infield hits in 1956.

Mickey and each of his Yankee teammates received a bonus of $8,715 for winning the World Series. Each Dodger received the loser's share of $6,934.

Mickey was voted the American League Most Valuable Player (MVP) in 1956 by a unanimous vote.

Mickey won the Triple Crown and was named the "Player of the Year" and the "Male Athlete of the Year" for 1956. Mickey led the American League in runs (132), walks (113), total bases (376), home runs (52), RBIs (130), slugging percentage (.705), and batting average (.353) in 1956.

Mickey appeared on the *Bob Hope Show* on December 28, 1956, which was filmed at an army base in Alaska in -46 degree weather.

Mickey recorded a song with singing artist Theresa Brewer, called "I Love Mickey." He received an advance payment of $2,000 for his part in the record.

Mickey purchased a bowling alley in Dallas, Texas. He also purchased a Holiday Inn in Joplin, Missouri, and renamed it Mickey Mantle's Holiday Inn.

Chapter Thirteen

RIDING THE CYCLE

In baseball, a hitter is said to have hit for the cycle when he gets a single, double, triple, and home run all in one game. Hitting for the cycle is just as rare as a pitcher throwing a no-hitter. Both events are newsworthy and earn the player a spot in the record books. Since the inception of baseball, there have been 271 incidences of batters hitting for the cycle, while 274 no-hitters have been thrown.

Going into the 1957 season, with six seasons under his belt, Mickey had a total of 2,944 at-bats, of which 555 were singles, 136 were doubles, 43 were triples, and 173 were home runs. He also had 524 walks, which are not included in the 2,944 at-bats. The equation to calculate the percentage of times that Mickey hit a single would be: 555 / (2,944 + 524) = 16.00%.

Therefore, every time that Mickey stepped to the plate from 1951 through 1956, there was a 16-percent chance that he hit a single. Performing the same calculation with other types of hits yields a 3.92-percent chance of a double, 1.24-percent chance of a triple, and a 4.99-percent chance of Mickey hitting a home run. Clearly, the triple is the toughest hit to achieve. Mickey had far more triples than the average player due to his amazing speed, which significantly increased his probability of hitting for the cycle.

As the Chicago White Sox arrived at Yankee Stadium on July 23, 1957, for the first of a three-game series, the Yankees were looking to increase their four-and-one-half-game lead over the second-place Chicago White Sox. The White Sox, however, were looking at this series as their last chance to stay in contention for first place.

Once again, Casey Stengel was trying to convince Mickey to ease up on his swing. During spring training, Stengel remarked, "One of these days he'll hit a ball so hard it'll burst, and all he'll get for his efforts will be a single." Swinging the bat hard increases a hitter's chances of hitting a home run, but it also increases his chances of striking out. Stengel was concerned that Mickey had struck out 99 times during his Triple Crown season and was averaging 96 strikeouts per season in his first six years with the Yankees.

The pitching matchup for the game was the Yankees' Don Larsen versus the White Sox's Bob Keegan. Mantle was batting third in the lineup behind Tony Kubek and Gil McDougald. Mickey entered the game in very strong contention for his second consecutive Triple Crown—no one yet had won the Triple Crown in consecutive years. Mickey held the second highest batting average in the American League at .360 (just one point behind Ted Williams). He was also second in home runs with 25 (two behind Ted Williams), and third in RBIs with 65. Just 10 days earlier, Mickey was leading the league in batting with a .370 average, but a stretch where he went 1-for-14 caused his average to drop 10 percentage points.

In the first inning, Mickey batting lefty off the right-handed Keegan, and hit a routine fly ball to center fielder Larry Doby, who lost sight of it in the twilight sky. The ball landed inches from Doby's feet, and by the time he threw it to the infield, Mickey was already standing on second base with a double. He then scored on a home run by Harry Simpson, which accounted for the Yankees' two runs in the first inning.

In the third inning, Mickey, facing Keegan once again, had a favorable hitter's count of three balls and one strike. Keegan delivered a fastball, which Mickey hit 465 feet into the second to last row of the bleachers in right center field just to the right of the massive Ballantine Ale and Beer scoreboard. It was Mickey's 26th home run of the season. He later described his blast saying, "I hit a fastball, and it was one of the hardest hit of my career."

Mickey led off the Yankees' sixth inning facing left-handed reliever Paul LaPalme. He singled for his third hit in the game in as many at-bats. With a single, double, and a home run under his belt, Mickey needed the toughest hit of all, the triple, in order to complete the cycle. At this point in his career, he had 43 triples in 2,944 at-bats, which is the equivalent of one triple in every 68.5 at-bats.

The Yankees entered the bottom of the seventh inning trailing the White Sox by the score of 6-4. After the Bronx Bombers scored twice to tie the game, Mickey came to bat with the bases loaded. Batting right-handed, he hit a vicious liner on the first pitch from lefty relief pitcher Jack Harshman to left field, over the outstretched hands of Minnie Minoso. Mickey raced around first and headed for second. As Mickey approached second base, he could see Minoso picking up the ball. Without breaking stride, he put his head back down and headed for third. Determined to get the triple, he poured on the speed, and slid into third base just as the ball was arriving from the outfield.

The umpire extended his hands and yelled, "Safe!"

The triple completed the cycle, in four at-bats, but also pushed three more runs across the plate to give the Yankees a 9-6 lead.

Mickey batted one more time, in the eighth inning, but grounded out. He ended the game going 4-for-5 with a homer, triple, double, and single to become the first American Leaguer to hit for the cycle since Larry Doby accomplished the feat for the Cleveland Indians back on June 4, 1952. After the game, Mickey stated, "As for the cycle, I hit for it with Kansas City at Toledo in 1951, but never before in the American League."

Mickey drove in four runs as the Yankees defeated the White Sox 10-6 and increased their lead over the Sox to 5½ games. The productive day at the plate raised his batting average to .367, once again bumping him ahead of Ted Williams to lead the league. He also led the league now with 69 RBIs, and was just one home run behind

Ted Williams. Mickey's race for his second consecutive Triple Crown was heating up.

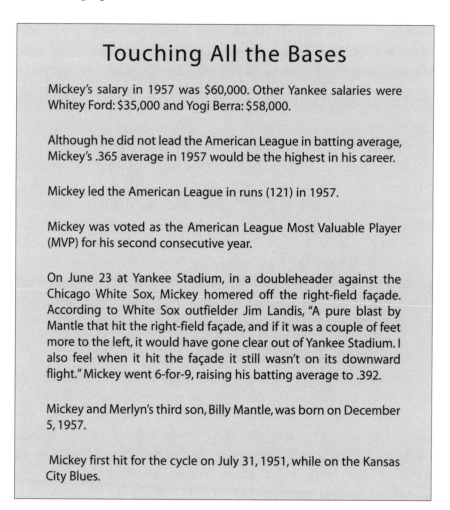

Touching All the Bases

Mickey's salary in 1957 was $60,000. Other Yankee salaries were Whitey Ford: $35,000 and Yogi Berra: $58,000.

Although he did not lead the American League in batting average, Mickey's .365 average in 1957 would be the highest in his career.

Mickey led the American League in runs (121) in 1957.

Mickey was voted as the American League Most Valuable Player (MVP) for his second consecutive year.

On June 23 at Yankee Stadium, in a doubleheader against the Chicago White Sox, Mickey homered off the right-field façade. According to White Sox outfielder Jim Landis, "A pure blast by Mantle that hit the right-field façade, and if it was a couple of feet more to the left, it would have gone clear out of Yankee Stadium. I also feel when it hit the façade it still wasn't on its downward flight." Mickey went 6-for-9, raising his batting average to .392.

Mickey and Merlyn's third son, Billy Mantle, was born on December 5, 1957.

Mickey first hit for the cycle on July 31, 1951, while on the Kansas City Blues.

Chapter Fourteen

LEADING THE WAY

After the first 32 games of the 1959 season, the Yankees were in last place in the American League for the first time since 1940 with 12 wins and 20 losses. They were 9½ games behind the first-place Cleveland Indians. The Yankees had gone from the most feared team in baseball to the biggest patsy. Mickey Mantle had the second highest batting average on the slumping Yankee team at .275.

In late May, the Yankees were in Baltimore for a four-game series with the Orioles. They lost the first game, 5-0 with only one hit off Hoyt Wilhelm. In that game, Mickey did something that he very rarely did: bat right-handed off a right-handed pitcher. He walked twice and grounded out twice. After the game, when asked why he batted right-handed, Mickey explained, "Because I hadn't been hitting Wilhelm's knuckleball anyway, so I figured I couldn't do worse no matter what I tried."

Manager Casey Stengel was becoming very concerned about the performance of his players. He said, "Some of them won't be around here long if they don't start winning." At the suggestion of coach Frank Crosetti, Stengel canceled the next day's pregame batting practice and ordered his players to sleep late in an effort to do something drastic to break the Bronx Bombers out of their spiraling nosedive. The Yankee players followed their skipper's orders and did not take the field for the second game of the series until 45 minutes before game time. This game and the next 14 would showcase Mickey Mantle's determination as both a leader and a winner.

On May 23, Mickey went 3-for-3 with a double, a home run, two RBIs, and scored three runs. He also stole third base and went home when there was a wild throw to third base. The Yankees won the game by the score of 13-5. After the victory, a pleased Casey Stengel said, "My players finally have found out which way is up from down in this league."

The Yankees and the Orioles played a doubleheader the next day. In the first game, the Yankees won 9-0. Mickey went 2-for-5 with another home run, four RBIs, and scored one run. In the nightcap of the doubleheader, Mickey was hitless in four at-bats as the Yankees lost 2-1.

The Yankees then traveled back home to New York to face the Boston Red Sox for two games. They were thoroughly routed in the first game by the score of 12-2. Mickey went 2-for-3 with an RBI. In the second game, in front of only 9,322 fans, Mickey was walked three times, and he stretched a single into a double with pure hustle. He also stole a base and scored a run as the Yankees defeated Boston 3-2. Mantle was now batting .305, but the Yankees were still stuck in last place.

The Baltimore Orioles then arrived for a short two-game series. In the first game, Mickey went 1-for-3 with two more walks and two more stolen bases. Even with his extra effort, the Bronx Bombers lost 5-0. In the second game, Mickey went 2-for-4, and stretched another single into a double. He drove in one run and scored one run as the Yankees triumphed 5-2. Mickey was now 11-for-23 in the last seven games for a .478 average. The Yankees had managed to win four of the last seven games.

The Yankees traveled to Washington to take on the Senators for a three-game series. As the Yankees' train pulled out of Baltimore, it came to a stop. "What's wrong?" Casey Stengel asked a passing trainman. "I dunno, Mr. Stengel, but the end of the train seems to be dragging something," said the train man. "Well, I can tell you what this is," said Stengel. "That's the Yankees. We're still in last place you know."

In a doubleheader with the Senators, the Yankees pounded them by the scores of 11-2 and 11-0, which gave the Yanks a three-game winning streak. Mantle went 4-for-4 in the first game with a home run, two RBIs, and scored three runs. In the second game, he was 1-for-4 with a scored run and stolen base. Yet the Yankees were still in last place.

In the third game with the Senators, a pitching duel was in progress between Yankee hurler Bob Turley and Washington's Camilo Pascual. The game was scoreless in the top of the ninth with two outs as Mickey stepped to the plate. He ignited a winning rally by doubling. Yogi Berra walked, and then Moose Skowron hit a three-run homer to give the Yankees their fourth straight victory with a 3-0 win. The double was Mickey's only hit in four at-bats, but he started the two-out rally and scored the winning run.

After the victory, the Yankees moved from last (eighth) place to sixth place. The next day, in the *New York Times*, sportswriter Arthur Daley wrote:

> The Yankee superstars of the past had the ability to keep the pressure on the opposition, applying it in an infinite variety of ways. They were leaders who led. The floundering Yankees of today needed such a leader. Maybe they've found him. As soon as Master Mickey Mantle came to life, the Bronx Bombers awakened, too. For most of this campaign the Stadium tenants have not had one hot ballplayer. They have one now, though. Mantle is sizzling. He's started to hit, and his antics on the base paths have been unsettling to the enemy. Not only has he stolen nine in ten tries, but he also drives pitchers crazy with the threat implied by his dancing tactics off first. They pay so much attention to the muscular Oklahoman that they can't concentrate on the batter. Moose Skowron won one recent game with a homer off a distracted pitcher.

The Yankees moved on to Detroit for a three-game series with the Tigers. Don Mossi tossed a four-hitter, and ended the Yankees' win streak by defeating them 2-0. Mantle was 0-for-3. In the second game, Mantle hit a ninth-inning home run of Tiger reliever Ray Narleski, to break a 5-5 tie and give the Yankees a 6-5 lead. It was Mickey's only hit of the game in three at-bats, but it was the game winner. Narleski later said that he had made a perfect pitch to Mantle, and he couldn't believe that he had hit it for a home run. Earlier in the game rookie Johnny Blanchard hit his first major league home run for the Yankees. The Yankees trounced the Tigers in the third game by the score of 14-3 as Mickey continued his torrid hitting pace, going 2-for-5, including a double. He also drove in a run, scored a run, and stole another base.

The Yankees then moved on to Cleveland for their next series against the Indians, who had just recently slipped from first to second place behind the Chicago White Sox. The Bronx Bombers routed the Indians in the first game by the score of 11-2. Mickey was walked three times and was hitless in three official at-bats. In the second game, Mantle was 1-for-3. His only hit proved to be the game-winner, driving in the second of two Yankee runs in a 2-1 victory over the Indians. After the victory, the Yankees were still in sixth place, but they had risen from nine and a half games games out of first place to get within three and a half games, with the help and leadership of Mickey Mantle.

In the 15-game stretch between May 23 and June 6, Mickey had batted .404 with five doubles, four home runs, 13 RBIs, six stolen bases, 16 walks, and had scored 16 runs. The Yankees had won 11 of those 15 games, and managed to climb out of the cellar into a more respectable sixth place and within striking distance of first place. Maybe the most amazing fact about Mickey's hitting surge is that he did it while his right leg was taped from the ankle to the hip, and his right shoulder was also taped due to a collision in the 1957 World Series. With all the tape that Mickey required, his teammates often said that Mickey resembled a mummy before he put on his pinstriped uniform.

Mickey's teammates were quick to praise him after his 15-game surge. "There's no question about it," said Gil McDougald. "The way he's playing has lifted the whole team."

"I've seen this guy do a lot of things I thought were great," said Hank Bauer, "but the last couple of weeks he's been better than ever."

"You might say," said Casey Stengel, "that he is making full use of his abilities, and therefore is playing better than anyone in this league for a long time." He admitted to letting Mickey steal bases because the team had not been hitting and he wanted to try to manufacture some runs in some way. "We weren't hitting, so I let him go. But it's taking too big a chance. One pileup somewhere on a close play, and then what do we do?"

"I like to run," says Mickey, "but he never let me go on my own before. There wasn't any need to steal when someone would usually drive you in. I guess now that we're hitting I won't do much running any more. I don't mind as long as I'm hitting."

Touching All the Bases

Mickey's salary in 1959 was $70,000. By comparison, Yogi Berra received $42,500 and Roger Maris earned $15,000.

The Yankees finished in third place with a record of 79 wins and 75 losses. It was their worst finish since 1925.

The next year, Don Drysdale of the Dodgers was asked if he thought lack of spirit explained Mickey's mediocre 1959 season. Don exploded, "How many big-league regulars would give their eye teeth to have the kind of season Mickey had last year? Me? Everybody says I should win 25 games. Mickey? Everybody says he should hit .350, hit 50 home runs and bat in 140 runs. My God, I try. Mickey tries. We try so hard it hurts, and it hurts even more when we read or hear that we don't care, that we don't try."

Mickey and Merlyn's fourth son, Danny Mantle, was born on March 20, 1960.

Chapter Fifteen

BUSHWACKED BY PIRATES

The 1960 season ended with a bang for the Yankees as they won their last 15 games. With an impressive record of 97-57, the Bronx Bombers easily finished in first place, eight games ahead of the second-place Baltimore Orioles. This marked the tenth time in the 12 seasons that 70-year-old Casey Stengel had managed his team to the American League Pennant. The power-hitting Yankees of 1960 set a new American League team record for home runs with 193, besting the old record of 190 also held by the Yankees (1956). With 7 world championships under his belt, Casey had his sights on number eight as his team prepared to battle the National League Champion Pittsburgh Pirates.

Mickey only missed three games during the entire season, making it the healthiest year of his career. He ended the season with a league-leading 40 home runs, in addition to 94 RBIs and a .275 batting average. As a right-handed hitter, his average was an outstanding .349; while as a left-handed hitter it was only .247.

Right after the Yankees clinched first place, Casey Stengel acknowledged Mickey's importance to their winning effort as he said, "It's amazin' what he's done with him a cripple playin' on one leg. Mantle has been my most valuable player." The reason for

Stengel's praise? Of Mickey's 40 home runs that season, 20 of them either won games or put the team within reach of a win.

"I've always been a better right-handed hitter than left," exclaimed Mickey. "But it wasn't until recently that I really got into a left-handed slump. I just don't seem able to pull the trigger, hitting left-handed. I have no excuse for it. It's not my legs or anything. The ball just gets up to me before I know it."

Mickey's left-handed hitting woes were evidenced by his strikeout record over the past three seasons, which turned out to be the worst three of his career in terms of strikeouts. These were the years immediately following the injury to his right shoulder, which he sustained during the 1957 World Series. Whether he publicly admitted it or not, the pain in his right shoulder definitely hampered his swing from the left side. The 100-plus point difference in his batting average was proof enough, but his left-versus-right strikeout ratios substantiate this claim—from 1958 through 1960, approximately 74 percent of Mickey's at-bats were left-handed, yet 82 percent of his strikeouts were left-handed.

The Yankees and the Pirates prepared to square off at Pittsburgh's Forbes Field for a World Series that would go down in baseball history as one of the most hard-fought and dramatic of all time. The Yankees were 7-5 favorites to win the Series. Just three days before the Series started, *The Los Angeles Times* published an analysis of Yankee players that had been carefully prepared by Pirates scouts. Regarding Mickey Mantle, the report stated, "Switch hitter, throws right. Batting left, pitch him high. Never slow up, because he murders changes of pace. Batting right, pitch him low fastballs and curves. Great outfielder and hasn't lost any speed."

Game 1 was played on October 5, in front of a standing-room-only crowd of 36,676. The pitching matchup was about as even as you could get—Art Ditmar, who held the Yankees' best pitching record, against the Pirates' Vern Law. During the regular season, Ditmar had compiled a record of 15-9 and a 3.06 ERA. Law's record was 20-9 with a 3.08 ERA. Both pitchers were right-handed hurlers and 6' 2" in height.

The two defining moments of the game occurred in the fourth inning. In the top of the fourth with no outs, Maris singled, and Mantle followed with a walk. Then Yogi Berra hit a vicious drive approximately 420 feet to deep right center field. Pirate center fielder Bill Virdon made an outstanding catch, keeping the Yankees from scoring. In the bottom of the fourth, Pirate third baseman Bill Mazeroski hit a two-run homer that proved to be the difference in the game. Although the Yankees out-hit the Pirates 13-8, they were outscored 6-4. During the Yankee loss, Mantle went 0-for-3 and walked once.

Game 2 was played on October 6, and featured another great pitching matchup of Bob "Bullet" Turley for the Yankees and Bob Friend for the Pirates. Just two years earlier, Turley was the American League Cy Young winner with a 21-7 record and a 2.97 ERA. He was also the World Series MVP in 1958. In the 1960 season, he had a 9-3 record and a 3.27 ERA. Friend had an 18-12 record and 3.00 ERA. When the game began, there were 37,308 people in attendance.

The Yankees unleashed a 16-run, 19-hit attack on the unsuspecting Pirates. Mickey and his team were holding on to a slim 3-1 lead in the top of the fifth inning. Fred Green, a rookie left-handed pitcher, had just replaced Buc starter Bob Friend. Mickey came to bat, hitting from the right side, with one out and a runner on first. He worked the count to two balls and two strikes. The 6-foot-4 Green went into his stretch and delivered a fastball. Mickey coiled his body, unleashed his mighty swing, and solidly connected. The ball rocketed into the air while Bill Virdon and Roberto Clemente raced back to right center field and watched helplessly as the ball landed in the seats approximately 400 feet from home plate. The two-run homer gave the Yankees a 5-1 lead heading into the sixth inning, but they weren't done with their attack. They scored seven more runs in the sixth inning, setting the score at 12-1.

Mickey was 1-for-2 as he stepped into the right-handers batter's box in the seventh inning with one out. Left-hander Joe Gibbon, the Pirates' fifth pitcher of the day, was on the mound. He had already given up singles to Tony Kubek and Joe DeMaestri before striking out Roger Maris. Gibbon delivered a fastball to Mickey that exploded off his bat even harder and faster than his first homer of the game. The ball flew over the 436-foot sign on the 15-foot-high ivy-covered wall in center field. In the 51-year history of Forbes Field, it was the first time a right-handed hitter had reached that remote area. The Bronx Bombers led by a lopsided score of 15-1, and Mantle now had five RBIs.

Mickey's last at-bat came in the ninth inning. With two outs and nobody on base, he stepped to the plate, greeted by an ovation. Righty reliever Tom Cheney walked him on four pitches. Mickey later scored the Yankees' 16th run. The Pirates managed to pick up two token runs in the bottom of the ninth before the game concluded. The final score was 16-3. Mickey ended the game with five RBIs—a feat that had only been accomplished by three other players in a World Series game. Mickey's two home runs increased his total World Series homer count to 13, just two behind the record held by Babe Ruth.

After the game, Pirate manager Danny Murtaugh was still thinking about Mickey's two blasts. He marveled to reporters, "Those two by Mickey were two of the hardest hit balls I've ever witnessed."

Meanwhile, in the Yankees dressing room, Mickey downplayed his two homers saying, "I wish I could have saved them for a time when they meant something—but in a 16-3 ball game. ... What in hell do two homers mean when the team scores 16 runs? Bob Turley did the real work. My homers didn't amount to a row of beans. My biggest day in a Series? Hell, no! I've hit homers that have won some Series games. They were much bigger as far as I'm concerned. I'm not kicking myself, though. It's better than what I did yesterday."

Reporters began asking Mickey if he thought he could break Babe Ruth's World Series home-run record of 15. Mickey replied, "I feel better than I have in years—no leg problems at all. But if I'm to get three more home runs, I'm afraid I'll have to get them right-handed. I can't hit a barn door left-handed. I do not know what's the matter. I have lost my confidence from that side."

Reporters from *The Tribune* went outside the ballpark to measure the exact distance of Mickey's second and longest blast of the day. Outside, just behind center field, patrolman Arthur McBride of the Pittsburgh police pointed his nightstick to the exact spot the ball landed—it had bounced off a tree into the hands of a departing fan. The distance from home plate to the point of impact was carefully calculated to be 478 feet.

As the Yankees got on their bus after the game, manager Casey Stengel was still talking to reporters about his prodigy, Mickey Mantle. He boasted, "I am more amazed about that fellah every day. You seen that one he hit over the center-field fence today. You've seen some of the left-handed shots he has made in Yankee Stadium. Now I tell you what amazes me so much; that fellah does all this on one leg. You noticed how that right knee is always wrapped. He plays on one leg. Only one leg, yet you've seen he plays in all the games, and even the doubleheaders."

After a travel day, the Yankees and Pirates squared off for Game 3 at Yankee Stadium on October 8. Herbert Hoover and Prime Minister Nebru of India were among the 70,001 fans packed into the "House that Ruth Built." The pitching matchup featured two left-handed pitchers. The Yankees sent veteran Whitey Ford to the mound, while the Pirates called on Wilmer Mizell whom they had acquired in mid-season from the St. Louis Cardinals. Newly retired Boston Red Sox legend Ted Williams tossed out the first pitch of the game.

Ford pitched a masterful shutout, only yielding four hits to the Pirates. The Yankees' offensive assault began in the bottom of the first inning, picking up right where it had left off in Pittsburgh. After singles by Bob Cerv, Mickey Mantle, Moose Skowron, and Elston Howard—plus a walk to Gil McDougald—the Bronx Bombers had two quick runs and the bases loaded. Bobby Richardson capped the inning off with a grand-slam home run, giving the Yankees a dominating 6-0 lead after only one inning.

Mickey singled again in the second inning off Fred Green, but his biggest blow came in the fourth inning when the Yankees tallied four more runs. With two outs and Whitey Ford on second base,

Mickey was batting right-handed against Pirates pitcher Green. Green's first offering was a knee-high fastball. Mickey slashed it deep into left center field, over the fence at the 402-foot sign over the visitor's bullpen, and careening into the spectators in the lower stands at some 425 feet from home plate. Mickey's blast was his 14th World Series home run, and it gave the Yankees an 8-0 lead.

Later in the second inning, Bobby Richardson hit a bases-loaded single, driving in two runs. Richardson now had six RBIs in the game, which established a new World Series record. When the smoke cleared after the fourth inning, the Yankees led the Pirates by the score of 10-0, which would prove to be the final score. In the fifth inning, Mickey hit a line drive that bounced into the right-field pavilion for a ground-rule double while batting left-handed off George Witt. He ended the day going 4-for-5 with two runs and two RBIs. His four hits in the game tied the record for most hits in one Series game.

In the dressing room, Mickey discussed his fourth-inning blast with reporters. "It was a fast ball, knee high, and I knew I hit it good enough to go out. In fact, I hit that one harder than I did the two in Pittsburgh the other day." Mickey then discussed his left-handed hitting woes as he said, "Let's face it, I just can't hit good from the left side. I haven't been able to do that since I hurt my right shoulder in the 1957 World Series."

After the first three Series games, the Yankees had an amazing team batting average of .397, and had out-scored the Pirates 30-9 in addition to out-hitting them 48-25. After their second straight crushing defeat of the Pirates, the Yankees became an unprecedented 5-1 favorite to beat the Bucs. The odds were so lopsided that some bookmakers stopped taking bets on the Series.

The Pirates out-hit the Yankees for the first time in Game 4 by 8-7 while edging out the Bronx Bombers by the score of 3-2. Mantle was 0-for-3 in the game with two strikeouts as he batted left-handed against right-handed pitchers Vern Law and Roy Face in front of 67,812 onlookers. The key play in the game came in the seventh inning. The Yankees were batting with one out and runners on first and second base, with the Pirates leading by the score of 3-

2 when Bob Cerv smashed a drive to deep right center field. Bill Virdon and Roberto Clemente frantically raced back to the wall. Virdon made a spectacular leaping catch for the second out, and the Yankee rally came to an abrupt end. The Series was now tied at two games each.

Game 5 was played on October 10 and proved to be another closely contested game. The Bucs defeated the Yankees by the score of 5-2. The Pirates seemed to have finally figured the secret of how to keep Mickey in check—they walked him three times. It was revealed after the game that Mantle had played despite a groin injury that he sustained in previous game.

The Series moved back to Pittsburgh for Game 6 with the Yankees down three games to two. Casey Stengel called on his left-handed ace Whitey Ford to pitch this crucially important game. Ford had shutout the Pirates in Game 3 so Stengel was hoping for a repeat performance from him. The Pirates skipper Danny Murtaugh sent Bob Friend to the mound to try to close out the World Series with a victory.

The Yankees returned to their winning ways, defeating the Bucs in front of 38,580 Pirate fans. Whitey Ford duplicated his masterful Game 3 performance by shutting out the Pirates again by the score of 12-0, and holding them to just seven hits that were all singles. Mickey was 1-for-4 with two RBIs despite his nagging groin injury. He was walked once, which set a new record of being walked eight times in a World Series.

With the Series tied at three games apiece, the stage was set for the decisive Game 7. Nobody could have anticipated the drama that was about to unfold. The game, witnessed by 36,683 fans, was simply one of the most exciting finishes in World Series history.

When Bob Turley arrived at the ballpark for Game 7 and opened his locker, he found a brand-new baseball resting in his shoe—that was Casey Stengel's way of telling a pitcher that he was starting. Stengel would often avoid telling a pitcher he was starting until the day of the game. Usually the starting pitcher had a good idea he would be pitching, but he never officially knew until he arrived at the ballpark and looked in his locker. Whitey Ford, the winner of

Games 3 and 6, was the Yankees pitcher with the best record; but he had pitched the previous day. Therefore, Stengel banked all of his World Series chips on the only other Yankee pitcher who had a victory in the Series. The Pirates pinned their World Series hopes on Vern Law, who was the winner of Game 1 and Game 4 of this Series.

The Bucs took a quick lead in the bottom of the first inning on a two-run home run by first baseman Rocky Nelson. They added two more runs in the second inning on three singles and a walk, which gave them a 4-0 lead over the Yankees. Vern Law dominated the Yankee hitters through the first four innings by yielding only two hits. Hector Lopez put the Yankees in the hit column, singling with two out in the third inning. The Yankees' next hit came in the fourth inning on a single by Mickey Mantle. The Pirates appeared to be coasting to victory with their 4-0 lead as the game entered the top of the fifth inning. Yankee lefty reliever Bobby Shantz, who entered the game to start the third inning, had effectively quelled the Pirate hitters. Shantz's strong performance stopped the bleeding long enough for the Bronx Bombers to begin their counterattack.

Moose Skowron started the fifth inning with a home run to reduce the Yankee deficit to 4-1. The Yankees tallied four more times in the sixth inning. Richardson singled, Kubek walked, and Mickey hit a single that drove in Richardson. Yogi Berra hit a three-run homer to give the Yankees the lead for the first time in the game. In the eighth inning, Casey's crew gave him two insurance runs as they padded their lead to 7-4. The Yankee pitchers were now just six outs away from giving Stengel his eighth World Series championship.

Bobby Shantz, who had been nearly flawless in his first five innings, was about to experience a severe change in his luck. With the Pirates batting in the bottom of the eighth, Gino Cimoli pinch hit for Roy Face and singled. Bill Virdon then hit what appeared to be a routine double-play ball to shortstop Tony Kubek. Just as the ball bounced in front of Kubek, it hit a rock in the infield dirt that changed its trajectory upward. Kubek had no time to react to the freak bounce. The ball struck him solidly in the Adam's apple as Virdon raced to first base for a single. While the team doctor attended to Kubek, who was laying on the ground coughing and spitting up blood, his teammates paced around nervously. Kubek's injury was so severe that he had to leave the game and be taken to a hospital.

That play was crucially important because instead of there being two outs and nobody on base, there were no outs, and runners were at first and second base. The Bucs took advantage of the bad bounce by scoring two runs on consecutive singles by Dick Groat and Roberto Clemente, which made the score 7-6. Pirate catcher Hal Smith was the next batter, and Jim Coates had a 2-2 count on him. The Yankees were one strike away from getting out of the inning and preserving their lead. Smith hit the next pitch over the left centerfield wall for a three-run home run to cap off a five-run outburst by the Bucs. They now held a lead of 9-7 as the game went into the ninth inning.

Bobby Richardson and pinch hitter Dale Long started the ninth inning by hitting singles. Roger Maris then fouled out. Mickey Mantle came to the plate for the fifth time of the game and batting right handed off lefty pitcher Harvey Haddix. Mickey was 2-for-4 in this game with two singles. He kept the Yankee rally going by hitting his third single of the game and driving in Richardson. Yogi Berra drove in the tying run on a groundout to first base before the rally came to an end. The score was now 9-9. The Yankees were confident, after coming from behind twice, that the game was theirs to win. Unfortunately, Bill Mazeroski hit a dramatic lead-off home run in the bottom of the ninth to give the Bucs the world championship.

Looking at the statistics for the Series, it seems impossible that the Yankees lost the Series. They had a team batting average of .338 compared to the Pirates' .256. The Yankees had out-scored the Bucs in the Series 55-27, out-hit them 91-60, and out-homered them 10-4. A total of 67 World Series records fell, and 27 more were tied during this Series—the Yankees had been involved in 87 of those new or tied records.

The Yankee players were shocked and devastated as they showered, but none more than Mickey Mantle. He had given his all in this Series offensively and defensively. He had 10 hits in 25 at-bats for a .400 batting average and an amazing .800 slugging percentage.

He also had hit three home runs, driven in 11 runs, and was walked eight times, which set a new World Series record. Mickey sat dejectedly in his locker. His eyes were wet and red as he tried vainly to brush away the tears. He spoke in an almost inaudible voice as he tried his best to respond to reporters. Here is a conversation that occurred between Mickey and a reporter.

Mickey: "How's Tony? They tell me his windpipe is broken."

Reporter: "No, it isn't broken, but there's internal bleeding. They've taken Kubek to a hospital."

Mantle: "I sure hope he's all right. He's a good kid."

Reporter: "You're pretty good yourself. You played a tremendous series, probably your best."

Mickey: "But we lost, that's all that counts. I never thought we would. We had it won, too. We got nobody to blame but ourselves. Years from now all they'll know is that we lost."

In his book *The Mick*, he wrote:

> In the locker room, all of us are wandering around in a trance, muttering, 'What happened?' I'm slumped on a stool, feeling so low I can hardly peel off my uniform. In all my World Series experience, that was the one time when I really thought the better team had lost.

Merlyn Mantle recalled Mickey's devastation vividly. "After the 1960 World Series, I was with Mickey on the airplane home and he cried all the way. He just could not stand to lose. He was devastated. He wanted to win. He didn't get over it for half the winter."

Tony Kubek remembered Mickey's anguish many years later. "In 1960, we lost the World Series in seven games to the Pittsburgh Pirates. Mickey was a hard loser and, also, a softy—he cried unashamedly. Several days after the defeat, Mickey called to see how I was doing. He was still down from the loss, but especially sad for Bobby Richardson, who was the MVP of that series. Mickey knew Bobby couldn't enjoy that award as much because we had lost. He always thought more about his teammates than himself."

Touching All the Bases

The Pirate players each received $8,417 as the winners' share of the World Series. The Yankee players each received $5,214 as the losers' share.

Roger Maris edged out Mickey Mantle for the American League MVP Award. Maris had received 225 votes to Mantle's 222.

Bobby Richardson was awarded the World Series MVP Award. It was the first time in World Series history that a player from the losing team was voted the MVP, and it has never happened again since.

In a 1968 interview, Willie Mays had this to say about Mickey's 1960 World Series performance: "[Mickey] didn't just beat pitchers, he broke their hearts. He hit two home runs off Fred Green in the 1960 World Series, and somehow Green was never that good of a pitcher again."

The *Guinness Book of World Records* shows that Mickey owns the record for the longest measured home run. It was hit in Detroit on September 10, 1960, and the ball is on record as having traveled 634 feet.

Chapter Sixteen

1 ARM, 2 HOMERS, 3-GAME SWEEP

Nineteen sixty-one was a historic year in several ways: April 17 newspaper headlines read, "Bay of Pigs Landing is Fiasco"; on May 5, the headlines read, "Alan Shepard first U.S. man in space", as both the Cold War and the "race to space" escalated between the United States and Russia. The 1961 baseball season proved to be a much needed escape for the country—it will always be remembered as one of the most exciting in the history of the game.

Ralph Houk replaced Casey Stengel as skipper of the Yankees beginning with the 1961 season. Houk immediately designated Mickey Mantle as the team leader. "I never believed in captains," said Ralph Houk, "but you do need leaders. I always was a Mantle man. Who wouldn't be? After I got the job, I went to Mickey and said, 'You're the leader of this ball club.' I did it because of his talent and his competitiveness. He wanted to win so bad."

From the very start of the 1961 season, Mickey Mantle and Roger Maris were clouting home runs at a torrid pace. (The Yankees won 10 of their first 16 games—seven of those were decided by the mighty bat of Mickey Mantle.) Fans and sportswriters began talking about the possibility of one or both of the men breaking the season home-run record of 60 home runs, which had been set in 1927 by the greatest, purest Yankee of all, George Herman "Babe" Ruth. Maris was not viewed as a pure Yankee because he had played for the

Cleveland Indians and Kansas City Athletics before the Yankees acquired him for the 1960 season. On the other hand, Mickey was viewed as a pure Yankee because he had played his entire ten-year career with the Bronx Bombers. Thus, when Yankees fans had to make a choice as to whom they would root for, that choice was overwhelmingly Mickey Mantle.

But the season would mark another important milestone for Mickey Mantle. It would mark the end of the boos and the beginning of the cheers.

In his first 10 major league seasons, Yankees fans regularly booed Mickey because, in their eyes, he had failed to live up to their expectations as the next Babe Ruth, Lou Gehrig, or Joe DiMaggio. Clete Boyer explained it this way, "Part of the reason for the booing Mickey took was that Casey had built him up so high. No matter how hard he tried or how much he did, he could never reach that potential. Nobody could."

Two famous sportscasters tried to rationalize the ridicule that befell Mickey. Mel Allen said, "The unfortunate thing about Mickey is that he followed DiMag' in centerfield. No matter who played centerfield after DiMaggio—that person would be booed. Fans resented perhaps that Mantle was supposed to be another DiMaggio. DiMaggio fans believed nobody could ever be another DiMaggio."

"Now Mantle is great," Red Barber observed, "but when he does not hit a home run people are mad. There's only one way to answer the fan. And that's with your bat. Should Mantle get hot for two weeks or so, then the booing will all be over."

Even with Mickey winning the Triple Crown in 1956 and being voted the American League Most Valuable Player in 1956 and 1957, the relentless boo birds continued. Casey Stengel didn't understand the incessant catcalls that Mickey received. Stengel commented during the 1952 season, "Only a month ago, they tried to boo my kid right outta town. Right here at Yankee Stadium, where I never thought I'd ever see it, they tried to boo him back to the bench. He doesn't have to make a bad peg or anything to get booed. He can do more things better than anybody else, but they give it to him, anyway. It's not right."

But all that was to change in late 1961.

The fans weren't the only ones who took sides—the players had opinions as well. According to Clete Boyer, "Truthfully, the players were all pulling for Mickey against Roger when they were both going after Ruth's record because Mickey was 'the Yankees.'" Moose Skowron described the feelings of the rest of the players: "I didn't give a darn who broke the record. I mean, as teammates we went out for one thing, and that was to win a pennant and participate in the World Series. I would say that the majority of our teammates—Mickey was the guy that hit the long ball, and we were pushing for Mickey Mantle to break Babe Ruth's record. Mickey got hurt, and all of a sudden the tide changed, and Roger started hitting home runs and everybody was hoping that Roger would break the record. Here's a guy that went through a lot of pressure. He was a great friend of mine. He was a great competitor, a great base runner, a great outfielder."

Roger Maris praised Mickey during the heat of the home-run race as he said, "Can you imagine what it means to have a Mantle on your side? I hope he hits a home run every time up—It helps me." Maris later added, "He's just about the best all-around ballplayer there is … period. When have you ever seen a better switch hitter with such power? He's also a great fielder and a helluva good base runner, although he doesn't think so himself. And he's got guts—the way he plays most of his games all bandaged up amazes me."

There was one very important person in baseball who didn't want either Mickey Mantle or Roger Maris to break the Babe's record—baseball commissioner Ford Frick. Nineteen sixty-one was the year in which the American League expanded from eight teams to 10 by adding the Minnesota Twins and the Los Angeles Angels. In order to re-balance the number of times each team played each other, the 154-game schedule was increased by eight games to a 162-game schedule. Frick was concerned that the extra eight games might allow players to break the home-run record that was previously set in 154 games. Therefore, on July 17, in order to protect Ruth's record, Frick issued the following ruling:

> Any player who may hit more than 60 home runs during his club's first 154 games would be recognized as having established a new record. However, if the player does not hit more than 60 until after his club has played 154 games, there would have to be some distinctive mark in the record books to show that Babe Ruth's record was set under a 154-game schedule and the total or more than 60 was compiled while a 162-game schedule was in effect. We also would apply the same reasoning if a player should equal Ruth's total of 60 in the first 154 games, he would be recognized as tying Ruth's record. If in more than 154 games, there would be a distinction in the record book.

As if the Ford Frick ruling was not controversial enough, the press tried to make a story about a feud between Mickey and Roger. The fact was that Mickey and Roger voluntarily roomed together in Queens along with Bob Cerv. The Yankees assigned roommates when the team traveled, but players could room with whomever they wished while staying in New York. Yankee catcher Yogi Berra also added, "Mickey and Roger were fighting for the home-run championship. You know a lot of people ask, 'Were you jealous of them?' Well heck no, we were pulling for both of them. They'd win games for us. Mickey never had no jealousy against Roger, and Roger didn't have it against Mantle. We were all pulling together."

"I think what I remember most," recalls Bob Turley, "is that when you start around August 1, until the end of the season, that's when Roger and Mickey were battling head to head to see who was going to hit over 60 home runs. And the crowds—everywhere we went there wasn't a ballpark that wasn't sold out. There wasn't a hotel that wasn't sold out. Fact is, we were flying towards the end of the season and when we would fly there would be two planes behind us. Two chartered planes, the press and TV people that were covering it. And then we'd come into the clubhouse after a ballgame, there'd be 25 ballplayers, but there'd be 100 press people in there. We didn't have a moment's peace to ourselves. We'd have to go to our rooms just to get away because everybody was looking for a special story. It was excitement time, like a World Series, all that last two months."

When the second-place Detroit Tigers came to Yankee Stadium for a three-game series beginning Friday, September 1, the eyes of a nation where glued on Mickey Mantle and Roger Maris. At the time, the Yankees held a narrow one-and-a-half-game lead over the Tigers for the American League title. Maris was leading the major leagues in home runs with 51, while hitting a modest .271. Mickey had 48 homers with a very respectable .324 batting average. The home-run lead had already exchanged hands between Roger and Mickey six times. The entire nation—and to a large degree, the world—was enthralled with the home-run race, which was going into the home stretch.

In the first game of the series, Mantle and Maris both went 0-for-4, but the Yankees managed to edge the Tigers by the score of 1-0 on a great combination pitching performance by Whitey Ford, Bud Daley, and Luis Arroyo. The win increased the Yankees' lead over the Tigers to two and a half games.

Game 2 pitted Yankees hurler Ralph Terry against Tiger right-handed ace pitcher Frank Lary. In the first inning, the Tigers jumped out to a quick 2-0 lead. In the bottom of that frame, Mantle walked and later scored to bring the Bronx Bombers within one run of the Tigers. In the fourth inning, Mickey showed that winning is more important than trying to hit another home run. He perfectly executed a squeeze bunt to score Roger Maris from third base and tie the score.

In the Yankees' sixth, with two outs, Roger Maris blasted his 52nd homer of the year to give the Yankees a 3-2 lead. Mickey then stepped up to the plate with intentions of going back-to-back with Roger in order to keep from falling further behind him in the heated home-run race. On a delivery from Lary, Mickey's body coiled and began its powerful swing. Halfway through the swing, Mickey realized the pitch was no good and tried to abort, but it was too late. The momentum of his powerful swing was headed in one direction while his body made a desperate attempt to put his arms in reverse. The result was similar to putting a car into reverse while traveling at a high speed. There was an explosion in his left forearm as a muscle painfully snapped. He was wrought with intense pain as he grimaced and gritted his teeth. Mickey could have easily taken himself out of the game at that point, but he finished the turn at-bat by grounding softly to second and, in disgust, did not run the ball out. The fans booed him because they didn't realize he was injured and thought he was just being lazy.

"They didn't understand," said manager Ralph Houk later. "If they did, they'd have cheered him. You gotta give Mantle lots of credit. He was in pain, and I was willing to take him out, but he volunteered to stay in there and play defense for me. He said he'd bunt the rest of the way, and that's what he did."

Mickey's next at-bat came in the eighth inning when the Yankees had just busted the game open by scoring four runs capped off with Roger Maris' 53rd homer of the season. The Yankees now led the Tigers by the score of 7-2. Mickey, still in much pain, did exactly as he had vowed to Houk he would do—he laid down a drag bunt to second base and beat it out for a single, but was stranded on first base as the Yankee rally later ended. The final score was 7-2.

After they learned about Mickey's injury, the New York press was writing him out of the home-run race, figuring he would be out for at least a week. "We'll have to wait until tomorrow to see," Gus Mauch, club trainer, said. "If he is able to play, he won't be able to swing hard."

Mantle sat somberly with his arm packed in ice and had very little to say. "They say it takes 24 hours sometimes to tell. It hurts now, but maybe by tomorrow it'll be all right. A muscle popped when I was batting in the sixth."

When reporters asked Houk what he planned to do without Mickey for the last game of the Detroit series, he shook his head and said, "Right now, I just don't know."

The next day, September 3, was the third and final game of the series with the Tigers. Houk did not have Mantle in the original lineup. Mickey went to Houk and said, "Play me." Houk, somewhat suspicious, asked Mickey, right there in the dressing room, to demonstrate that he could swing the bat. Mick picked up a bat, somehow concealed the pain and convinced Houk that he could swing. Mickey then went out and took batting practice with Houk watching closely. Finally, Houk said, "OK, you're playing." The stage was set for one of the most courageous performances in baseball history.

Yankee Stadium was packed with 55,676 fans, setting a new all-time record for the Stadium for a three-game series as the Yankees drew a total of 171,583 fans. The Tigers took a 1-0 lead off Bill Stafford in the first inning, but the Yankees stormed back in the bottom of the frame as Roger Maris lined a single to center field to start the rally. Mickey then stepped to the plate, batting lefty, using a bat that he borrowed from teammate Bob Cerv. Mickey normally used a 33-34 ounce bat, but wanted to use Cerv's heavier 36-ounce bat in order to force him to slow his swing down because of the pain in his forearm. Mickey took the first two pitches for balls. On the next pitch, Mickey swung and fouled back into the backstop. He must have been in intense pain because he went down on one knee, grimacing. Jim Bunning's next delivery was a ball outside. The fans grew impatient, and began to boo Bunning for pitching around Mickey. Mickey fouled the next pitch straight back to make the count full. Bunning's next pitch was a low fastball, and Mickey began his swing using his right arm to pull the bat through the strike zone, using his painful left arm to guide. With his right arm fully extended, the bat made perfect contact with the ball as it rocketed from his bat and headed to deep right field. The right fielder ran back to the warning track and then helplessly watched as the ball sailed into the stands approximately 400 feet from home plate. It was a two-run blast and his 49th homer of the season. On the very next pitch from Bunning, Yogi Berra also belted a homer to right field, giving the Bronx Bombers a 3-1 lead.

In the Yankees half of each inning, Mickey kept his left forearm packed in ice when he wasn't batting. The purpose of the ice was two-fold: it minimized additional swelling, and it numbed the pain. According to teammate Tony Kubek, "As the game went on, Mickey's arm seemed to get worse." Mickey struck out in his next two plate appearances in the fourth and sixth innings, and it looked like he would be done for the day.

Stafford was great for seven innings, but he had to leave in the top of the eighth. The sweltering heat had made him sick to his stomach. Houk then handed the ball to Luis Arroyo who gave up a run in the eighth, and two more in the top of the ninth to give the Tigers a 5-4 lead.

In the bottom of the ninth, Mickey stepped to the plate as the leadoff hitter to face 41-year-old right-handed sinker and knuckleball thrower Gerry Staley. Staley had begun the 1961 season with the Chicago White Sox and was later traded to the Kansas City Athletics before being acquired by the Tigers.

As the catcher made his throw down to second base, Mickey stepped into the batter's box. He must have been wondering if he had one good swing left. His teammates had to be asking themselves the same question after witnessing Mickey strike out in his last two at-bats. One the other hand, the fans were totally unaware of the pain that he was suffering or the ice treatments that he was taking between innings. Staley delivered his first pitch outside, and Mickey took it for ball one. On the next pitch, Mickey summoned every ounce of courage and strength as he launched his one-armed swing, again using his left arm purely for guiding the bat. For the second time of the day, his bat made perfect contact with the ball. The ball shot from his bat and headed deep right center field. The ball soared approximately 400 feet for his second homer of the day and 50th of the season.

Mickey's clutch homer (No. 370 of his career) was significant in that it tied the game at 5-5, but it also put him in eighth place in the all-time home run list. It put him two games ahead of Babe Ruth's home-run pace of 1927; and for the first time in the history of baseball, one team owned two sluggers of 50 or more home runs. A few batters later, Elston Howard would end the game with a dramatic two-out, towering walk-off three-run homer as the Yankees came back in the bottom of the ninth to hand the Tigers their third straight defeat at Yankee Stadium with a final score of 8-5. The win increased the Yankees' lead over the Tigers to a commanding four and a half games. The Yankees went on to win the next 10 games, giving them a 13-game winning streak as they ran away with the American League pennant.

After the game, Mickey was icing his forearm when he said, "Give the iceman an assist. The arm pained me considerably, especially when I swung and missed. The ice really helped between innings. I was trying to swing hard most of the time. But the times I did swing hard, I missed the ball. Both times I really tried to swing easy, the ball went out of the park."

An impressed Ralph Houk stated, "He's an amazing player and a superb competitor. I know very well he was in more pain than he cares to admit. For a guy who was hurting like that, he had one helluva day."

Mickey's arm significantly stiffened overnight. The next day, even after two hours of physiotherapy treatment before a doubleheader with the Washington Senators, he was unable to play. When the Yankee fans read about his injury, they realized that they had witnessed one of the most courageous efforts ever displayed in sports history.

For 11 seasons they had mercilessly booed Mickey Mantle, but his home-run streak and his appearance in the game changed their attitude. On September 8, the unjustified boos finally came to an end when Mickey his 52nd home run of the season. The Yankee Stadium fans actually stood up and gave him a thunderous ovation as he rounded the bases. Afterwards, a pleasantly surprised Mickey commented, "Those fans! They've changed. I never heard so much cheering in all my years with the club. For the first time, I felt like I was playing before a home crowd, before *our* fans. Before, it was like we were playing on the road. They've never been so good to me. It seems too nice."

Roger Maris acknowledged the favoritism to his teammate. "If that's the way it is, okay," he said. "At least they finally appreciate what a great thing they have in Mickey."

Years later, Mantle said, "After Roger beat me in the home run race in 1961, I could do no wrong. Everywhere I went, I got standing ovations. All I had to do was walk out on the field. Hey … what the hell? It's a lot better than having them boo you."

Touching All the Bases

Mickey hit his 1,000th career hit—a home run—on July 2 at Yankee Stadium.

Roger Maris hit is 61st home run on the last day of the season (the 162nd game). Therefore, due to the Ford Frick ruling, he was not considered to have broken Babe Ruth's record and an asterisk was put by Maris' feat in the record books.

The book *Mickey Mantle: The Indispensable Yankee* by Dick Schaap was released in 1961.

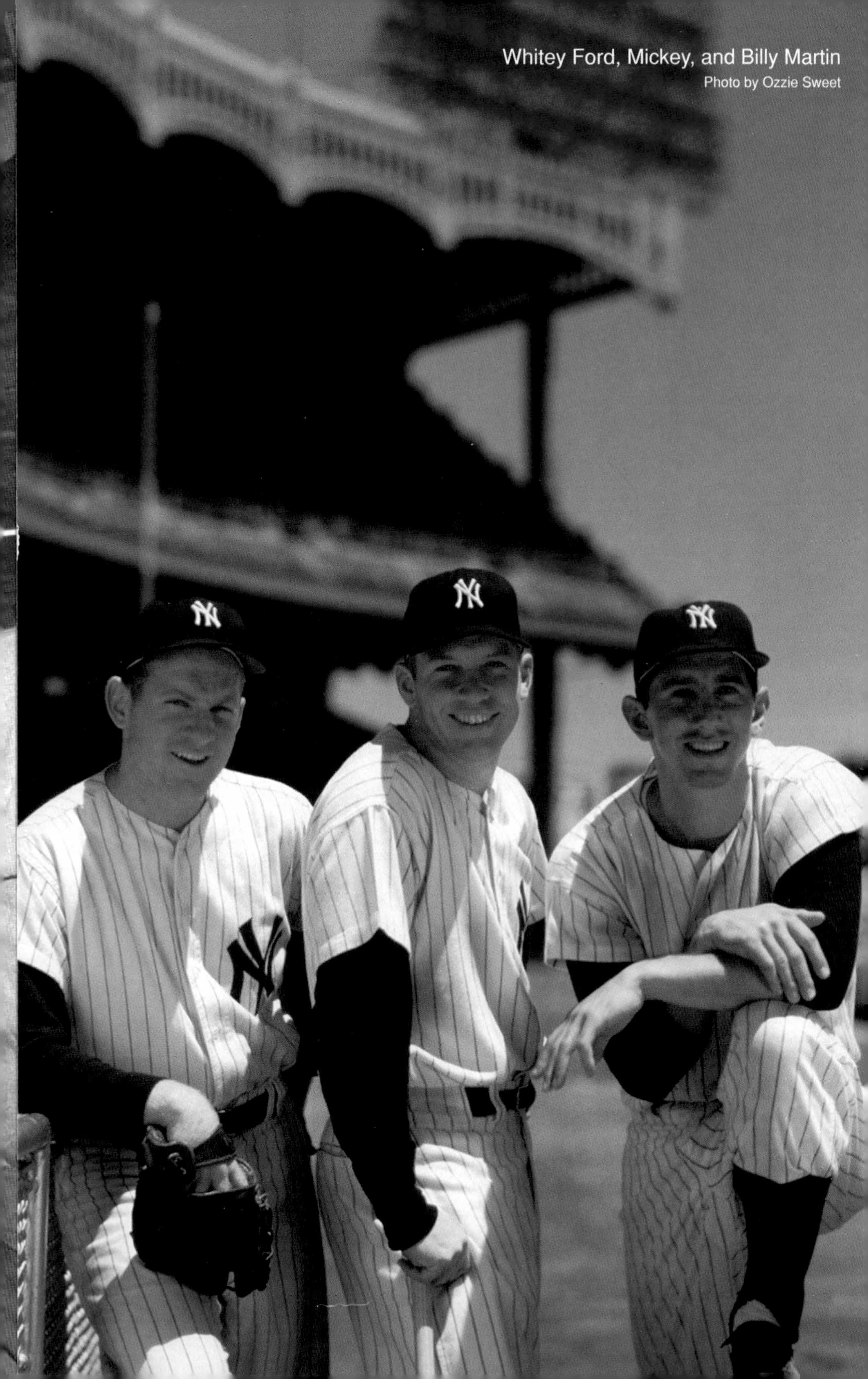
Whitey Ford, Mickey, and Billy Martin
Photo by Ozzie Sweet

WCBS
CHICAGO

Mickey with Mickey Jr.
Photo by Ozzie Sweet

Mickey and Billy Martin
Photo by Ozzie Sweet

Photo by Frank Bauman

Photo by Frank Bauman

Photos by Ozzie Sweet

Photos by Ozzie Sweet

Chapter Seventeen

BLEEDING SINGLE

In September of 1961, the intensity of the home-run race between Mickey Mantle and Roger Maris reached a fever pitch as they neared Babe Ruth's record of 60 home runs in one season.

"We needed special cops to escort us in and out of the ballparks," recalled Mickey. "We couldn't enter a dining room or a hotel lobby without having a horde of writers, photographers, TV and radio people, everybody breathing down on our necks. The tension was unbelievable."

The immense stress took a toll on Mickey and Roger. They never had privacy; different reporters were constantly asking them the same questions; someone always wanted an autograph; and—worst of all—Maris was receiving hate mail and death threats at an alarming rate. The pressure had been so intense that Maris had started losing clumps of his hair.

On September 10, after a doubleheader with the Cleveland Indians, the total attendance for the year at Yankee Stadium was 1,657,031 people. This was the highest total in 10 years, most likely caused by the home-run race. On September 14, after going 0-for-7 in a doubleheader against the Chicago White Sox, Mickey conceded his race to beat Ruth's record. He was stuck at 53 homers after 147 games, with only seven games left to break the record according to Ford Frick's guidelines.

"I don't see how I can make it now. When we came to Chicago, I decided I'd have a chance if I could hit a couple here. They stopped me cold. I haven't got a chance now—even in 162 games. I'm just plain tired. I haven't got much pep anymore," Mickey had said after the second game of the doubleheader. He was physically and emotionally drained, and came down with a bad cold over the next couple of days.

On September 18, Ralph Houk decided to sideline Mickey for the four games in Baltimore. Mickey did get a pinch-hit appearance in the first game, but struck out. From Baltimore, the Yankees traveled to Boston for a short two-game series. Mickey somehow managed to play in both games. He was 2-for-4 in the first game, including a three-run homer—his 54th for the season. Mickey went 0-for-3 in the second game.

"When we left Boston, I think I was only like two home runs behind Maris, something like that," said Mickey. "And I had a real bad cold, in fact it was almost walking pneumonia. We took the train from Boston back to New York. On the way back, one of the people on our train told me he knew a doctor in New York that he thought could cure me since those antibiotics weren't doing me any good. So I go to this doctor and later on find out that they call him 'Dr. Feel-good'. I don't know what he gave me, but he gave me a shot in the hip and it was too high and it hit the bone. The next morning I woke up with a 104-degree temperature and I called Ralph and I told him I couldn't come to the ballpark."

The shot that Mickey had received developed into a bad abscess. As a result, he was admitted to Lenox Hill Hospital on September 28, to remove the abscessed tissue in his upper right hip. Johnny Blanchard remembered, "They cut a cross—a three-inch cut and then a three-inch cut across the other way. When it opened up, it opened up like a flower. They took Sulfur powder and sprinkled that in. It had to heal from the inside out. You couldn't stitch it together so they packed it with sulfur powder and gauze and then they put tape over it."

The extremely painful wound caused Mickey to miss the remaining five games of the season. He ended the season with a .317 batting average, 54 homers and 128 RBIs. Maris went on to clout his 61st home run during the last game of the regular season, thereby breaking Babe Ruth's record of 60 homers. Since it took Maris 162 games, Ford Frick enforced the asterisk besides Maris' feat in the record books. The Yankees, as a team, hit an amazing 240 home runs for a new major league record.

The Yankees finished the season in first place with 109 wins and 53 losses, eight games ahead of the second-place Detroit Tigers. They were now preparing for the upcoming World Series with the National League champions, the Cincinnati Reds, amid much concern about Mickey's playing condition. Mickey was no stranger to misfortune regarding his health at World Series time. Even though his efforts had been a huge factor in getting the Yankees to the Fall Classics, Mickey was forced to miss a significant portion of the 1951, 1955, and 1957 World Series contests due to injuries. Even though his status for the 1961 Series was in question, nobody—especially Mickey—was counting him out.

Mickey was released from Lennox Hill Hospital on Monday, October 2, just two days before the Series was set to begin in New York. He described his treatment: "I thought they would just lance it. Instead they cut a hole so big you could put a baseball in it. The wound is still open. I was told it's nothing to worry about. It's not a matter of life and death. Under normal conditions, it would heal in two or three weeks once it has drained."

Mickey's illness had greatly weakened him, and he had lost five pounds. After suiting up and walking around the field Mickey said, "I'm weak, sore, and still in pain. I came here hoping to work out today, but I can't. If I feel Wednesday like I feel today, I don't see how I possibly can play."

On the same day, the Cincinnati Reds were working out when first baseman Gordon Coleman commented on right field in Yankee Stadium. "It looks real close, but I found out in practice that it takes a pretty good pop to put one in the seats. When somebody pointed out where Mantle hit the façade above the third deck it was hard for me to believe."

In the October 3 edition of the *Washington Post*, Bob Addle wrote, "Mantle is the untitled team leader. He is admired by his teammates for his courage in playing against tremendous physical odds, and they're a different ball club when he's not in there." Yankee catcher Elston Howard also voiced his feelings: "He'll play if he can walk. Nobody has the guts Mickey has. He's a player. He wants to play in this Series real bad." Unfortunately, by the time the World Series had started, Mickey still had no appetite and had lost a total of seven pounds. There was no way he could play.

Game 1 of the World Series was played in front of 62,397 fans at Yankee Stadium. Those fans paid $10.50 for box seats, $7.35 for reserved seats, $4.20 for standing room, and $2.10 for bleacher seats. Despite Mickey's absence, the Yankees won 2-0. Whitey Ford had pitched his third consecutive World Series shutout backed by home runs from Moose Skowron and Elston Howard. Ford now had his sights set on Babe Ruth's record of consecutive scoreless World Series innings of 29 ⅔. Whitey was just three innings away from the record.

Game 2, also at Yankee Stadium, drew 63,083 fans as the Reds bounced back to defeat the Yankees by a score of 6-2. Ralph Terry took the loss for the Bronx Bombers while Joey Jay picked up the win for the Reds. The Series was now even at one game each as the teams moved to Crosley Field in Cincinnati for Games 3, 4, and 5. Crosley Field, with a seating capacity of approximately 30,000, was probably one of the most unique ballparks in the major leagues. The dimensions were 328 feet down the left-field line, 390 feet to center field, and a long 366 feet down the right-field line. The unusual characteristic of the field was the lack of a warning track, which had been replaced by an incline. The ground level at the fence was approximately five feet higher than the rest of the playing field. About 25 feet from the fence, all around the outfield perimeter, the grass sloped up toward the fence. The slope not only made catching balls more difficult, it also made throwing balls from the hill (or terrace as they called it) a challenge.

Bleeding Single

The day before Game 3 at Crosley Field, the Yankees worked out and became familiar with the sloping outfield. Mickey drew a lot of attention from the fans and players as he stepped into the batting cage to take batting practice from the left-handed side of the plate. He was wearing a thick bandage that was about eight inches by eight inches to cover his open wound. The first swing caused him great pain as he stepped away from the plate, gritted his teeth, bent over, and banged his bat on home plate for a few seconds before stepping back in to hit. He took 13 swings, and hit six of those over the fence for home runs. As Mickey stepped out of the cage, the roughly 2,000 fans who had shown up early to watch batting practice erupted in applause for his gutsy performance.

Teammate Bobby Richardson jokingly challenged Mickey to a home-run contest for Cokes. Mantle just smiled and said, "I'll take you on next spring, but not today."

Moose Skowron recalled, "Mickey was taking batting practice at Crosley Field, and the blood was coming out of his pants. You can see it on the World Series film. You could put a golf ball in that [abscess]. Mickey knew I took biology in college and whenever they changed his bandage, he would tell the trainer, 'I want Moose to come and see this.' So I'd go in there and see it. The infected area was about the size of a golf ball and I'll never forget that. That's courage."

Game 3 was the first World Series game played at Crosley Field in 21 years. Bill Stafford took the mound for the Yankees, and Bob Purkey for the Reds. The game was witnessed by 32,589 fans who saw Johnny Blanchard contribute a clutch two-out pinch-hit home run in the eighth inning. It was Blanchard's first World Series home run of his career. Roger Maris then hit the go-ahead solo shot in the top of the ninth to give the Yankees a 3-2 victory. Yankee reliever Luis Arroyo picked up the win, while Bob Purkey took the loss for the Reds. Despite Mickey's pain, he started the game in center field and was given a nice ovation from the crowd as he stepped up to the plate in the second inning. Mickey flew out to left center field and ended the day going 0-for-4, with two fly outs and two strikeouts. The Yankees now had a two game-to-one lead in the Series as they looked toward Game 4.

During batting practice for Game 4 on October 8, Mickey drew another big round of applause from the Cincinnati fans, hitting a home run on virtually every swing. Houk had Mickey in the starting lineup for the second game in a row, once again playing centerfield and batting cleanup. Prior to the game, Yankee physician Dr. Sidney Gaynor described how he prepped Mickey for the game: "I put on an extra-heavy dressing to prevent the blood from seeping through. It's not a bad situation, but it's very painful."

Cincinnati's lefty Jim O'Toole was on the mound for the Reds while Whitey Ford was taking the mound for the Yankees with his sights set on breaking Babe Ruth's consecutive scoreless innings pitched in the World Series. With the Reds batting in the bottom of the first inning with two out, Vada Pinson hit a fly ball to center field. Mickey made the catch for the out, but showed obvious signs of painful distress. His first at-bat came in the second inning, with nobody on base and no outs in a scoreless game. He swung hard and slapped a ground ball to third base. On his way to first base, he pulled up suddenly, hobbling the rest of the way. Later, Mickey revealed that he had aggravated the injury on that swing. Dr. Gaynor explained that Mickey's powerful swing had stretched the granulation tissues surrounding the wound and forced some bleeding.

After Whitey Ford completed his third scoreless inning of the day, he had increased his consecutive World Series scoreless streak to 30 innings, thereby breaking Babe Ruth's record, which had stood since 1918. There was no score for either team starting the fourth inning when Maris led off with a walk for the Yankees. Mickey stepped to the plate batting right-handed. O'Toole positioned himself on the left side of the pitching rubber for the purpose of giving him a better throwing angle to the right-handed hitter. Mickey worked the count to two balls and one strike. O'Toole then took his next sign from catcher Darrell Johnson, checked Maris at first base, and then delivered a belt-high pitch to Mickey, who banged a sharp liner between Vada Pinson and Wally Post into deep left center field. Maris raced to third base on the play, but Mickey hobbled to first base with only a single. Ralph Houk could see blood seeping through Mickey's pants, so he sent Hector Lopez in to run for him. Elston Howard grounded into a double play, but Maris scored the first run of the game, giving the Yankees the early 1-0 lead.

Whitey Ford recalled Mickey coming to bat, "When he got up to hit that inning, I saw the blood on the bench. I didn't say anything because I knew how badly Mickey wanted to play." Teammate Johnny Blanchard also recalled the moment, "Oh gosh, about the fourth inning, he was in a lot of pain, but everything was all right. And then the blood spot came out on the back of his pants. Well, he didn't know it. It got to be the size of a silver dollar. Houk spotted that and said, 'Mick, I'm gonna have to take you out. You're bleeding.' Mick said, 'What are you talking about?' So Houk showed him the blood. Mickey just stared at him and after a moment said, 'Ok'. Maris then went to center and Lopez went to right."

The one run in the fourth inning would prove to have been enough, but the Yankees added another in the fifth inning, two in the sixth, and three more in the seventh inning to complete a 7-0 shutout of the Reds. Whitey Ford was removed in the sixth inning, after topping Ruth's record by amassing 32 scoreless World Series innings. The victory gave the Yankees a commanding 3-1 lead over the Reds. The odds had the Yankees as 12-to-1 favorites to win the Series.

After the game, Mickey told reporters, "I could see the blood coming through the uniform and I knew I had to quit. I just couldn't play anymore. It hurt like the devil. It felt bad all day. I guess I shouldn't have played at all, but I kept thinking it might get better. But it got worse instead. When I ran to first base on that ground ball in the second inning, I knew I couldn't finish the game. I told Houk the pain was getting worse. He said he would let me bat once more and then take me out even if I got a hit." When asked about his current playing status, Mickey said, "It still hurts. I don't think I'll play any more, but if Houk wants to use me as a pinch hitter, I'll be ready. It's a shame. You play all year, you play even when you don't feel good, just to get into the World Series, and then you can't play in it."

Manager Ralph Houk said, "I consider Mantle's hit the turning point of the game. It was very important because it got us that first big run. Mickey's right hip was hurting so badly I had to take him out. It hurt more than it ever did before."

The Yankees won Game 5 by the score of 13-5, regaining their title as world champions. Johnny Blanchard batted cleanup for the first, and only, time of his career. He responded favorably by going 3-for-4 with a home run and three RBIs.

After that game, Elston Howard walked into the clubhouse where Mantle was face down, receiving treatment for his open abscess. He said four simple words to that reflected the feelings of the entire Yankee team: "You're a great man."

The unequaled courage that Mickey demonstrated toward the end of the 1961 season, and his courageous performance in the 1961 World Series endeared Mickey to the Yankee fans and his teammates for the rest of his life.

Touching All the Bases

The same day that Mickey was released from Lennox Hill Hospital, he and Roger Maris participated in the taping of the *Perry Como Kraft Music Hall* show. The show would air on October 4, 1961.

Mickey's salary in 1961 was $70,000, while Roger Maris earned $37,500. Mickey and each of his Yankee teammates received a $7,389 bonus for winning the World Series. Each Cincinnati Red received $5,356 as the losers' share.

Mickey, Roger Maris and Bob Cerv shared a $250-a-month apartment in Jamaica, Long Island, for the 1961 season.

In 1961, Mickey led the American League with 132 runs.

In the September 20 edition of *The Los Angeles Times*, it was pointed out that based on age, Mickey was 99 homers ahead of Babe Ruth's lifetime homer pace. By the Babe's 30th birthday, he had hit 274 home runs. Mickey would not turn 30 until October 20, but he already had 373 home runs.

Chapter Eighteen

COMPETITIVE COMPULSION

On February 20 of 1962, John Glenn became the first American to orbit the Earth, completing three revolutions. By May 17, the Yankees' season was 39 games old and they were completing great feats as well. After beating the Boston Red Sox, 2-1, the Bronx Bombers were tied with the Cleveland Indians for first place. The Minnesota Twins were in third place, but only by one-half game. Mickey Mantle was already having a stellar season, hitting .326 with three doubles, one triple, seven home runs, 17 RBIs, and an impressive slugging percentage of .628. The guys in pinstripes had just returned to Yankee stadium to face the Minnesota Twins for an important four-game series.

At 8 p.m. on May 18 at Yankee Stadium, a crowd of 20,112 fans gathered to watch the Yankees take on the Twins. With the pitching of Whitey Ford, the Yankees held on to a slim 3-2 lead after six innings. Harmon Killebrew soon erased that lead when he slammed a two-run homer in the top of the seventh to give the Twins a 4-3 lead. The Yankees had failed to score in the seventh and eighth innings. Going into the ninth, Yogi Berra was announced as a pinch hitter for Bobby Richardson. Tom Tresh was on deck, and Joe Pepitone was in the hole.

Berra grounded out to shortstop, followed by Tom Tresh who singled. Joe Pepitone then hit a 440-foot fly ball to deep center field where Bill Tuttle caught it for the second out. Tom Tresh taggedup and easily made it to second base on Pepitone's long out, but the Yankees were down to their last out with the tying run in scoring position. It was up to Mickey who stepped to the plate to bat left-handed off the righty Don Lee. Twins manager Sam Mele called a time out and went to the mound. He ended up calling on left-handed relief pitcher Dick Stigman to face the menacing Mickey Mantle.

Mickey's speed was legendary amongst baseball players. One year after injuring his knee in the 1951 World Series, he was clocked at 3.1 seconds from home plate to first base from the left side of the plate, and 3.4 seconds from the right side of the plate. In 1953, *The Sporting News* actually proposed that Mickey Mantle and Washington Senators speedy centerfielder Jim Busby compete in a 100-yard race as an attraction at the All-Star game that year. Both Busby and Mantle were willing, but manager Casey Stengel vetoed the idea saying, "I'm not running a track team. I know Mantle is fast enough for us around the bases. I don't want to prove anything by running him against another fella and maybe getting him hurt."

Then in 1959, Washington Senator pitcher Pedro Ramos outran Philadelphia Phillie Richie Ashburn by eight yards in a 70-yard race and immediately challenged Mickey Mantle. Again Stengel vetoed the idea. Ramos continued to challenge Mickey over the years. In 1961, when Casey Stengel was no longer the Yankee manager, Mickey called up Ramos and told him that he was ready to race provided there was a $1,000 purse. Ramos shot back quickly, "My manager, Sam Mele, won't let me run. Besides, I don't know where I'd get $1,000." Mantle was still extraordinarily fast, even after multiple leg injuries. So fast, in fact, that opposing infielders had little time to spare when Mickey hit a ground ball to them. This sense of urgency often forced infielders to rush a catch or a throw and end up making an error.

So, with two outs in the bottom of the ninth and the tying run on second base, Stigman delivered his pitch. Mickey swung and ripped a low line drive between shortstop and third base that looked like it would be a base hit. The Twins' shortstop, Zoilo Versalles, darted quickly to his right and made an outstanding backhanded grab as the ball took its first hop. In his haste to gather up the ball and make a quick throw, he momentarily bobbled it. Mantle, racing to first base, saw Versalles bobble the ball and sensed an opportunity to keep the game going, so he put on a last-second extra burst of speed. Mickey always ran at 100 percent, but when he really needed extra speed, he would bear down extra hard. The risk factor of sustaining another injury was always high when he ran all out, so he reserved the extra efforts for emergency situations such as this. About five steps short of first base, Mickey's right leg locked and he fell headlong to the ground, coming down hard on his left knee. He was out at first base and the game was over.

The crowd rose to its feet in shocked silence while the entire Yankee team quickly gathered around Mickey. A stretcher was brought out, but Mickey left the field with the help of two of his teammates. He was taken to Lenox Hill Hospital, where doctors determined that he had severely torn a muscle in his right upper thigh and strained ligaments behind his left knee. It was a hard loss for the Yankees. Not only had they lost their star center fielder for approximately four weeks, they also fell into third place behind the Indians and the Twins.

Before leaving for the hospital, Mantle recalled his ninth-inning ground ball saying, "I saw the shortstop was having trouble with the ball, and so I put on an extra burst of speed. I tried to stride and it pulled. It felt like somebody took a knife and stuck it in there. The leg was up in the air and it wouldn't go down."

Vic Power, the Twins' first baseman said, "If Mantle hadn't fallen, I don't know if we'd got him. It was going to be real close. Boy, he was coming! Really coming!"

Mickey had torn the adductor muscle leading from his upper right thigh to the groin area. He had also injured his left knee when it took the brunt of his fall. Nine days later, Mickey went to Clint Houy, trainer for the National Football League Dallas Cowboys, for a series of treatments to his thigh. Houy prescribed lots of heat, massage, and whirlpool; and estimated that Mickey would be able to play in about two to three weeks.

After splitting a doubleheader with the Minnesota Twins on May 30 (12 days after Mickey's injury), the Yankees had lost five of their last seven games. The reasons for their losses were twofold: the lack of timely hitting and inability to get pinch hits. The Yankee pinch hitters had a collective .070 batting average after going 3-for-43 during the season so far. Despite their losses, the Yankees were still just one-half game out of first place behind the Cleveland Indians; while the Minnesota Twins were just one-half game behind the Yankees. After the doubleheader, manager Ralph Houk discussed the fact that Mickey was going to be joining the team in Los Angeles for the series against the Angels: "Under no circumstances will I use Mantle, least of all as a pinch hitter, until I have been assured he has fully recovered. Much as we may need him, we're running no risks. He won't play until we're certain he's absolutely sound. Even having the guy around and just sitting on the bench is bound to pep up our fellows."

Houk was absolutely right. Mickey joined the team in Los Angeles on June 1 and actually took two sessions of batting practice, batting right-handed, and managed to belt two home runs into the left-field bleachers. Mickey commented after his batting practice, "I really only started walking around a couple of days ago. However, the legs are beginning to feel better, although I can't tell how much longer it will take before I can play. We'll just have to try it out slowly."

Having Mickey on the bench, and the thought of him playing soon energized the Bronx Bombers. They won six of their next seven games, regaining first place in the American League. The fans were missing Mickey too. By June 8, Mickey had received over 2,500 get-well messages.

On June 15, the Yankees traveled to Cleveland to play the Indians in an important four-game series. After the Yankees dropped the first game of the series, they were in a three-way tie for first place with the Cleveland Indians and the Minnesota Twins. Mickey was not in the starting lineup and was not anticipated to appear during the game. Since his injury on May 18, he had missed a total of 30 games.

In the second game of the series, the Indians had jumped out to a quick 6-0 lead in front of a home crowd of 50,254. The Yankees fought back as they scored two runs in the fourth, fifth, and seventh innings. The Indians scored an additional run, giving themselves a slim 7-6 lead. Johnny Blanchard and Roger Maris led the Yankee comeback by each hitting two-run homers.

Entering the top of the eighth inning, the Yankees were still trailing the Indians by the score of 7-6 and flirting with their second consecutive loss to the Tribe. A second loss would bump the Yankees to one game out of first place, and possibly put them into third place. Moose Skowron led off the inning by grounding out to third base for the first out. Hector Lopez then pinch hit for Joe Pepitone and promptly doubled to left field. Tom Tresh then worked Indians pitcher Bob Allen for a walk to put runners on first and second with one out. Yankees pitcher Marshall Bridges was due up next when Ralph Houk called on Mickey Mantle to pinch hit for him. Ralph Houk had been quoted numerous times over the past couple of weeks insisting that he would not use Mickey as a pinch hitter until he was absolutely sure that he was ready. Houk, feeling first place slipping away, turned to Mickey with the hope that after sitting out a full month he could somehow pull off a much needed miracle. Houk instructed Mickey, "Go on up and hit for Bridges. But if you hit it on the ground, don't bother to run. Give 'em the double play."

The Cleveland fans were shocked to see Mickey step out of the dugout with a bat in his hands, but they welcomed him with a warm round of applause. Mickey modestly touched his cap in response to the cheers. Indians manager Mel McGaha, feeling a potential threat and also sensing the urgency of the situation, went to the mound and replaced left-handed pitcher Bob Allen with right-handed reliever Gary Bell. The stage was set as Mickey dug into the batter's box from the left side of the plate.

Bell took his sign from catcher Johnny Romano and delivered his first pitch, which Mickey took for a called strike. Bell took his next sign and delivered the next pitch—a fastball. Mickey unleashed his powerful swing and connected solidly with the pitch. The ball soared approximately 450 feet over the railed fence in right center field for a home run. The ball landed in front of the Indians bullpen for a clutch three-run homer, which now gave the Yankees a 9-7 lead. Mickey was mobbed by his teammates as he returned to the dugout.

The Yankees eventually lost the game 10-9, but Mickey's performance added yet another exciting chapter to his legendary career. He would later recall his pinch-hit, clutch homer in his book, *The Mick*:

> I was out for a month. When I finally returned, it was to pinch hit in Cleveland. I got a long home run off Gary Bell, which put us ahead. The icing on the cake was hearing those fans cheering me around the bases. After that, Ralph Houk used me in a few more pinch-hitting roles. It's a hard job. You come in fresh off the bench, and there's only one chance to show yourself. You strike out, you're a bum. Get a base hit and win the game, you're a hero. No in-between.

By July 25, Mickey was hitting .342 and was obviously back to top form. Elston Howard praised him: "When Mickey's going good like he has, his actions kind of spill over on everybody. Just to know he's in the lineup, ready to swing with somebody on base, gives a ball team like ours a lift it needs. He's the kind of player who has more determination and guts than you'll ever know. He's a great fighter on the field. He loves to win."

Four years later, in a 1966 TV interview with Howard Cosell, Mickey was asked about the game against the Twins when he ran to first base and severely pulled a leg muscle.

> **Cosell**: "There's something within you that doesn't apply just to pleasing your own teammates, Mickey. And this is not by way of ego gratification for you. But, for instance in 1962, vividly, I recollect your hitting a ground ball against Minnesota. Versalles trapped the ball. You had no chance in the world to beat that hit out. Yet you went down to first base with everything you had, overexerted yourself in fact, crossed the bag and fell to the ground like a shot rabbit. Do you remember that?"

Mantle: "Uh huh. That was the last out of the game."

Cosell: "That's right. What is the compulsion that makes you do that when you know in your heart and mind you can't succeed?"

Mantle: "Well, you don't really know. If he bobbled the ball and I was trotting and he threw me out, can you imagine how you would feel if you had trotted down there and got thrown out on a bobbled ball? So I think the best thing to do is just run as hard as you can and then if you're out, why…"

Cosell: "But you knew the risk to your legs. Even in 1962 your legs were like that."

Mantle: "Well, you don't know you're going to do something like that. I mean, I ran every ball out that night and it didn't happen before, so…"

Cosell: "Well, isn't it true, Mickey? Isn't it true that Stengel and Houk, and Berra and Keane have all told you, cut back on your running, Mick. When you know you can't make it, cut back. And yet you're not capable, emotionally, of cutting back. Is that not true?

Mantle: "You don't think—when you hit the ball, Howard, you don't think. I've had all four of those managers use me to pinch hit, and they'll say now if you hit the ball just trot to first. Well the first thing, just as soon as you hit a ball you don't think trot to first, the first thing you do is start running, and you don't think, you know, until it's—until you get there, and then you think, oh, I should have trotted. It's like that. But I guess it's—I don't know what they call it."

Cosell: "I'd say it's competitive compulsion that was born in you. Wouldn't you?

Mickey: "Maybe. I don't know."

Touching All the Bases

Mickey's 1962 salary was $90,000. Relative salaries were Roger Maris: $72,000; Whitey Ford: $50,000; and Yogi Berra: $52,000.

On June 22, Mickey returned to the starting lineup in the second game of a doubleheader against the Detroit Tigers. He would get one hit (his ninth home run of the year) in four at-bats as the Yankees lost by the score of 5-4.

On August 19, in a game against the Kansas City Athletics, Mickey got three hits in four at-bats; including a single, double and a grand-slam home run. Mickey had seven RBIs as the Bronx Bombers bombed the A's by the score of 21-7.

In a five-day stretch between July 2 and 6, Mantle hit seven home runs in 12 official trips to the plate. Two of those came in his last two at-bats on July 5, and two more came in his first two at-bats on July 6 to tie a major league record of consecutive home runs with four. Only 11 other players had accomplished the feat, including Mickey's teammate and good friend, Johnny Blanchard, the previous year.

Even though Mickey missed 39 games during the season due to injuries, he was awarded the Most Valuable Player award for the third time in his career. He batted .321, with 30 home runs and 89 RBIs in the 123 games.

Mickey won the Gold Glove Award in 1962, with a fielding percentage of .978.

In 1962, Mickey was awarded the Most Courageous Athlete Award by the Philadelphia Sports Writers Association.

June 14 marked the premier of the new movie *Touch of Mink* which starred Doris Day and Cary Grant. The movie also contained cameo appearances by Mickey Mantle, Roger Maris, and Yogi Berra. In their brief cameo appearances, the slugging trio was ejected from a Yankees game due to Doris Day, who was sitting in the dugout and harassing the umpires!

In 1962, the movie *Safe at Home* premiered. It starred Mickey Mantle and Roger Maris.

Chapter Nineteen

WALK-OFF THE FACADE

Prior to the start of the 1963 season, Mickey received a $10,000 raise in salary, which boosted him to $100,000. Mantle commented on his new salary: "I don't feel any special pressure on me because of the contract, but there are some things I want to do for personal reasons. I want to drive in more than 100 runs. And I'd like to hit 600 home runs before I'm through."

During spring training, Mickey issued an ultimatum to all American League pitchers as he said, "I've been taking too many pitches the last few years. This year, I'm going to be up there swinging more. I'm going to forget about cutting down on my strikeouts. Every year I say I'm going to cut down on them, and I still strike out 100 times. Now I'm going to do it my way and see what happens."

Mickey and the Yankees started the season winning 19 of their first 32 games. It was already a very tight race in the American League as five teams were within one game of first place. The Baltimore Orioles and Chicago White Sox were tied for first place. The Yankees, the Boston Red Sox, and the Kansas City Athletics were all one game out of first place and tied for third place. Mickey was hitting .292 with six homers.

The big news item around the world was the successful return of Maj. L. Gordon Cooper on May 16. He had splashed down in his

Mercury capsule, Faith 7, after orbiting the Earth a record 22 times over his 34-hour historic space flight. Cooper's 593,885-mile trip began from pad 14 of Cape Canaveral at 8:04 a.m. Central Time, the day before and ended in the Pacific Ocean near Midway Island near Hawaii.

The Kansas City Athletics came to Yankee Stadium on May 21 for a short two-game series with the Bronx Bombers. In the first of the two games, Mickey single-handedly defeated the A's as he belted two home runs and drove in five of the Yankees' seven runs in the 7-4 win. The Orioles and White Sox both won their games, so the Yankees remained one game out of first place with Boston and Kansas City now two games out.

On May 22, the second game between the Yankees and the A's started at 8 p.m. in front of a meager crowd of only 9,727 fans. The starting pitchers were Ted Bowsfield for the A's and Bill Stafford for the Yankees. The Bronx Bombers busted loose for seven runs in the second inning and took a commanding 7-0 lead. The score remained unchanged until the eighth inning when the A's put six runs on the board, and then added another tally in the ninth, with two outs, to tie the game at 7-7.

In the bottom of the ninth, Kansas City manager Eddie Lopat called on his 32-year-old right-handed reliever, Bill Fischer. Fischer entered the game with six wins and no losses as a relief pitcher. He was enjoying new success after Lopat had taught him two new pitches—a slow curve and a fast curve. Before the game, Lopat bragged on his star pupil: "I taught Fischer the slow curve that [Ted] Lyons had taught me, and before the season was over he'd added a fast curve too." Lopat pointed out that Fischer's record last year was four wins and 12 losses, but with his two new pitches, Fischer had a perfect 6-0 record.

Mickey led off the bottom of the ninth inning by walking for his third time in the game. Elston Howard then laid down a successful sacrifice bunt, moving Mickey to second base. The A's intentionally walked Roger Maris in order to set up a possible double play. Joe Pepitone flied out to left, and Tony Kubek struck out which sent the game into extra innings.

The game went into the bottom of the 11th inning with the score still tied 7-7. As Fischer took his warm-up pitches, Mantle loosened up in the on-deck circle with a 35-inch, 33-ounce bat that he had borrowed from Yankee reserve first baseman Dale Long. The Yankees were already upset that they let a 7-0 lead slip away and were at risk of losing ground in the early pennant race. Mickey went to the plate with one thought in mind: Home run.

Fischer and his catcher, Haywood Sullivan, had easily sensed that Mickey wanted to end the game, so Fischer tried out one of his new pitches—the slow curve—in hopes of fooling Mickey. Fischer delivered the ball and Mickey swung so hard that he nearly came out of his shoes, missing the ball for strike one. The A's bench gave Mickey the business and now he was embarrassed and very mad. Next, Fischer tried to sneak a fastball by him. Mickey must have been pumped up on adrenaline, because what happened next was incredible. Mickey unleashed a perfect swing at just the precise moment, with his bat speed at its maximum point in the swing, the baseball struck the dead center of the sweet spot of his bat and took off like a bullet heading for the right-field roof.

Mel Allen, the "Voice of the Yankees", called that pitch in his radio broadcast as follows:

> Right-hander Bill Fischer out on the mound for Kansas City. He's looking in to get the sign. Mickey Mantle digs in at the plate swinging that dangerous bat of his around batting left-handed against right-handed pitching. Fischer all set to go—goes into the windup. 'Round comes the right arm. In comes the pitch. Mantle swings. There's goes a long drive going to deep right field! It's soaring up high! It's going! It's going! It is gone! A home run for Mickey Mantle, and it almost went out of the ballpark. Mickey Mantle for the second time in his career has come within a few feet of becoming the first man to hit a ball clear out of Yankee Stadium.

A's manager Eddie Lopat recalled the sound of Mickey's bat as it made contact with the ball saying, "I'm a pitcher. I know the sound. I just turned my back." Lopat was referring to the sound a bat makes when a powerful hitter connects the sweet spot of the bat to the sweet spot of the ball—it is a unique and unforgettable sound.

Within a couple of seconds of making contact with the bat, the ball struck the façade over the upper deck of the stadium at a point that was 367 feet from home plate, and 108 feet above the ground for a game-winning, walk-off home run. The ball was only a few feet from clearing the stadium roof, and becoming the first ball ever to exit Yankee Stadium in fair territory. It was the first and only time that Mickey stood at home plate watching the flight of the ball. By all eyewitness accounts, the ball had not yet begun to drop when it hit the façade with such force that it bounced almost all the way back to the A's second baseman Jerry Lumpe.

When Mickey hit the ball, Yogi Berra jumped off the Yankee bench yelling, "My God! That's it!" The ball soared in a straight path toward the right-field roof. As Mickey circled the bases in his standard fashion, with his head down, players, and fans both gazed in disbelief at what they had just seen. In the 40 years that Yankee Stadium had been in existence, nobody had ever come close to hitting a fair ball out of the stadium—even Babe Ruth and Jimmy Foxx had never achieved this.

After the game, Mickey described his historic blast, "As hard a ball as I had ever hit in my life. That was the only homer I ever hit that the bat actually bent in my hands. I watched it. I saw it in the haze that comes over the roof when the lights are on. I knew it was going places. I wouldn't have been surprised if it had gone out of the joint."

Bobby Richardson commented, "That would take four of my best shots."

Whitey Ford jokingly said, "I hit 'em that hard. Only they don't go that far."

Frank Crosetti, who had played back in Babe Ruth's days proclaimed, "That's the hardest I've ever seen anyone hit a ball—Jimmy Foxx, Ruth, anybody. I don't believe a man can hit a ball harder. It went out like it was shot out of a cannon."

Manager Ralph Houk joked, "I wish it could have been cut into singles and we would have had enough hits for a week."

Over in the A's dugout, Kansas City catcher Haywood Sullivan explained his strategy for calling the pitch saying, "We were trying to keep Mantle off balance. On the second strike Mickey had been fooled on a slow curve and had swung so hard that he almost went down. Fischer blazed one. Then the lightning came."

Norm Siebern, the A's first baseman said of Mickey, "He ought to have a league of his own. He's too much for everybody else."

Pitcher Bill Fischer commented, "He gets $100,000 a year. I get $10,000. He has to be making it for some reason."

The next day in the newspapers, the reporters didn't quite understand the significance of Mickey's blast. In the *Chicago Tribune*, an article headline read "YANKEES WIN ON MANTLE'S HOMER IN 11th". In *The Los Angeles Times*, the headline "Mantle's Clout in 11th Sinks Athletics, 8-7" appeared. The *New York Times* article headline was "MANTLE'S HOMER SUBDUES A'S, 8-7". It would take another day before the significance would sink in to the newspaper reporters. In the May 24 editions, the *Los Angeles Times* article headline read "Mantle Space Clout His Mightiest" while the *New York Times* article headline read "MANTLE'S HOMER VIEWED WITH AWE".

Mickey had hit the Yankee Stadium façade on one other occasion back on May 30, 1956. The difference between that blast and this one is that his 1956 homer was on its way down when it struck the façade. The home run, hit on May 21, was still rising as it impacted the façade, which raised the question of how far the ball would have actually traveled if its flight would not have been interrupted by the façade. Dr. James E. McDonald, a physicist at the University of Arizona, issued a report on May 29 regarding Mantle's mammoth blast. In his report, he assumed that the ball was at its summit when it impacted the façade despite the fact that witnesses claimed it was still rising. Based on that assumption, McDonald estimated conservatively that the ball would have traveled at least 620 feet, and left Mickey's bat at the speed of 155 mph. He also acknowledged that if the ball had been still rising upon impact with the façade, it would have traveled much farther.

Even 40 years later, Yankees shortstop Tony Kubek can still vividly recalled the legendary blast. Kubek said, "I do remember a few things about the '63 home run by Mickey. When a home run is hit, especially because of the sound they made off Mickey's bat, one popped pretty quickly off their seat in the dugout. Many of his home runs had an unusually loud crack. I guess that goes along with the distance he hit them. In my mind's-eye view, I do not recollect it bouncing all the way back to second base. I can picture it landing on the outfield grass in right field about halfway from the low outfield fence and the dirt portion of the infield. It rolled, by my estimate, another 15 yards and stopped before it reached the outer edge of the infield. The thing I recall most was that the ball appeared to be still rising on impact. Now—and memories play tricks—but I do know this, the ball was NOT coming down when it hit the tower. This was NOT a fly ball! This was a high line drive like no one else could hit 'em."

Some 42 years after the historic homer by Mickey, Bobby Richardson recalled, "I don't remember much about the game, but I do remember that it's been a conversation piece through the years. People saying, 'You should have seen the one Mickey hit off Bill Fischer. It was still going up when it hit the top of the façade.'"

Touching All the Bases

Baseball bats have what hitters call a sweet spot. The sweet spot is an area on the barrel of the bat that starts about six inches from the end of the bat and is about two to three inches long, depending on the density of the wood used in the bat. To further complicate matters for a hitter, the batter must hit the ball exactly perpendicular to the grain of the wood in order to avoid breaking the bat. Envision an area on the barrel of the bat that is less than three inches long, and less than a half-inch in height—that's the sweet spot. When a hitter manages to contact the ball precisely in that area, he can barely feel the bat and ball make contact, and the ball will travel the maximum distance possible based primarily on the hitter's bat speed. It is a feeling that hitters love and they know instantly when they have achieved it.

Hitting the ball on the bat anywhere other than the sweet spot usually results in an out, and certainly limits the distance the ball will travel. It has been said that hitting the ball 1/8 inch or more above the sweet spot will result in a fly out or pop out. Hitting the ball 1/8 inch or more below the sweet spot will result in a ground ball. Now, consider that the ball, which is approximately 2.75 inches in diameter, coming toward the batter at between 80 and 90 mph. Also consider that the pitcher can vary the speed of the ball, the location of the ball, and the movement on the ball, from pitch to pitch. As Ted Williams once said, hitting a baseball is the hardest thing to do in any professional sport, but guys like Williams and Mickey Mantle often made it look easy.

Chapter Twenty

A LEGEND IS BORN

During spring training for the 1963 season, Mickey Mantle was asked by a reporter if he had any particular objective in the season ahead. He playfully replied, "Yes. I have an objective. My objective is to stay in one piece." By the beginning of June, Mickey had managed to avoid injury. *New York Times* reporter Arthur Daley, impressed with Mickey's physical condition and appearance, later wrote, "Mantle looks like the perfect physical specimen. Muscles ripple all over him as he moves around the clubhouse. He has the physique of a Hercules, but more vulnerable points than Achilles."

As the Yankees arrived in Baltimore on June 4 for a three-game series at Memorial Stadium, they were in first place, holding on to a slim half-game lead over the Baltimore Orioles and the Chicago White Sox. The Yankees lost the first game of the series by the score of 3-1. Mickey went 2-for-4 and raised his batting average to .298. He also drove in the Bronx Bombers' only run of the game with his 11th homer of the season. The Yankee loss put Baltimore into first place.

In the second inning of the second game, the Orioles jumped out to a 2-0 lead on a home run by Jack Brandt. The Yankees countered in the top of the third inning with a run on a single by Whitey Ford and a double by Phil Linz. The score remained 2-1 until the top of the sixth inning, when, with one out, Mickey doubled and Roger Maris hit his 200th career homer to put the Yankees up 3-2. In the bottom of the sixth inning, with two outs, Orioles third baseman Brooks Robinson lofted a fly ball to deep center field. Mickey was determined to make the catch and, as Casey Stengel had taught him long ago, kept his eyes fixed on the ball as he ran toward the eight-foot-high wire mesh center-field fence. Unfortunately, there was no warning track where the ball was headed in center field. As Mickey approached the fence at full speed, he leapt in a desperate attempt to keep the ball from being a home run. He crashed into the center-field fence as the ball sailed over it. A metal spike in the sole of Mickey's left shoe stuck in the fence, causing him to twist his leg as he fell to the ground in obvious pain. Robinson was still rounding the bases as the entire Yankee team, as well as many of the Orioles, sprinted out to Mickey's aid. He was taken off the field in a stretcher and rushed to Union Memorial Hospital for X-rays.

The Yankees rallied for a run in the eighth inning to take a 4-3 lead. After the inning ended, an announcement was made over the PA system that Mickey had suffered a broken foot and would miss four to six weeks. The 24,924 fans, still disappointed that the Baltimore Orioles had relinquished their lead, actually cheered the news of Mickey's diagnosis. The Yankees held on to win the game, regaining first place over Baltimore. The next day in the *Baltimore Sun*, the headline read, "BALTIMORE FANS CHEER MANTLE INJURY." The fans' undignified behavior was the subject of conversation in Baltimore for the next few days.

Mickey had fractured the third metacarpal bone in his left foot. This was his first broken bone in his 12-year career. Yankee manager Ralph Houk pledged, "We've lost the best player in the league, but that doesn't mean we're going to lie down and die." Mickey's injury would cause him to miss the next 61 games. During that time, Ralph Houk had made good on his pledge.

On August 2, 1963, the Baltimore Orioles went to Yankee Stadium for a four-game series. By this time, the Yankees had built up an eight-game lead over the second-place Chicago White Sox, and a nine-game lead over the third-place Baltimore Orioles. Mickey was still on the disabled list, so he sat out for the first three games, of which the Yankees lost two and won one.

The 38,555 fans that were on hand to watch the doubleheader on Sunday, August 4, had no idea that they were about to witness one of the most dramatic events in baseball history. The second game of the doubleheader moved into the bottom of the seventh inning with one out and the Yankees trailing the Orioles by the score of 10-9. Pitcher Steve Hamilton was scheduled to hit, but Ralph Houk called on Mickey to pinch hit. It was his first plate appearance since his injury. As Mickey stepped out of the dugout, the fans welcomed him with one of the greatest ovations in Yankee Stadium history. Mickey later said, "The ovation actually chilled me. I was shaking. I could feel the bumps rising on my arms. I told myself, 'I'll settle for a single.' I'll admit I was really scared. I didn't want to strike out and look foolish."

Batting right-handed against the southpaw George Brunet, Mickey took the first pitch for a called strike, giving Mickey a chance to collect his thoughts after the tremendous ovation. "Don't strike out," he recalled telling himself. "I never had a crowd going for me like that in my life. I had to make contact. I'd have settled for anything." He must have collected himself by the second pitch, which was a curve ball, because he belted the ball over the railing of the lower left-field stands 390 feet away for his 12th home run of the season to tie the game at 10-10. The first ovation that Mickey had received, when he stepped out of the dugout, was dwarfed by comparison as he circled the bases. As he approached home plate, he was still favoring his injured left foot. His teammates had lined the top step of the dugout to greet Mickey has he returned.

Mickey recalled the moment, "On August 4, Ralph Houk sent me in to pinch hit against Baltimore pitcher George Brunet. They had a 10-9 lead and the crowd noise in Yankee Stadium turned into a big welcoming roar when I came off the bench. I was hoping to hit a hard grounder, a single, anything, as long as I didn't strike out. Brunet's first pitch was a fastball below the knees. Then he threw a curve. I pulled it into the left-field stands. I don't know if I ran fast or slow or what. I didn't see it go into the seats, but I saw the umpire signal and I told myself, 'I'm a lucky stiff. Gee, but I'm a lucky stiff.' As I touched home plate, I tipped the bill of my cap, responding to the fans. They were up on their feet, cheering and whistling, a whole chorus of yells, 'Mick ... Mick ... !' My teammates surrounded me in the dugout, everybody showing how happy they were for me. Bobby Richardson had tears in his eyes. Yogi stuck out his paw saying, 'Nice, nice...'"

Three days later, Ralph Houk was quoted in the *Washington Post* as saying, "The ovation Mickey got was enough to give me one of the greatest thrills I ever had. I mean the ovation before he hit his homer. I didn't want Mantle to look bad. It would have been hell if he struck out after that reception. When he hit the homer, I just had a feeling that comes from away down deep. Mickey was white when he came back to the dugout. It was the doggondest ovation I ever heard."

It was poetic justice that Mickey would get his home run off the team whose fans cheered after learning he had broken his foot. As it turned out, fate was not yet finished with Mickey's revenge. The next time that the Yankees returned to Baltimore was for a three-game series beginning on August 30. At this point, Mickey still had not started a game and had been put back on the disabled list. The Yankees won the first two games by the scores of 4-1 and 5-3. In the third game on September 1, the Yankees were trailing 4-1 in the eighth inning with one out. Clete Boyer singled; the pitcher, Metcalf, was due to hit next. Ralph Houk decided that it was a good time to use Mickey as a pinch hitter. He asked Mickey if he was up to the task. Mantle responded with, "What are you talking about? I'm not even on the active list." Houk replied, "Yes you are. You went on the active list this morning."

As Mickey stepped out of the Yankee dugout and kneeled in the on-deck circle, he was greeted by a rousing ovation from the Baltimore fans. It must have been their way of apologizing to him for the unforgivable way they had treated him back in June. As Mickey walked to the plate to face left-hander Mike McCormick, the fans cheered him again, this time even louder. Baltimore's manager, Billy Hitchcock, called time out, walked to the mound to discuss the situation with his pitcher, and then returned back to the dugout. McCormick's first pitch was a high fastball. Mantle lashed it over the left-field barrier for his 13th homer of the season and brought the Yankees to within one run of the Orioles. After Bobby Richardson singled, Tom Tresh homered for his second time in the game to give the Bronx Bombers a 5-4 lead that held up for the win. Mickey had sparked a game-winning rally.

The next day in the *Baltimore Sun*, Bob Maisel described how Mickey's teammates responded to his unbelievable feat: "The Yankees acted as if they were celebrating New Year's Eve. Whitey Ford raised his hands over his head, then lowered them to the ground as though he might be worshiping some god."

A year later, Bobby Richardson would recall Mickey's dramatic home run in Baltimore, "When he comes into the lineup, we are a different ball club," says Richardson. "Last year in Baltimore, he came up for only the fourth or fifth time in three months after breaking his foot. We're behind by three runs, but he pinch hits a homer with a man on, and we come from behind to win. Things like that, they make you feel that when he's in there, nobody's going to beat us."

Touching All the Bases

Mickey's 1963 salary was $100,000 compared to Roger Maris' $65,000.

Mickey hit his 400th career home run on September 4 against the Detroit Tigers' pitching ace Hank Aguirre. The homer, which traveled 450 feet, put Mickey in seventh place on the all-time home run list.

The book *Mickey Mantle—Mister Yankee* by Al Silverman was released in 1963.

Chapter Twenty-One

WORLD SERIES WALK-OFF

On September 17, 1964, the Yankees defeated the Los Angeles Angels, becoming the first-place team in the American League for the first time since August 6. In that game, Mickey collected his 2,000th hit (a single), as well as his 450th home run. As he was standing on first base, Angel first baseman Joe Adcock wanted to openly congratulate Mickey, but instead said, "I'd shake hands with you, but it would look kind of funny."

Just one month earlier, on August 12, Mickey had hit the longest home run that ever landed within Yankee Stadium. It was off right-handed hurler Ray Herbert of the Chicago White Sox during the fourth inning. Mickey, batting left-handed, blasted the ball over the 461-foot marker in center field, over the 22-foot screen, and 15 rows deep into the center-field bleachers. The ball traveled a total of 502 feet. It was only the second time in the history of Yankee Stadium that a home run had been hit into the bleachers in dead center field. It too was hit by Mickey, back in June 21, 1955, but it had not gone quite as far as this particular blast. Mickey also hit a right-handed homer, and ended the game 3 for 4.

The game marked the 10th and final time that Mickey would homer from both sides of the plate in the same game. Afterwards, he talked about his prodigious blast saying, "I never expected it to travel that far. If fact, I threw my bat down in disgust thinking it was just a big out. Then I saw [center fielder Gene Stephens] turning around and running as hard as he could. I still didn't believe it would clear the wall."

The Yankees had spent most of August in third place behind both the Baltimore Orioles and the Chicago White Sox. They reclaimed first place in September and never looked back as they finished the season with 99 wins and 63 losses. Despite an 11-game winning streak near the end of the season, the Bronx Bombers finished just one game ahead of the second-place White Sox.

Mickey finished the season fourth in the American League in batting with an average of .303. He was also third in home runs with 35, and fourth in RBIs with 111. Mickey only missed 19 games during the 1964 season due to injuries, which is far better than the 97 games he missed the year before.

On October 7, in St. Louis, the American League-champion New York Yankees took on the National League-champion St. Louis Cardinals in Game 1 of the World Series. This was the Cardinals' first World Series in 18 years, while it was the 15th for the Yankees in the same amount of time. This World Series pitted brothers against each other—Clete Boyer of the Yankees and Ken Boyer of the Cardinals. Ironically, both were third basemen. Mickey Mantle entered this Series tied with Babe Ruth for the record of most World Series homers (15). This was Mickey's 12th World Series appearance in his 14 years in the major leagues, and he had amassed 206 at bats in the October Classics.

In Game 1 of the Series, 30,805 St. Louis fans showed up to watch the Cardinals defeat the Yankees 9-5. The game clincher was a dramatic eighth-inning two-run home run hit by Mike Shannon. Whitey Ford took the loss, while Ray Sadecki got the win for the Cardinals. Mickey, who played right field for the entire Series, was 2-for-5 with two singles.

Game 2 drew a crowd of 30,805 to watch the pitching matchup of Yankee hurler Mel Stottlemyre and Bob Gibson for the Cards. After being swept by the Dodgers in the 1963 World Series, the Yankees broke their five-game World Series losing streak by defeating the Cardinals 8-to-3. Mickey had a double in four plate appearances, and he drove in two of the Yankees' eight runs. The Series was tied at 1-1, and heading to Yankee Stadium for Games 3, 4, and 5.

On October 10, Yankee Stadium was packed with 67,101 fans for Game 3. Twenty-five-year-old Jim Bouton was on the mound for the Yankees, against Al Simmons of the Cardinals. The Yankees jumped out to a 1-0 lead in the bottom of the second inning in what turned into a pitching duel between Bouton and Simmons. The Cardinals tied the game in the fifth inning when Tim McCarver singled to Mickey in right field. The ball hit his glove and rolled between his legs, giving McCarver the chance to advance to second base. Then Mike Shannon, the Cardinal hero from Game 1, lined out to Mickey. McCarver, respecting Mantle's arm, did not attempt to tag and remained on second base. Dal Maxvill then grounded out, advancing McCarver to third. Pitcher Al Simmons followed with an infield single to drive in McCarver for the tying run.

Bouton and Simmons continued their impressive pitching performances into the ninth inning with the score still tied 1-1. Bouton had spread out six Cardinal hits over eight innings, while Simmons had yielded only four hits to the Bronx Bombers. With one out and two men on base, due to an error and a walk, the Cardinals called on Bob Skinner as a pinch hitter for Al Simmons. Skinner flied out, and Curt Flood lined out to end the Cardinal threat and send the game to the bottom of the ninth.

Mickey was the lead-off hitter for the Yankees in the bottom of the ninth. He was 1-for-2 so far with a double in the sixth inning. Cardinal manager Johnny Keane sent 38-year-old, right-handed, knuckleballer Barney Schultz to replace Simmons who had been pulled for a pinch hitter in the top half of the ninth. The Cardinals had called up Schultz in August from the minor leagues. In 49 innings pitched during the regular season, he had only given up one home run, but in Game 2 he had also given up one to Phil Linz.

Schultz was a right-handed pitcher, which meant that Mickey batted lefty. This was a very calculated move by Johnny Keane, who realized Mickey had only hit .241 from his left side compared to .424

from his right side during the regular season. Also, Mickey's home-run ratio right-handed had been once in every 10 at-bats, but only once every 16 at-bats left-handed.

The Yankee scouting report on Schultz was that he liked to get the first pitch over, because it is important for a knuckleball pitcher to not get behind in the count. To accomplish this, Schultz would throw the first pitch a little harder than usual to reduce the movement and give him better control of the pitch. Mantle was well aware of the scouting report as he grabbed his bat and prepared to step out of the dugout.

As Mickey was about to step into the on-deck circle, manager Yogi Berra gave him specific instructions. "Get up there and hit one. I'll meet you inside." As Mickey exited the dugout, he passed Elston Howard who was in the on-deck circle preparing to bat. Mickey told Howard, "Elston, you might as well go on back to the clubhouse, because I'm going to hit the first pitch out of here for a home run." Mickey then walked toward home plate and stopped about 12 feet short of his destination and stood with both hands in his back pockets as he closely studied Schultz's warm-up tosses. As Mickey stepped into the batter's box, Jim Bouton later recalled murmuring to himself on the bench, "Come on, Mick. Hit a home run. I don't want to go out there again." Bouton had already pitched 123 pitches and wasn't looking forward to extra innings.

Schultz took the sign from Tim McCarver and delivered his first pitch, which floated in about knee-high. Mickey's eyes were intensely fixed on the flight of the ball as his right foot strode forward to begin his classic swing. As his right foot stepped forward, his body followed, but his hands were fixed in space. With perfect timing, he sprung his muscular arms forward, rotated his hips, and snapped his wrists. When the bat made contact with the ball, it made the sound that pitchers know and fear.

Curt Gowdy called the play-by-play. He described the hit: "There's a high drive into deep right—and forget about it! It is gone. The ballgame's over! One pitch and Barney Schultz, when he just saw that bat connect, he just shook his head and started for the dugout. He knew it was gone. It was a patented Mickey Mantle drive, a towering home run that landed up in about the third or fourth row of the third tier in right field."

Elston Howard was first to greet Mickey at the plate followed by Tom Tresh and Joe Pepitone before the rest of the jubilant Yankees swarmed him. Mickey had just pulled off a miraculous 2-1 victory. Once again, with this 460-foot homer, Mickey had proven his amazing ability to help the Yankees win important games and the ability to come through in the clutch.

In the locker room, Jim Bouton raced over to Mickey and shouted, "Man, you belted the devil out of that one! You're the greatest!" Berra beamed, "I told Mantle he was going to hit one. When Mick went out I told him, 'I'm going to stay right by the runway so I can go quick because you're going to hit one.' Man, he did. I didn't even have to look when I saw him hit it. I knew it was going out right away. But I had to come back anyway to congratulate him."

Reporters swarmed Mickey, his hands still shaking as he spoke to them, "It wasn't a very good knuckle ball. It was a knuckler that floated in. It looked too good to miss. I had no idea I'd hit a home run when I swung, and I was afraid the wind might kick it foul. I was looking for a knuckler all the way. I'd have had the horns if I hadn't hit that home run, wouldn't I? We'd have been in the clubhouse before this if I hadn't missed that ball." Mickey was referring to the fact that if he hadn't have hit a homer, he would have perceived himself as the 'goat' of the game for making the error that allowed the Cardinals' lone run to score. With his home run, which was fair by approximately 40 feet, he felt redeemed. It was Mickey's 16th Series homer, which set a new World Series record by shattering Babe Ruth's old record of 15 Series long balls.

By winning the game, the Yankees now took a 2-1 lead in the Series. Barney Schultz later said of his first and only pitch to Mantle, "It had to be a knuckle ball. It was, but not a good one. Just think. You throw just one ball—and it's gone. The ball I threw was right down the well. It was knee high and across the plate. It didn't break. It's a shame I had to throw one pitch like that."

Cardinal manager Johnny Keane was asked if Schultz's pitch had anything on it as it was delivered. Keane replied with a grin, "Yes, I guess it did—when it came off Mantle's bat." Keane was then asked if the ball got a good piece of the plate, to which he replied, "It sure got a good piece of the bat."

Cardinal catcher Tim McCarver said, "You have to give Mantle all the credit in the world. He hit the ball real good. That wasn't the first knuckler he's ever hit either."

In the third inning of Game 4, Mickey walked and advanced to second base on a walk to Elston Howard. Cardinal shortsop Dick Groat chatted amiably with Mickey while he was on second base about the dramatic game-winning home run the game before. While chatting, Groat slipped behind him and executed a successful pick-off play from pitcher Roger Craig. After the game Groat reflected, "I thought to myself that I have such respect for Mantle—playing on those bad legs—that this is one of the most unfair things I've ever done in baseball." The Cardinals won the game 4-3 on a grand-slam home run from Ken Boyer, which tied the Series at two games apiece.

The Yankees lost the Series to the Cardinals in seven games. Mickey hit two more home runs—a solo shot off Curt Simmons in Game 6, and a three-run blast in Game 7 off Bob Gibson.

Years later, Mickey felt that hitting the walk-off home run in the 1964 World Series against the Cardinals was one of the biggest thrills in his life. He stated, "I hit a home run off Barney Schultz. When I came back, all of the ballplayers ran up to home plate, you know, and hugged me and all that. And I think that gives me a bigger thrill than anything, is to please my own players. And it makes you feel good to make them happy, you know."

Touching All the Bases

Mickey's salary in 1964 was $100,000. Other Yankee salaries were Roger Maris and Whitey Ford, who both earned $60,000.

Although the Yankees lost, Mickey had a great World Series. He batted .333 with three home runs, eight RBIs, and scored eight times.

In addition to setting the record for most World Series home runs during the 1964 Series, Mickey set the record for most Series played for an outfielder (12), most games played by an outfielder (63), most runs scored (42), most RBIs (40), most total bases (123), most long hits (26), most extra bases on long hits (64), most walks (43), and most strikeouts (54).

The Cardinals' winning World Series share per player was $8,622, while the Yankees' losing share per player was $5,309.

The book *The Quality of Courage* by Mickey Mantle was published in 1964.

Chapter Twenty-Two

MICKEY MANTLE DAY

On April 9, 1965, the Yankees were in Houston, Texas, to face the Houston Astros in the brand-new Astrodome, which had been proclaimed the "Eighth Wonder of the World." This game, witnessed by 47,876 fans, was historic because it was the first indoor competition in the major league. Yankee manager Johnny Keane honored Mickey Mantle by making him the first batter in the game, and Mickey responded with a single—the first hit in the new stadium. The game went scoreless until he led off the sixth inning with the first indoor home run. The fly ball traveled 406 feet over the head of Astros center fielder Jimmy Wynn to dead center field. As Mickey rounded the bases, the million-dollar scoreboard displayed "TILT!" He left the game after the eighth inning, having gone 2-for-3 with a walk. The Astros won the game in 11 innings by the score of 2-1.

During the 1965 season, Mickey's legs continued to plague him as they had throughout his entire career. When a reporter asked how his legs were doing, Mickey replied, "They feel good this year. They get stiff when the weather is cold. They get real stiff when it's cold and wet." Although Mantle's legs had already plagued him for 14 years, his right shoulder had become his biggest liability. He had sustained a shoulder injury back in the 1957 World Series when Red

Schoendienst fell on him during a pickoff attempt at second base. Although the injury had somewhat healed, Mickey re-aggravated it during the off-season while playing touch football with his sons. Through pure guts and determination, he had continued to play, but then, after a few hard throws from the outfield, the pain in his shoulder became unbearable.

It became nearly impossible for Mickey to throw or bat left-handed. The Yankees did their best to guard this information so that the other teams could not take advantage of his injuries. Mickey's teammate and close friend Moose Skowron recalled, "I remember when he played when he couldn't throw a ball from here to my refrigerator in my kitchen, but we held secrets so that nobody took advantage of him. He played when he was hurt. That's why we respected him all the time because he played any time you wanted."

Bob Turley recalled, "There were games where Mickey's shoulder bothered him so much that he'd have to swing with one hand, and he'd still get hits. Or else, if it was really bad, I remember him bunting for a hit."

In June of 1965, Yankees management feared that Mickey was at the end of his playing days so they announced that September 18 would be "Mickey Mantle Day" at Yankee Stadium. At that time, only four other Yankees had received such an honor. Babe Ruth had a day when the Yankees learned he was dying from throat cancer. Lou Gehrig had a day when the Yankees learned he was dying. Joe DiMaggio had a day after he announced he was retiring from baseball, and Yogi Berra had a day shortly before becoming the manager of the Yankees. Mickey agreed to the ceremony under the sole condition that all the proceeds from the event be donated to the Mickey Mantle Hodgkin's Disease Foundation at St. Benton's Hospital in New York.

That gesture by the Yankee organization led fans and teammates to believe that Mickey was nearing the end of his baseball career. Elston Howard alluded: "It's great to give Mick a day. Nobody deserves it more than he does, but I hope it doesn't mean anything more than that." Ralph Houk tried to remain optimistic: "I know nothing of Mickey's personal plans. As far as the club is concerned,

Mickey Mantle Day is something that is long overdue." Mantle was asked if he was contemplating retirement after the season and he responded, "It all depends on what happens this year."

After the Yankees announced Mickey's special day, sportswriters began to express their love and respect for Mickey. Sidney James of *Sports Illustrated* wrote, "Almost everyone who has done a story on Mantle, like almost everyone who has played baseball with or against him … has much the same feeling for him: a mingling of affection and awe."

Dick Young of the *New York Times* phrased it well when he wrote the following passage:

> [Mickey] gave more to his teammates because he had something more to give than strength in his arms and his shoulders. He had strength in his will, and today, at the last stage of the Mantle comet, he has it greater than ever, because it takes a special kind of strength to keep a man going when there is less and less to go on. … The fans cheer him now, more than ever, all around the league. Perhaps they realize what they are about to lose. Perhaps they regret, just a little, that when he was at his peak they booed him, and cursed him, and some of the things they said were terribly unfair.

Phil Pepe wrote:

> What is most impressive about Mickey is he never complains. The pain can rattle him to his teeth, but he will never ask out of a game. Often, he will get to the park and head straight for the trainer's room. He will sit there several hours, getting rubbed, dipping his aching legs in the whirlpool, getting taped. He will miss batting practice and outfield practice and drag himself out just in time for the game. And he will play with pain and then he will drag himself off the field and into the trainer's room again. More often than not, he will be the last one out of the clubhouse. He will sit around, afraid to move because the pain is so great. Two hours after the game has ended, he will lug himself out and head home.

As the special day grew close, Mickey grew increasingly terrified of the speech that he was expected to deliver. This became public knowledge and, not surprisingly, many professional speechwriters offered to help him, but Mickey turned them down. He told them, "This is something I have to do myself."

On September 18, "Mickey Mantle Day" at Yankee Stadium, 50,180 fans passed through the turnstiles to pay tribute to The Mick. Mayor Robert Wagner had proclaimed this day as Mickey Mantle Day in New York. The day was also Mickey's 2,000th major league game. Weeks earlier, he had asked Yankee manager Johnny Keane if Mickey Mantle Day could coincide with that milestone game. Keane had carefully planned the number of off days for Mickey so that his request could be met.

Game time was set for 2 p.m., and Mickey's ceremony was scheduled to begin 45 minutes prior to that. When Mickey arrived at the stadium, an army of reporters immediately swarmed him. One reporter asked if he was more nervous than on his wedding day. Mantle replied, "Today. On my wedding day I only had to say two words, 'I do.' But today…" Mickey then confessed that he hadn't slept well the previous night because he had been worrying about his big day.

Hoping to avoid more interviews, Mickey skipped batting practice. Instead, he remained hidden away in the clubhouse. However, even that didn't protect him from the hordes of reporters and well-wishers. Mickey eventually retreated to the sanctuary of the trainer's room, which was forbidden territory to all except the Yankee players. Moments before the ceremony was to begin, Whitey Ford tried to break the tension as he lugged a stretcher into the dugout saying, "This is to carry you off in case you collapse out there."

Yankee Stadium was full of signs and banners honoring Mickey. Messages like, "Don't leave us, Mickey we need you", "Mickey MVP forever", "We've been cheering since '51, not '65", and "Ruth, Gehrig, DiMaggio, Mantle" adorned the massive stadium. As the ceremony began, Walter "Red" Barber, the master of ceremonies, read a congratulatory telegram from President Johnson. Also on hand were Joe DiMaggio, Bobby Kennedy, Mickey's wife, Merlyn, along with their oldest son, Mickey Junior.

DiMaggio introduced Mickey to the crowd, which was one of the largest of the season. Mickey stepped up to the microphone and delivered the following speech:

> Thank you very much, Joe. I think just to have the greatest baseball player I ever saw introduce me is tribute enough for me in one day. Today's game will be my 2,000th game with the Yankees. I've been very nervous in this ballpark many times in the last 15 years, but never any more nervous than I am right now. To name everyone who has helped me through my career would be impossible. So I'm gonna take this opportunity to say to them one and all, that I certainly appreciate everything they've done for me and hope that I've lived up to their expectations. To have any kind of success in life I think you have to have someone behind you to push you ahead and to share it with if you ever obtain it. And I certainly have that in my wife Merlyn, little Mickey who's here, and I have three little boys at home that didn't get to come but they're watching on TV: David, Billy, and Danny. And also a wonderful mother who is here.
>
> As you all know, all the donations for this day are turned over to the Hodgkin's Disease Fund at St. Benton's Hospital, that was founded in the memory of my father who died of Hodgkin's disease. I wish he could have been here today. I know he would be just as proud and happy at what you all have done here as we are. There's been a lot written in the last few years about the pain that I've played with. But I want you to know that when one of you fans, whether it's in New York or anywhere in the country, say "Hi Mick! How you feeling?" or "How's your legs?", it certainly makes it all worth it. All the people in New York, since I've been here, have been tremendous with me. Mr. Topping, all of my teammates, the press and the radio and the TV have just been wonderful. I just wish I had 15 more years with you. Thank you very much.

A deafening ovation followed. An article in the *Washington Post* the following day described Mantle's reaction: "Mantle didn't quite know what to do. The muscles around his jaw tightened and he brushed at the tears in his blue eyes a little awkwardly. He pawed at the grass with his spikes and then put his arm around his attractive platinum-haired wife, Merlyn, and his red-haired, oldest son, Mickey Jr."

A check for the proceeds, approximately $10,000, was presented to the Mickey Mantle Fund for Hodgkin's Disease. American League President Joe Cronin followed by presenting a check to the fund on behalf of the other nine teams in the American League.

The actual game between the Yankees and the Detroit Tigers was meaningless since the Minnesota Twins had already run away with the American League pennant weeks earlier. The Yankees were in sixth place, 21 ½ games out of first place. The Tigers started the day in fourth place, 11 ½ games out of first.

Joe Sparma, a right-handed pitcher, was on the mound for the Tigers. This was unfortunate for Mickey because he would have to bat left-handed and bear the pain of his right shoulder. In the first inning, Yankee pitcher Al Downing managed to retire the Tigers. In the bottom of the first Bobby Richardson grounded out to third base, and Bobby Murcer struck out. As Mickey Mantle stepped to the plate, he received an ear-splitting ovation from the crowd. That's when Tiger pitcher, Joe Sparma, did something unprecedented in major league baseball—he stepped off the mound, walked to home plate, and shook Mickey's hand in open admiration. Sparma later said, "He's been my hero since I was a little boy and I just wanted to let him know." He then walked back to the mound, and the game resumed.

The crowd was anxious with anticipation. They hoped Mickey would hit a home run, but instead he flew out to left field. Home-plate umpire Bill Haller stopped the game and presented Mickey with that ball as a memento from his 2,000th game as a Yankee. In Mickey's last at-bat of the game, in the ninth inning, he walked and was then replaced with a pinch runner. As Mickey jogged back to the dugout, the fans gave him a prolonged standing ovation.

After the Yankees played the Minnesota Twins on the September 26, Mickey's batting average had slipped to .266. It was obvious now, even to the other teams, that Mickey was hurting. Knowing that it was no longer a secret, Mickey informed reporters about his shoulder problems. "The shoulder is so sore I can hardly return the ball to the infield. I'm doing the best I can, but I'm not helping this club much."

The Yankees went on to finish in sixth place, their worst record in 40 years. It was also Mickey's worst season in his 15-year career. He missed 40 games, most of which were toward the end of the season. His batting average plummeted to the lowest point in his career at .255 as he managed only 19 home runs and 46 RBIs.

Playing with a Yankee team that had no hopes of finishing in first place taught Mickey something: "Losing is no fun. When we were on top, every day used to mean something. When I was hitting .350 and fighting Ted Williams for a batting title, I used to think that he was lucky not to have the pressure of the pennant race every day. How nice it would be, I thought, to be free of it just one year, to just worry about your own hitting. I was wrong. It's harder to play without pressure."

Touching All the Bases

With his sore shoulder, Mickey went 0-for-3 on Mickey Mantle Day. The Yankees lost to the Tigers 4-3.

In 1965, Mickey played in 122 games and only completed 36 of those.

Chapter Twenty-Three

GIFT OF A TIGER

In January of 1966, Mickey told Yankees general manager Ralph Houk that he was going to retire. He revealed, "When I came to New York a few days ago, I was seriously thinking about quitting. My shoulder hurt so much that I couldn't even throw a ball, my legs will never be any better, and I was pretty discouraged. But Ralph Houk talked things over with me and told me what the people and the team expect, and now I feel better about it and I'm willing to try."

Houk explained how he convinced Mickey to go another year:

> Well, he was down, all right, when he came here. He was saying things like, 'If I had to play under these conditions . . .' and 'I don't want to go out as a bad player.' I told him that no one would want him to go out that way; that he didn't realize what he meant to the public, the Yankees, and his fellow players. Just having Mickey Mantle on the team has been a great influence on all of us. And I told him he didn't realize how good he was. Mickey has the feeling that he must play every game for the Yankees and that he sometimes did things that hurt them. But I certainly think he has some years left in him, if he handles himself in the right manner. If he established in his mind that he could still contribute, then Johnny Keane could pick the shots for him—like not playing him the day after a night game, or the

> second game of a doubleheader. I think the Mickey Mantle Day at Yankee Stadium showed him what the public thinks, and I told him so.

At Ralph Houk's suggestion, Mickey visited Mayo Clinic in Rochester, Minnesota, to have his troublesome shoulder examined. Doctors found a bone chip and recommended surgery. Mickey agreed, and the surgery was performed on January 25, 1966. Johnny Blanchard described the sequence of events: "The Yankees sent Mickey to Mayo Clinic for his shoulder surgery. I live 80 miles from there, so I drive down and have dinner with him a few days after the operation. He's staying at the Kaylor Hotel across the street from Mayo Clinic. So I get down there and go right up to his suite. I go in there and it's just me and him, and he says, 'Hey Blanch! You want to see this thing?' With one hand, he pulls his T-shirt up and shows me. He explained to me what they did. It was cut like a half circle and down his arm by his bicep. And they had to bore a hole into that bone and they took the tendons and run them through that hole and tied them in a knot.

"We went to a steakhouse about a block away and he couldn't cut the steak. The waitress came over and he looked up at her and he asked, 'Would you cut this for me? I can't raise my arm.' For him to say that, it took a lot of guts because he did everything his way. You couldn't help him for nothing. You couldn't help him out of a cab or nothing. She cut it up and he ate the steak left-handed. He was a warrior. Opening day, in April, he was on the field. He had more balls than 20 men."

He started out very slowly in March of 1966 at spring training but by the eighth day, he was back to banging balls over the fences. Elston Howard said, "It's good just to see him on the field. He's our leader. He can give us the big hit when we need it but so can some of the rest of us. It's more than that. When you see how he has had to play, what he's done to play, those legs, now the arm – you've got to be proud of him, proud to play with him. You play harder with him around." On March 25, the Yankees while still in spring training, traveled to play the Philadelphia Phillies. Before the game, Phillies manager, Gene Mauch, could not deny his respect for Mickey as he excused himself from a dugout conversation saying, "I want to watch Mickey Mantle take batting practice. I get a thrill out of that."

Mickey had somewhat of a comeback year in 1966. He hit .288, had 23 home runs, and 56 RBIs over the course of the 108 games in which he played. In 1967, the Yankees moved Mickey to first base in order to protect his legs from more 'wear and tear' and prolong his career as much as possible. Under these conditions, he only missed 18 games in each of his last two seasons (1967 and 1968). However, in 1967 his batting average dropped to a new low of .245, while his lifetime batting average dropped to .302. The highlight of the year for Mickey was clouting his 500th home run on May 14 at Yankee Stadium off Baltimore's Stu Miller. Mickey hit that home run with a bat that he had borrowed from teammate Joe Pepitone.

The 1968 season was a long one for Mickey and the Yankees as they spent most of the season bouncing between seventh and eighth place in the American League. After a 10-game winning streak in September, the Yankees climbed to third place, but were still 17 games behind the Detroit Tigers. Mickey had flashes of his old brilliance during the season. On May 30, he went 5-for-5, with two home runs and drove in five runs as the Yankees clobbered the Washington Senators 13-4. On June 29 against the Oakland Athletics, he hit a clutch pinch-hit double in the eighth inning to drive in the winning run in a 5-4 victory.

On September 19, the Yankees were in Detroit playing the first-place Tigers in the third game of a three-game series. The Tigers had won the first two games 9-1 and 2-1, and had extended their winning streak to eight games. In the Tigers' 2-1 victory, they clinched first place in the American League. At an earlier time in Mickey's career, he might have been upset that the Yankees had failed to capture first place themselves. He might have sat in his locker and cried. But somewhere along the way, Mickey had grown up. His comments in a diary that he kept in the final part of that season for *Look Magazine* reveal a different side of Mickey—a more mature and mellow side. In the diary, he described how the town of Detroit celebrated its league championship. He wrote, "Whitey and I started the ride back to the hotel. All the way, we kept looking at the happiness on the people's faces; you couldn't believe it. My room was on the 12th floor, and I sat by the window for at least an hour just watching the people; they were really genuinely happy. They weren't just a bunch out to dirty up a town. Some drivers would stop their cars and get out to shake one another's hands. Color of skin made no difference that night in Detroit. It made me feel great. I was proud that Detroit won the pennant, and to see the way the people in Detroit acted. It made me feel good."

The third game of the series had 24-year-old Denny McLain on the mound for the Tigers, and Mel Stottlemyre for the Yankees. Even though the Yankees were floundering this year, Stottlemyre was enjoying a great year with 20-9. But this record paled in comparison to his mound opponent's record. McLain entered the game with an astonishing record of 30-5.

The game appeared as if it was going to be another Tiger victory as it headed into the top of the eighth inning with the Tigers leading by the score of 6-1. McLain was pitching another great game. Mantle had singled in the first inning, and walked in the fourth and sixth innings. Now, in the top of the eighth, Jake Gibbs led off the inning grounding out to third base. Mickey Mantle strolled to the plate. What followed next was something unprecedented in major league baseball.

As Mickey stepped to the plate, the crowd of 9,063 gave him a standing ovation since it would be his last at-bat of the year, and possibly the last at-bat of his career at Tiger Stadium. Mickey later recalled the moment saying, "The crowd suddenly gave me a standing ovation; it made me feel so good, the way they screamed and yelled. It made me nervous. Even though I've been playing 18 years, I got goose bumps. They seemed to sense that this might be the last time they'd see me."

McLain waited for the cheers to subside, and then called Tiger catcher Jim Price halfway to the mound to talk things over. After a short discussion, McLain walked back to the mound while Mickey and Price had a brief conversation at the plate as Mickey dug in batting lefty. McLain looked in, wound up and delivered his first pitch—a fastball right down the heart of the plate. Home plate umpire yelled, "Steeeeeerike!" McLain smiled as he prepared to throw his next pitch. It too, was another fastball right down the heart of the plate. This time Mickey took a fierce cut at the ball and fouled it straight back. Strike two. Mickey then signaled to McLain that he would like the next pitch about letter high! McLain smiled again.

What follows is a transcript of the play-by-play call from Yankee announcers Phil Rizzuto and Frank Messer, heard by thousands of Yankee radio listeners that day.

> **Rizzuto**: "[McLain] said to Mick, I think he said it, 'I'm gonna lay one right in there for you. Hit it.' And sometimes when you know what's coming it's tough to hit it."
>
> **Messer**: "They were all grinning, Mickey, McLain, and the catcher Jim Price a moment ago."
>
> **Rizzuto**: "There it goes! Awwwww, he did it! You gotta give that McLain some credit! I want to tell you! He's grinning a mile wide! Boy, I tell ya, you think these ballplayers don't have heart, Frank? And look! Mickey's nodding to him thanking him! Boy I tell ya, I've never seen anything like this in my life! Mantle has now gone ahead of Jimmy Foxx 535 home runs ... and now Pepitone says, 'Lay one in for me,' and McLain is shaking his head at him and says, 'No sir!'"

Mantle had lined the ball into the upper deck in right field, just inside the foul pole, for his 17th homer of the year, and the 535th of his career, which moved him into third place behind Babe Ruth and Willie Mays. What was more amazing is that Denny McLain, out of his love and respect for Mickey, grooved three pitches to him in hopes that he would hit a home run on his last at-bat at Tiger Stadium. As Mickey rounded the bases, McLain had saluted him as if to say, "Congratulations" while the Tiger fans gave Mickey another thunderous standing ovation. All of the Tiger players in the Detroit dugout stood and applauded Mickey.

The Tigers beat the Yankees 6-2 that day, but all the talk in both locker rooms after the game was about the Mickey's home run. In the locker room, Mickey had this to say, "I got a feeling he wanted me to hit it. I think it was just a straight fastball. After the first pitch I had a feeling he was going to let me hit it. I have no doubt about it. It's got to be one of the best thrills I've had in baseball. … McLain has made a fan of me for life."

In the Tiger locker room, McLain was besieged by reporters who wanted details. McLain replied with a smile, "I think you guys think I gave it up on purpose. You don't think I'd deliberately throw him a home run ball do you? There would be a scandal and an immediate investigation of baseball. I didn't throw it to him. It was a good pitch, a fastball low. Mickey has been my number-one idol since I was a kid, but I didn't groove it for him. I wanted to finish the game because I'd gained about 10 pounds from all the celebrating over our pennant the last two days and I wanted to work it off. But that Mantle—he was my idol. Still is. Baseball is going to be sad when he leaves it."

The questions continued to come almost faster than McLain could respond. "What went through your mind when Mantle hit the homer?" asked one reporter. "I said, 'O God, another one.' None of them gopher balls are special. This one I'll remember a little bit more." When asked if he expects Mantle to retire, McLain replied, "I hope so. I get tired of him hitting home runs off me." Tiger manager Mayo Smith added his own comment: "No pitcher likes to have a home run hit off him. If someone had to hit it, I'm glad it was Mantle. Our bench even rose up and applauded him."

A week later in the *New York Times*, writer Arthur Daley was pointing out the difficulty of hitting a home run, even if you know what pitch is coming. "It was a romantic gesture that McLain made, but the propriety of the move always can be questioned, even though he did get away with it. However, Mantle still had to connect for distance, fat pitch or not. This is not as easy as it sounds. A homer contest was held at the Stadium the other day and every pitch was fat. Yet Mantle propelled only two of 10 fair balls into the stands, while Carl Yastrzemski of the Red Sox contrived to hammer in only one. Three of 20 present rather low percentages." Daley continued, "From the standpoint of propriety, McLain acted unwisely, but it was such a human touch that he can readily be forgiven for his beau geste."

Seventeen years later, Mickey would describe the memorable moment in his book, *The Mick*, but he mistakenly recalled the Tiger catcher to have been Bill Freehan. The official box score from that game showed the catcher to actually have been Jim Price.

> The Tigers were playing us and I was struggling to pass Jimmie Foxx at 534. By then, what with my right leg as shaky as a wet noodle, when I got up to hit against Denny McLain, the Detroit crowd thought this would be my last turn at bat. So we're losing, 6-0. McLain strolls toward the plate, beckons his catcher, Bill Freehan, then says loud enough for me to hear, 'I'm gonna let him hit one.' Freehan comes back and I say, 'Did I hear that right? He's gonna let me hit a pitch?' Freehan grins. 'Yeah.' He snaps down his mask. The first pitch is a fastball for a strike. I let it go by. Denny gestures as if to say, 'What's going on here?' I look at Freehan. 'Don't shit me, Bill. Is he setting me up for something?' 'No, Mick. He wants you to hit one.' The next pitch is another juicy fastball. I foul it off. Freehan gets a new ball, rubs it up, throws it to Denny, crouches behind the plate, and says to me, 'Here comes another one.' Sure enough, it's another fastball, right down the middle. This time I hit it as well as I ever hit a baseball—my 535th home run into the upper deck.

Joe Pepitone was the next batter after Mickey. He recalled, "I stepped up next and, figuring McLain was in a good mood, signaled with my bat where I'd like a pitch. McLain smiled, went into his windup, and fired a fastball that hopped about a foot over the inside corner of the plate—a pitch *nobody* could hit. The players on both benches roared."

Touching All the Bases

On July 21, after going 1-for-4, Mickey's lifetime batting average dropped below .300. He ended the 1968 season with a .298 lifetime batting average, which was one of his biggest career disappointments.

Mickey would hit his 536th and final home run of his career on September 20, 1968, against the Boston Red Sox at Yankee Stadium in front of a crowd of 15,737.

Chapter Twenty-Four

THE MICK BOWS OUT

As the fifth-place Yankees arrived in Boston for the last series of the 1968 season, they were 22 games behind the league-leading Detroit Tigers. The Boston Red Sox were 18 games behind, in third place. The only significant thing about the series was that the bonus for finishing third place was $1,600 versus only $800 for fourth place. The Yankees would receive $300 per player for fifth place, but nothing if they finished in sixth place or below. There was another reason other than money that was driving the Yankees to win. Mickey Mantle told reporters: "We went to Boston, where we had to win two of the three games to take fifth place. The money amounted to $300, which certainly wasn't much to the fellows who had been with the Yankees for a while. But winning meant a lot to us because Ralph had wanted it, and all the boys would try to do anything to please Ralph."

Despite the team spirit, the Yankees were just a shadow of the team that Mickey had played with for most of his career. All of his close teammates had either retired or been traded. Moose Skowron had been traded to the Los Angeles Dodgers at the completion of the 1962 season. Yogi Berra retired after the 1963 season. Johnny Blanchard was traded in 1965 to the Kansas City Athletics. Tony Kubek retired after the 1965 season. At the conclusion of the 1966 season, Bobby Richardson retired, Roger Maris was traded to the St. Louis Cardinals, and Clete Boyer was traded to the Atlanta Braves. Elston Howard was traded to the Boston Red Sox during 1967, and Whitey Ford retired that same year. The supporting cast that had led the Yankees to the World Series 12 times between 1951 and 1964 no longer surrounded Mickey. The game just wasn't the same anymore.

In the latter part of the 1968 season, *Look Magazine* asked Mickey to keep a diary. In one entry, he revealed his frustrations: "The last month is always the longest. For the last few seasons, if I had been forced to make up my mind in September about playing the following spring, I would have quit five years ago. But by February, my legs wouldn't hurt so much, I'd be tired of loafing around the house, and I'd get an itch to play again. But this time, there was a difference. My legs were worse than ever, and a man has to face up to his age sometime. I just feel like I've gotta quit, and I feel like I've waited a little too long already."

On September 27, Mickey received a standing ovation from 28,796 Boston fans as he stepped to the plate in the first inning. It was almost as if the crowd sensed that his career was coming to an immediate end. Mickey flew out and went 0-for-3; the Yankees lost 12-2. On September 28, a crowd of 25,534 fans gave Mickey a standing ovation in the first inning just as they had done the day before. Righty Jim Lonborg was on the mound for the Red Sox as he faced Mantle, who was hitting left-handed. Mickey flied out to Rico Petrocelli in short left field, breaking his bat. This would be the last time Mickey played in a major league game because Yankee manager Ralph Houk had agreed to let him skip the last game. Mickey later recalled his last at-bat, "I came up in the first inning, made an out, and returned to the bench. Ralph sent Andy Kosco in to replace me. I sat back and watched the kid limber up. I knew I had reached the end of the line. After a few moments I headed through the runway into the locker room, took off my uniform, and went home."

Boston right fielder Ken "Hawk" Harrelson recalled the details of Mickey's last game on September 28, 1969, in a *Baseball Digest* article:

The Mick Bows Out

The game that stands out most in my mind outside of the '67 pennant winner is the next to last game of the 1968 season because it was the last game ever played by Mickey Mantle (Saturday, September 28, 1968).

It was the next to last day of the '68 season at Fenway Park and the game didn't mean much because both the Yankees and Red Sox were way behind the Tigers, who had clinched a week or two earlier. Still, there were about 30,000 in the park that day, and I think a lot of them must have sensed this might be Mickey's last game.

I had talked to Mickey before the game, as well as a couple of days before, and he'd sort of hinted he would hang it up. He said he felt pretty good, but that his reflexes weren't what they'd been after 18 years in the American League. He was hitting around .240 and had moved to first base, but you could see he was struggling. He told me he wasn't going to stay around for the last game of the season, but was flying to Dallas that night.

In any event, I knew pretty well this would be the final game of his career, though he wasn't going to announce anything until the next spring training.

Manager Ralph Houk put him in the lineup at first base, and he came to bat in the first inning. The ovation was tremendous. He always got a tremendous ovation in Fenway Park. It was a great thing about the New England fans that they always appreciated the play of other teams and the milestones. They went wild when Mantle walked up there.

I don't remember exactly what Mantle did, except he went out. I was standing in right field and tears were running down my cheeks because Mickey was always my idol and that of 90 percent of the ballplayers in the American League. I looked around to left field and centerfield and Yaz (Carl Yastrzemski) and Reggie (Smith) were wiping their eyes too.

It was a very emotional moment, and it was the end of something that was good for all of us because the man was such a great player and man as well as a credit to the game of baseball. I don't now how many players would arouse such a feeling among those who play with or against them, but Mickey Mantle … well, he was Mickey Mantle.

We all had known for several years that the end of his career was coming and what he was going through to be able to play as long as he did. I can recall several close games in which Mickey had laid down bunts and had had to run hard down the first-base line. He'd run past first base another 80 or 90 feet

> because he didn't want to cause any more pain to the leg that was shortening his career. By the time he came back to the bag he'd have tears in his eyes from the pain. Yet, he kept on playing through the hurt.
>
> You see these things over the years and see how hard he played, and then, all of a sudden it's his last game, his swan song. You realize that one of the greats of the game is in the last game he's going to be playing in.
>
> I remember that after Mantle batted in the first inning, Houk sent in Andy Kosco to play first base and—as it worked out—Kosco hit the home run to beat us.
>
> But what I remember most is seeing Mantle go into the dugout for the last time as a player and the way we all felt about it. It was a very meaningful moment for all of us as well as for him. I would say that was the game that sticks out even more so than the World Series or an All-Star game for me.
>
> There are a lot of guys who are in their last games as you go along in your career, but there is only one Mickey Mantle.

Soon after Mickey's final game, he revealed another significant insight to his personality and career. While discussing the fact that Ralph Houk allowed him to miss the last game of the season, Mickey said, "Letting me go home early was like Ralph Houk. He was the best thing that ever happened to me. Casey Stengel was my first manager, and he gave me my start. He had enough confidence in me to talk George Weiss into keeping me when I first came up. But when Houk took over, he told everybody that I was the leader of the Yankees. I think I came of age because of the way Ralph put stuff on me, said I was good, built up my confidence."

Looking back, Stengel really was like a father to Mickey, and very much in the way that Mutt had been—no matter how good Mickey did, Stengel seemed to always have constructive criticism for him. Mickey had great respect for Stengel, but he certainly disagreed with some of his opinions. For example, Mickey wanted to swing with all of his might at every pitch, but Casey repeatedly scorned him for doing so. In one instance in early July of 1953, Stengel publicly censured Mickey for trying to hit tape-measure home runs instead of producing singles and runs. Mickey answered him a few days later on July 6, in a pinch-hit appearance by hitting a 450-foot grand-slam homer completely out of Shibe Park.

One could argue that Mickey was underappreciated by Casey Stengel and Yankee fans for the first 10 years of his career. Even after Mickey had proven himself in 1956 by winning the Triple Crown, Stengel kept criticizing and the Yankee fans kept booing. In Mickey's book titled *The Quality of Courage*, Mickey wrote, "But I think I was always a disappointment to Casey. He wanted me to be the greatest player in the world, and I wasn't. One of Casey's ways to get a man to play better was to criticize him. It's hard to say that that system doesn't work—after all, Casey has those 10 pennants as proof—but sometimes it makes me feel pretty low."

Mickey hungered for acceptance, appreciation, and respect; but received very little. During these rough years, Mickey relied on his teammates. They understood and appreciated his greatness; but more importantly, they could relate to the way Stengel treated him. Surprisingly, Mickey could always rely on the fans outside of New York showing him more respect and love than the Yankees fans did.

When Ralph Houk became the Yankee manager in 1961, everything changed for Mickey. His management style was completely different from Stengel's. Houk appreciated Mickey for who he was, and he didn't try to force him to be something he wasn't. In *The Quality of Courage*, Mickey wrote, "When Ralph took over as manager, he didn't say anything at all about hoping that I would finally develop into the outstanding player I should be. Instead he said that I was an outstanding player right now; that I was a player the other players on the team respected and looked to as a leader. That might not seem like very much, but to me it meant a great deal."

Mickey continued this sentiment in an interview with *The Sporting News*, "It made me feel real good when Ralph started bragging on me. How I would be the team leader and all that. It made me believe in myself. I found I could take the boos better. I could take the bad days better. Ralph Houk is the man who brought out the very best I had."

As it turned out, Houk was exactly what Mickey needed—someone to recognize his accomplishments and appreciate his abilities, and let him play the game the way he wanted to play the game. Under Houk's guidance, Mantle flourished.

As the 1968 season neared an end, Houk easily sensed that Mickey was tired and frustrated and ready to retire. His move to let Mickey go home early was not only a show of faith, respect, and friendship; but it was also a calculated attempt to get him to play another year.

The 37-year-old Mantle reported to Ft. Lauderdale for spring training in 1969 on February 28, three days after the rest of the regular players had arrived. He had a long phone conversation with Ralph Houk that night, and then breakfast the next morning with Yankee president Michael Burke. Mickey and Houk sat side by side at the press conference in which Mickey was to announce his retirement from baseball. Mickey sat with his arms crossed, his eyes and stern face had a distant and dejected look as he made the following statement:

> The main reason I'm quitting is I can't hit any more. I feel bad that I didn't hit .300. But there's no way that I could go back and get it over .300 again. I can't hit when I need to. I can't go from first to third when I need to. There's no use trying. I can't contribute to the team any more. I can't give the fans what they might expect of me. I'm really glad I decided to do it. I'll probably go to the ballpark on Monday, but I'm not going to put on a uniform again. I'll probably sit around and talk to the guys. I don't know how I'll feel not playing ball. I've been playing ball for twenty years and I'll probably miss it like crazy. I don't know how my four boys feel about it, but my wife has been after me to quit for three years. I know she's happy.

Reporters then asked Mickey what he liked about his 18-year career and he replied, "I liked those 536 home runs I hit. But I didn't like those 1,700 strikeouts, 1,710 actually."

In the next few days, praise for Mickey started coming from all directions: Yogi Berra said, "If Mickey had been healthy, there's no telling what he might have done." Gil Hodges, who played for the Brooklyn Dodgers said, "I have three words for him. Hall of Fame. There's never been any player like him as a switch hitter with power.

Besides that, when he hit right-handed he was the equal of any right-hander in the game, and when he swung left-handed he was the equal of any left-hander." J.C. Martin, catcher for the White Sox, said, "I'll never forget the day in Yankee Stadium when I was catching and Ray Herbert was pitching. Mantle was batting left-handed, and we got two strikes and one ball on him. The next pitch was perfect—a fast sinker ball tailing away from him as it caught the outside corner of the plate. He hit it over 460 feet to center field and it landed 15 rows back. Later in the game, Frank Baumann was pitching for us and Mantle batted right-handed. Frank pitched him low and away too, and Mantle bombed one into the right-field seats." Tommy Agee, center fielder for the White Sox, added, "Once in Yankee Stadium, he hit a ball right-handed to right field and broke his bat. He was so mad that he took the handle and pounded it on the ground. While he was doing that, the ball kept carrying into the seats for a home run."

Tom Tresh had spent seven years in the locker next to Mickey. He sadly reminisced, "Mickey's locker is next to mine in the Stadium. After every game, I'd go and get a beer for both of us, and we'd sit and discuss the game. And I used to ride up to the ballpark with Mickey when we stayed in the same hotel. I'll miss him as a friend." Steve Hamilton had this to say: "Mickey Mantle gave us an aura of respectability. It made us all feel better to be associated with someone of his stature. I used to look across the locker room at him, I guess I was awed too. He just had a special style about him. I played six years with him, and I still got a thrill out of seeing him here. I'm really going to miss him."

Mickey Mantle was the Yankees' last link to greatness and power. Since 1920, when Babe Ruth began the Yankee dynasty, there has been someone great to carry the torch. First there was Ruth, then Gehrig, then DiMaggio, and then Mantle. For almost 50 years, the Yankees had been able to boast that they had greatest player in baseball, but this was no more. Mickey Mantle's retirement marked the end of an era.

Touching All the Bases

Mickey played his last game at Yankee Stadium on September 25, 1968, against the Cleveland Indians. Luis Tiant one-hit the Yankees on his way to a 3-0 victory. Mickey had the lone base hit for the Yankees.

It is interesting to note that Mickey ended his major league career the same way that he started it—with a broken bat. He broke his bat in his very first major league at-bat on April 17, 1951; and he broke his bat in his very last major league at-bat on September 28, 1968.

The Yankees finished in fifth place in the American League in 1968.

Chapter Twenty-Five

A DAY TO REMEMBER

Early in the 1969 season, the Yankees polled over 20,000 fans in order to find out who they thought was "The Greatest Yankee Ever." Babe Ruth won the voting with 60 percent of the vote. Mickey Mantle came in second place with 25 percent of the vote, Joe DiMaggio was third with eight percent, and Lou Gehrig in fourth place with six percent of the votes. This proved that Mickey had left his mark on the New York people during his 18-year career.

In April, writer Dick Young of *Sport Magazine* expressed his admiration for Mickey: "Some stars are envied, some tolerated, some despised. Mickey Mantle has been worshiped. By his mere presence he leads them, and that is where the biggest void will be for the Yankees. Long after the legs and the reflexes are gone, the inspirational leadership remains."

The Yankees found themselves besieged with requests from fans that Mickey Mantle be honored at Yankee Stadium as he had been on September 18, 1965, when they held "Mickey Mantle Day." Thus, on May 19, the Yankees announced that they would retire Mickey's uniform No.7 on Sunday, June 8, between the games of a doubleheader against the Chicago White Sox. The Yankees had only previously retired three other uniform numbers. The Yankees retired Lou Gehrig's No. 4 on July 4, 1939; Babe Ruth's No. 3 on June 14,

1948; and Joe DiMaggio's No. 5 on April 18, 1952. Furthermore, only five uniform numbers had been retired in all of baseball history.

On June 8, 1969, a near-capacity crowd of 60,096 turned out for the doubleheader between the Yankees and the Chicago White Sox. It was the largest baseball crowd that Yankee Stadium had since 1967. The Yankees won the first game by the score of 3-1 on a three-run homer by Joe Pepitone. Before the game was over, fans were already chanting, "We want Mickey. We want Mickey."

As the long awaited and much anticipated ceremony began, 12 giant pennants were laid on the outfield grass to represent each of Mickey's championship seasons. Frank Messer, the master of ceremonies, addressed the highly excited crowd saying, "Good afternoon, ladies and gentlemen. This truly is a historic occasion. We are here to honor one of the greatest of all Yankees, Mickey Mantle—and to officially retire his No. 7 uniform. Ladies and gentlemen, as you know, Mayor Lindsay has proclaimed today, Sunday, June 8, 1969, 'Mickey Mantle Day' in New York City." This was followed by an ovation.

Messer then introduced one representative player from each of those 12 championship teams as they formed a line between second base and third base. The teammates included Ed Lopat (1951), Gene Woodling (1952), Joe Collins (1953), Phil Rizzuto (1955), Jerry Coleman (1956), Gil McDougald (1957), Whitey Ford (1958), Bobby Richardson (1960), Elston Howard (1961), Tom Tresh (1962), Joe Pepitone (1963), and Mel Stottlemyre (1964).

Mel Allen, the longtime voice of the Yankees who had stopped announcing five years earlier, introduced Mickey, "This is one of the proudest moments I've ever had on this hallowed baseball ground. And I'm terribly privileged to have the honor to, once again, call from the dugout one of the all-time Yankee greats. The magnificent Yankee, the great No. 7, Mickey Mantle!"

Mickey, who had been standing on the dugout steps, came out of the dugout and began walking toward the mound. Everyone in the stadium jumped to their feet and let out a mighty roar. Mickey took his place near the battery of microphones and waved to the crowd as the noise level grew in intensity until it was deafening. He stood solidly in his dark blue suit and tie as he soaked up the love and admiration. After about two minutes, Mickey raised his arms in a polite attempt to quiet the crowd, still on its feet, producing a deafening roar. The crowd cheered even louder. After three solid minutes of ovation, Frank Messer tried to quiet the crowd but to no avail. Mickey shook his head in disbelief as the crowd was still on its feet, waving hats and banners while screaming for their hero. The thunderous ovation was now five minutes long, and Yankee president Michael Burke approached the microphone, but the fans would not give up the ovation. Mickey became embarrassed as he tried, once again, to quiet the crowd, only to cause them to raise the noise level yet another notch. A teenage boy climbed out of the stands and made his way to congratulate Mickey before being escorted off the field by police. After a continuous six-minute ovation, Frank Messer was finally able to convince the fans to quiet down in order to continue the ceremony.

Messer then introduced other noted guests, including Tom Greenwade, the scout who discovered Mickey; George Weiss, the Yankees former general manager; Harry Craft, Mickey's manager on the 1949 Independence Yankees and the 1950 Joplin Miners; George Selkirk, Mickey's manager on the 1951 Kansas City Blues; along with Ralph Houk and Yogi Berra. Next, Messer introduced Mickey's wife, Merlyn, his mother Lovell, and his mother-in-law, Reba Johnson.

The following is an excerpt from the festivities:

> **Frank Messer**: "Ladies and gentlemen, there was only one man who could make this next and most significant presentation. Mickey's predecessor in centerfield as well as in the Hall of Fame, the Yankee Clipper, Joe DiMaggio!"
>
> **Joe DiMaggio:** "Thank you ladies and gentlemen. Mickey, I know just how you feel out here today. This is a nervous moment, but it is also a very thrilling one too. I'd like to present you with this plaque, which will be right along in a modest spot out there in center field. The Yankees have also asked me to see that you fans are invited to see this with its great achievements after every ballgame. Congratulations, Mickey. It's nice to be here along with all these fans."

DiMaggio then gave Mickey a replica of the plaque that was going to hang in center field along with those of Ruth, Gehrig, Miller Huggins, Ed Barrow, and Jacob Ruppert.

> **Frank Messer:** "And now to make this next presentation to Mickey, most appropriately, here is his good friend and longtime teammate, Whitey Ford."
>
> **Whitey Ford:** "Mickey, we've had a lot of fun playing here all these years at Yankee Stadium. It's my honor to thank you on behalf of your teammates for the many thrills you have given us. Those clutch hits, booming home runs, great catches, and an occasional strikeout."

Whitey had to pause as the crowd exploded with laughter. Mickey practically bent over double trying to contain his laughter.

> **Whitey Ford:** "And for all you did in the clubhouse and on the bench to make those real great Yankee teams click. Now No. 7 is being retired. The Yankees have asked me to give to you this uniform."

Whitey presented Mickey with No. 7, a duplicate of the number framed for posting in the Stadium Club.

> **Frank Messer**: "Ladies and gentlemen. Another uniform of Mickey's will be given to the Baseball Hall of Fame at Cooperstown, New York. And now, Mickey Mantle, Yankee Stadium is all yours!"
>
> **Mickey Mantle**: "Thank you very much. Before I make any personal comments, I have one last task here. Joe gave me a plaque they're going to hang on the center-field wall. And certainly, if they give me one, his has gotta be hanging just a little bit higher than mine. To the greatest Yankee that I ever saw, it's gonna be a great honor for me to present him with this plaque. Thank you very much."
>
> **Joe DiMaggio**: "Ladies and gentlemen. Thank you, Mickey. I just want to add this certainly is a pleasant surprise. I had no idea this was going to happen. I just want to say I'm out there with great company. Thank you so much."
>
> **Mickey Mantle**: "When I first walked in here 18 years ago, I felt much the same as I do right now. I don't have words to describe how I felt then or how I feel now. I'll tell you one

> thing. Baseball was real good to me and playing 18 years in Yankee Stadium before you folks is the best thing that could happen to a ball player. To think that the Yankees are retiring my No. 7 with numbers 3, 4, and 5 tops off everything that I could ever wish for. I've often wondered how a man who knew he was going to die could stand here and say he was the luckiest man in the world. But now I think I know how Lou Gehrig felt. This is not just a great day for me, it's a great day for all of the Mantles, my wife Merlyn, my four boys, my mother and I wish my father could have been here but. ... It's been a great honor. I'll never forget it. God bless you all and thank you very much."

Mickey then stepped into the Yankee bullpen golf cart. It was decorated in Yankee pinstripes and the license plate read: 'MM-7'. Yankee Stadium groundskeeper Danny Colletti slowly drove Mickey around the perimeter of the field as he waved to the fans in every section of every deck.

After the ceremony, Mantle sat down in the press room and fondly recalled the moment. "That last ride around the park. That gave me goose pimples. But I didn't cry. I felt like it. Maybe tonight, when I go to bed, I'll think about it. I wish that could happen to every man in America. I think the fans know how much I think about them—all over the country. It was the most nervous I've ever been—but the biggest thrill. The thing I miss most is being around the clubhouse. Not the way I played the last four years—that wasn't fun. I've got some guys on this team that are almost like brothers to me—Pepi, Tresh, Stottlemyre. I'm probably their biggest fan. First thing I do every morning is pick up the paper and see how they did."

Touching All the Bases

Mickey made his debut as a baseball television commentator on April 12, with NBC in a nationally televised game between the San Francisco Giants and the San Diego Padres. "Maybe I should make a comeback," boasted Mickey. "The game looks easy from up here."

On April 23, Mickey played golf in a pro-amateur preliminary to the Byron Nelson Golf Classic. On the dogleg 440-yard 14th hole, Mickey hit a tee shot that landed only 32 yards from the green for a whopping drive of 400 yards. Professional golfer Martin Roesink witnessed the drive and stated, "I saw it, yet I can hardly believe the distance the ball traveled."

Chapter Twenty-Six

ENSHRINED IN COOPERSTOWN

On January 16, 1974, in his first year of eligibility, Mickey Mantle's name was on the ballot for induction into baseball's Hall of Fame. The 365 members of the Baseball Writers Association of America would determine his fate and that of several other players, including Mickey's great friend Whitey Ford. In order to be inducted, a player needs 75 percent of the votes. Only six players had ever been inducted in their first year of eligibility—Ted Williams, Stan Musial, Jackie Robinson, Bob Feller, Sandy Koufax, and Warren Spahn.

After the voting was tallied, at the age of 42, Mickey became the seventh player in Hall of Fame history to gain admission on his first try with 322 votes (89.4 percent). His buddy Whitey Ford also got in with 284 votes (77.8 percent). The election marked the first time two players from the same team were elected in the same year.

"Probably the biggest thrill I ever had," said Mantle, "is that Whitey and I both made the Hall of Fame together. He's the best pitcher I ever saw. I'm closer to Whitey than to any other man in the world. I talk to Billy Martin a lot now that he lives in Dallas, and I talk to Yogi Berra on the phone. But Whitey and I were roommates for 12 years, and it wouldn't have been any fun getting into the Hall of Fame without Whitey. It's nice the two of us made it together—

we have always been great friends. Our families are very close. When you're playing, especially if you were alone or if you'd struck out a couple times, you'd say, 'What the h---'s it all for, anyway?' But if you hit a home run and your teammates jumped all over you, you knew what it's all for. And when you're elected to the Hall of Fame, you know it's really worth it then."

Mantle was somewhat surprised that the sportswriters voted him into the Hall: "A lot of them thought I was arrogant. It wasn't that at all. I was scared. I was afraid to say anything. They thought it was aloofness. It wasn't. It was just plain scaredness."

Casey Stengel recalled when Mickey went to his first spring training in Arizona, "He could have embarrassed my writers if it turned out he could not hit the curve ball. They had him in Cooperstown in knickers." He then praised Mickey, "You'd see him, he'd go down the dugout steps and his knees would shake. But he was the greatest hitter for distance I ever managed. The distance of those balls were outstanding. He hit one in Washington one day and they had to send a cab after it."

Sportswriter Jim Murray wrote, "Mantle's career could have been traced in X-rays. He had more cartilage and bone taken out of him than most people have. He was built like something that should have horns. He had to be careful on hunts. Even the moose thought he was one of them."

David Condon, another sportswriter, wrote, "It was fascinating to watch Mickey progress from rookie to elder statesman of the Yankees. God gave Mickey many gifts. The most precious of all was class."

At 10 a.m., August 12, on the porch of the National Baseball Library, six people were inducted into the National Baseball Hall of Fame in Cooperstown, New York, which included Mickey Mantle, Whitey Ford, Jim Bottomley, Cool Papa Bell, Jocko Conlan, and Sam Thompson. The six new members increased the Hall of Fame membership total to 146. On hand for the induction where other baseball greats such as Roy Campanella, Joe Cronin, Bill Dickey, Charley Gehringer, Lefty Grove, Buck Leonard, Monte Irvin, Joe Medwick, Casey Stengel, and Stan Musial.

Enshrined in Cooperstown

As the ceremony unfolded in front of approximately 2,500 onlookers, the baseball commissioner, Bowie Kuhn, prepared to introduce Mickey Mantle. He first read some of Mickey's many accomplishments such as his numerous World Series records for most home runs (18), RBIs (40), runs scored (42), and total bases (123). Kuhn then read a list of awards such as AL MVP in 1956, 1957, and 1962. The crowd then gave Mickey a warm ovation as he stepped to the microphone and read his prepared speech:

> Thank you very much, Commissioner. I would really like to thank you for leaving out those strikeouts. He gave all those records, but he didn't say anything about all those strikeouts. I was the world champion in striking out and everything, I'm sure. I don't know for sure, but I'm positive I must have had that record in the World Series, too. I broke Babe Ruth's record for all-time strikeouts. He only had, like, 1,500 I think. I ended up with 1,710. So that's one that no one will ever break probably, because, if you strike out that much, you don't get to play very long. I just liked to.
>
> One of the reasons I'm in the Hall of Fame right now is not because of my speaking, so everybody be patient here. I know it's hot and I'll try to get through with what I gotta say real fast here. I was named after a Hall of Famer. I think this is the first time it's ever happened that a guy's ever come into the Hall of Fame that was named after one. Before I was born, my father lived and died for baseball, and he named me after a Hall of Famer: Mickey Cochrane. I'm not sure if my dad knew it or not, but his real name was Gordon. I hope there's no Gordons here today, but I'm glad that he didn't name me Gordon.
>
> He had the foresight to realize that someday in baseball that left-handed hitters were going to hit against right-handed pitchers, and right-handed hitters were going to hit against left-handed pitchers; and he taught me—he and his father—to switch-hit when I was at a real young age, when I first started to learn how to play ball. And my dad always told me if I could hit both ways when I got ready to go to the major leagues, that I would have a better chance of playing. And, believe it or not, the year that I came to the Yankees is when Casey started platooning everybody. So he did realize that that was going to happen someday, and it did. So I was lucky that they taught me how to switch-hit when I was young.

We lived in a little town called Commerce, Oklahoma, and my mother, who is here today—I'd like to introduce her right now ... Mom. We didn't have a lot of money or anything. She used to make my uniforms and we would buy the cleats or get 'em off of somebody else's shoes or somethin' and then we would take 'em and have 'em put onto a pair of my street shoes that were getting old. So that's how we started out. We lived in Commerce till I can remember I was about in high school, then we moved out to a farm. We had a 160-acre farm out in White Bird, Oklahoma, I remember. I had three brothers, but one of them was too little. My mom used to have to make the twins come out and play ball with me. We dozed a little ballpark out in the pasture, and I think that I probably burnt my twins out on baseball. I think by the time the twins got old enough to play ball they were tired of it, because I used to make 'em shag flies for me and play all day, which I'm sorry of because they could have been great ballplayers.

My dad really is probably the most influential thing that ever happened to me in my life. He loved baseball, I loved it and, like I say, he named me after a baseball player. He worked in the mines, and when he came home at night, why, he would come out and, after we milked the cows, we would go ahead and play ball till dark. I don't know how he kept doing it.

I think the first real baseball uniform—and I'm sure it is—the most proud I ever was, was when I went to Baxter Springs in Kansas and I played on the Baxter Springs Whiz Kids. We had—that was the first time—I'll never forget the guy, his name was Barney Burnett, gave me a uniform and it had a BW on the cap there and it said Whiz Kids on the back. I really thought I was somethin' when I got that uniform. It was the first one my mom hadn't made for me. It was really somethin'.

There is a man and a woman here that were really nice to me all through the years, Mr. and Mrs. Harold Youngman. I don't know if all of you have ever heard about any of my business endeavors or not, but some of 'em weren't too good. Probably the worst thing I ever did was movin' away from Mr. Youngman. We went and moved to Dallas, Texas, in 1957, but Mr. Youngman built a Holiday Inn in Joplin, Missouri, and called it Mickey Mantle's Holiday Inn. And we were doin' pretty good there, and Mr. Youngman said, 'You know, you're half of this thing, so why don't you do something for it.' So we had a real good chicken there and I made up a slogan. Merlyn doesn't want me to tell this, but I'm goin' to tell it anyway. I made up the slogan for our chicken and I said, 'To get a better piece of chicken, you'd have to be a rooster.' And I don't know if that's what closed up our Holiday Inn or not, but we didn't do too good after that. No, actually, it was really a good deal.

Also, in Baxter Springs, the ballpark is right by the highway, and Tom Greenwade, the Yankee scout, was coming by there one day. He saw this ball game goin' on and I was playing in it and he stopped to watch the game. I'm making this kind of fast; it's gettin' a little hot. And I hit three home runs that day, and Greenwade, the Yankee scout, stopped and talked to me. He was actually on his way to Broken Arrow, Oklahoma, to sign another shortstop. I was playing shortstop at that time, and I hit three home runs that day. A couple of them went in the river—one right-handed and one left-handed—and he stopped and he said, 'You're not out of high school yet, so I really can't talk to you yet, but I'll be back when you get out of high school.'

In 1949, Tom Greenwade came back to Commerce the night that I was supposed to go to my commencement exercises. He asked the principal of the school if I could go play ball. The Whiz Kids had a game that night. He took me. I hit another home run or two that night, so he signed me and I went to Independence, Kansas, Class D League, and started playing for the Yankees. I was very fortunate to play for Harry Craft. He had a great ball club there. We have one man here in the audience today who I played with in the minors, Carl Lombardi. He was on those teams, so he knows we had two of the greatest teams in minor league baseball at that time, or any time probably, and I was very fortunate to have played with those two teams.

I was lucky when I got out. I played in Joplin. The next year, I came to the Yankees. And I was lucky to play with Whitey Ford, Yogi Berra, Joe DiMaggio, Phil Rizzuto—who came up with me—and I appreciate it. He's been a great friend all the way through for me. Lots of times I've teased Whitey about how I could have played five more years if it hadn't been for him, but, believe me, when Ralph Houk used to say that I was the leader of the Yankees, he was just kiddin' everybody. Our real leader was Whitey Ford all the time. I'm sure that everybody will tell you that.

Casey Stengel's here in the Hall of Fame already and, outside of my dad, I would say that probably Casey is the man who is most responsible for me standing right here today. The first thing he did was to take me off of shortstop and get me out in the outfield where I wouldn't have to handle so many balls.

> At this time, I'd like to introduce my family. I introduced my mother. Merlyn, my wife; we've been married 22 years. That's a record, where I come from. Mickey, my oldest boy, David, Billy, and Danny. That's my family that I've been with for so long.
>
> I listened to Mr. Terry make a talk last night just for the Hall of Famers, and he said that he hoped we would come back, and I just hope that Whitey and I can live up to the expectation and what these here guys stand for. I'm sure we're going to try to. I just would—before I leave—would like to thank everybody for coming up here. It's been a great day for all of us and I appreciate it very much."

Years later, in an interview, Mickey spoke about the implications of being inducted into the Hall of Fame, "The turnaround was in 1974. Maybe it called people's attention to who I was and what I'd done. I don't know, but things started to change. I think I'm more popular now than when I was playing. People come to me in the streets, they spend fortunes for my baseball card—I tell you, it's flattering to be remembered, but I'm kind of worried. I could be overexposed—people get tired of some guys after a while, you know?"

Mickey Mantle's plaque that hangs in the Hall of Fame reads: Mickey Charles Mantle. New York A.L. 1951-1968. Hit 536 home runs. Won league homer title and slugging crown four times. Made 2,415 hits. Batted .300 or over in each of 10 years with top of .356 in 1957. Topped A.L. in walks five years and in runs scored six seasons. Voted Most Valuable Player 1956-57-62. Named on 20 A.L. All-Star Teams. Set World Series records for homers, 18; runs, 42; runs batted in, 40; total bases, 123; and bases on balls, 45.

Chapter Twenty-Seven

A HERO TO THE END

In January of 1994, at age 62, Mickey Mantle publicly admitted that he was an alcoholic and entered himself into the Betty Ford Clinic in Palm Springs, California for treatment. His close friend, Pat Summerall is commonly credited as the one who convinced Mickey to undertake the 32-day treatment. Mickey had been suffering from memory loss and blackouts over the past six years. During his stay at the Betty Ford Clinic, he was no longer Mickey Mantle—he was the guy in Room 202.

On March 12, 1994, Mickey's youngest son, Billy, died of a heart attack at the age of 36. Billy had suffered from drug dependency and Hodgkin's disease. This tormented Mickey: "I often wondered why the disease had skipped me after it had felled so many in my family. I had been expecting it all my life. For that matter, why had it spared my brothers, my sister, and their children? Why had it picked Billy? I wish it had been me. I wish I could have taken the cancer from him."

After suffering from severe stomach cramps for several weeks, Mickey was taken to Baylor University Medical Center by ambulance on May 28, 1995. The doctors quickly discovered that Mickey had liver cancer. The cancer had resulted from Hepatitis C that he had contracted from a blood transfusion in one of his multiple surgeries due to baseball injuries. Mickey's heavy drinking had fueled the cancer. Without a liver transplant, doctors estimated that he had two to four weeks left to live. The problem was that the drugs necessary to keep his body from rejecting the new liver, suppresses the immune system and tends to make cancer cells grow more quickly. The doctors recommended an experimental regimen of grueling chemotherapy to supplement the liver transplant. Mickey responded with, "I want to do whatever we have to do. It goes back to my days as a ballplayer. I never give up."

The press's interest in Mantle's illness was unprecedented. Jennifer Coleman, Vice President of Public Affairs for the Baylor Health Care System marveled, "I have been here 15 years, and have handled stories ranging from the exhumation of Lee Harvey Oswald, to celebrity patients, including Barbara Bush, Marilyn Quayle, and John Tower. This case has probably generated the biggest press crush."

When the medical center's clip service used the key words "Mantle" and "Baylor" to search the database, all 18,000 sources that they monitor had run a story on Mantle at least twice. The cumulative tape of the television coverage was already over eight hours long.

After a 3.3-day wait for a donor, the 63-year-old, 225-pound Mantle underwent a liver transplant during a six-and-one-half hour operation on June 8. Mickey was moved from intensive care on June 10, and his condition was upgraded to "serious but stable." After the surgery, Dr. Goran Klintmalm described the operation to the press, "This donor contributed seven organs that have gone into six different people. It shows how he made a contribution to humanity." One sportswriter asked him, "Well, is the donor alive?" The audience broke into laughter while Dr. Klintmalm struggled to maintain his composure as he replied, "So, you're a sportswriter, Mike?" Jennifer Coleman later pointed out, "It showed how we were dealing with reporters who were medical writers and who knew all about liver transplants, and we had a group of sportswriters who know only Mickey Mantle."

During his recovery, Mickey received tens of thousands of cards and letters. The letters of hope, inspiration, and gratitude came from men and women, boys and girls, professional people including doctors, lawyers, businessmen, and blue collar workers, from every state, Canada, Mexico and around the world. One of the more noted letters read, "Dear Mickey: Hillary and I were so sorry to learn of your health problems. You hold a special place in the hearts of Americans across the country, and I hope that all of our thoughts and prayers will bring strength to you during this difficult time. Sincerely, Bill Clinton."

Mickey experienced a slight rejection of his new liver on June 22. Doctors said it was common, and treated the rejection with high doses of steroids. After being hospitalized for exactly one month, and approximately forty pounds lighter, Mickey was released from the hospital on June 28.

In a press conference held on July 11, a gaunt and frail Mickey made a public statement in which he pleaded, "Don't be like me. God gave me a body and the ability to play baseball. I had everything and I just ... " His voice faded off as his eyes became misty. Mickey composed himself and then added, "I've been so lucky. I owe so much to God, to the American people, to Baylor University. I think they saved my life. I'll never be able to pay it all back to all you people. But as soon as I get more stable, I'll try to make up for stuff."

Regarding his alcoholism, Mickey said, "All you got to do is look at me to see it's wasted. I want to get across to the kids not to drink or do drugs, everything. I think that moms and dads should be the role models."

Talk show host Rush Limbaugh was impressed with Mantle's public statement and had this to say about it, "I never met Mickey Mantle and saw him play only once, so I leave commentary on his career to others more qualified. I will, however, never forget Mickey's press conference following the transplant surgery. He said he wasted all the blessings bestowed upon him. 'Don't be like me,' he warned kids. This was, to me, as valuable as anything he inspired by playing. His point was that he could have been even better that he was had he only taken his life more seriously. On that day, Mantle's journey to manhood was completed. Mickey Mantle, role model for millions, transcended the confines of mere athletic prowess by reminding us of one simple fact we often neglect: that we can all excel beyond our own self-imposed limitations and actually live our dreams. It is up to us."

On August 1, doctors announced that Mickey's cancer had spread to his right lung. A couple of days earlier, Mickey had recorded the following public announcement,

"Hi, this is Mick. When I left Baylor University Medical Center about six weeks ago, I felt great. I started working out on the treadmills, bicycles, etc. and I was doing great. I came back to the hospital for check-ups. About two weeks ago, the doctors found a couple of spots of cancer in my lungs. Now I'm taking chemotherapy to get rid of the new cancer. I'm hoping to get back to as good as I was right after the transplant. I'd like to again thank everyone for all the thoughts and prayers. And if you'd like to do something really great—be a donor. Thank you."

Doctors downgraded Mickey's condition to "serious" on August 9, when they revealed that the cancer had spread beyond his lungs to his pancreas and bowels. Dr. Goran Klintmalm, medical director of transplant services at Baylor said, "This is the most aggressive cancer that anyone on the medical team has ever seen. But the hope in this is that Mickey left behind a legacy. Mickey and his team have already made an enormous impact by increasing the awareness of organ donation. This may become Mickey's ultimate home run."

Mickey's condition worsened so quickly that the Mantle family decided to ask his teammates to come visit him one last time. Whitey Ford was the first Yankee visitor, and he lifted Mickey's spirits tremendously. The following day, Moose Skowron, Hank Bauer, and Johnny Blanchard visited Mickey. After the visit, Blanchard sadly stated, "My heart just sank. I remember this guy carved out of granite. And to see his face withered and shrunk—my Adam's apple was as hard as a rock." Mickey's last teammate to visit him was Bobby Richardson, a lay minister. With Richardson's help, Mickey accepted his death with grace. Mickey told Richardson, "Bobby, I want you to know I've accepted Christ as my savior."

A Hero to the End

Mickey's gastroenterologist, Daniel DeMarco marveled at Mickey's courage as he said, "Somebody is lying on their deathbed, and you disturb or awaken them, and the first thing they do is smile at you. I've never really seen anyone do that. And then he would lift his hand up and shake your hand."

Mantle was in and out of consciousness over his final 48 hours. He awoke for the last time around 12:30 a.m. CDT, held the hands of his wife, Merlyn, and son, David, then lapsed back to sleep. He died at 1:10 a.m. CDT on August 13.

Later that day at Yankee Stadium, on a perfect baseball afternoon, the crowd of 45,866 once again cheered wildly for Mickey Mantle as the DiamondVision screen played a seven-minute tape of highlights from his career. All the flags and pennants around the rim of the stadium were at half-staff. Just prior to the video, Bob Sheppard, who had become the Yankee announcer the same day that Mickey played his first game as a New York Yankee, announced, "Today is a sad day for the Yankee family and Yankee fans. Today we have lost one of our own, and one of the greatest players in the history of baseball. Please join now for a few moments of silent prayer as we all remember Mickey Mantle." The moment of silence was followed by a two-minute standing ovation.

Bobby Murcer praised Mantle, "Mickey, the reason people loved him so much is that he portrayed the innocence of what we all want to be. I don't think to this day Mickey ever realized how people felt about him and how he touched their lives. We've truly lost not only an American hero, but a person that portrayed the innocence and the honesty that we would all like to have." The New York Yankee players wore black armbands and some honored Mickey even further by marking a No. 7 on their caps.

Funeral services were held at Lovers Lane United Methodist Church in Dallas, Texas, on Tuesday, August 15. The church only accommodated 1,500 people, but over 2,000 mourners showed up—some as early as 5 a.m. in order to get a seat. People from all walks of life came to pay tribute to their hero. Two governors were present, including Texas Governor George W. Bush. Many of Mickey's teammates attended, including Yogi Berra, Whitey Ford, Hank Bauer,

Moose Skowron, Bobby Richardson, Johnny Blanchard, and Bobby Murcer. Other notables present were members of the Roger Maris family, Reggie Jackson, and Billy Crystal.

Flowers surrounded the casket and the podium area. A beautiful spray of white flowers on a bed of greenery covered the stately mahogany casket. Next to the podium was an arrangement of blue flowers bordered by white flowers, forming Mickey's famous number 7. Pastor William J. Bryan III began the ceremony with prayers. Bobby Richardson read passages from the Bible and then introduced Bob Costas who delivered a powerful and eloquent eulogy. Richardson then called upon country singer Roy Clark to sing "Yesterday When I Was Young". Mickey had first heard Roy Clark perform the song at a charity golf tournament at Preston Trails in Dallas. He had thought that it depicted his life so well that he asked Roy to sing it at his funeral. As Clark stepped up to the microphone, with his guitar in hand, he said, "Well, a promise is a promise. It just wasn't supposed to happen this soon."

As Bobby Richardson stepped back to the podium to give his eulogy, he said, "Roy, I was told that when you played that song, Mickey would always end up crying." He then delivered the eulogy, which included several humorous stories about Mickey:

> I want to make a transition now from crying and sadness to laughter, because if you know Mickey, he was always laughing and he enjoyed playing football in the back yard with the boys. He enjoyed golf games at Preston Trails with the boys, and their traveling to autograph sessions with him. But the teammates that are here today will also know that he always kept all of us laughing. I remember the Mongoose in Detroit in the clubhouse. I remember the snake that he put in Marshall Bridges' uniform in Kansas City before he was dressing that day. He always ran out of money, [so] he borrowed money from Yogi, and Yogi would charge him 50 percent—no, that's not in there. I'm sorry. I take that back Yogi. Yogi flew in today on Bob Hope's plane, and he's flying out tomorrow with President Ford's plane.
>
> Yogi was a manager in 1964. The Yankees lost four games in a row in Chicago. Tony Kubek had bought some harmonicas. He gave one to Phil Linz. Phil didn't play in any of those

ballgames, but on the bus, with Yogi in the front, he chose this time to learn how to play his harmonica. Well, he played for a while and Yogi took as much as he could and finally he jumped up and he said, 'Put that thing in your pocket!' He didn't use those words, but something to that effect; and Phil was in the back of the bus and he didn't hear what [Yogi] said, and he said, 'What did he say?' And Mickey was sitting over across the isle and he whispered back, 'He said he couldn't hear you. Play it again!'

And Yogi was the manager in '64 when Whitey Ford and Mickey started talking about how good they were in other sports, basketball in particular. And it ended up we played the cadets at West Point. Whitey was to have the pitchers and catchers, and Mickey was to have the infielders and outfielders; and there would be a great game at the gymnasium at West Point after the regulars got out of the lineup. Well, Yogi said, 'Somebody's gonna get hurt.' Well, Mickey did it right. He had uniforms for his players, he had a limousine, he had a chauffeur. He did like this, and they took players on Mickey's team over to the game and came back. And it was a great game. Mickey's team won! Tommy Tresh was voted most valuable. Yogi was right. Steve Hamilton—the only one that played professional basketball—turned his ankle, and he was hurt.

But you know so many good things that Mickey did that people never heard about. I remember that he flew across the country for Fritz Packel when he was dying with cancer. In this church, right here, he did a benefit for Missions Outreach. And over the years he very seldom said no. He came to my hometown on numerous occasions, but in particular for the YMCA. We had a great banquet. There was a highlights film. And then we went out to the ballpark and Mickey was to give a batting exhibition. Something you just can't imagine him doing. Tony Kubek was there. Tony throws straight overhanded, same speed all the time. He was chosen to pitch to Mickey. Everything was all set, but Tony changed up on Mickey on the first pitch, and he swung and missed and pulled his leg; and if he could have run he would have chased Tony around the outfield. Tony made up for it though. He hit one in the light towers in right field in the old-timers game that followed that.

But underneath all of Mickey's laughter and kindness there was a fear of death and an emptiness that he tried to cover and fill, sometimes with harmful choices. Remember Bob [Costas] when he said on his interview, 'There's still an emptiness inside.' The last game that Mickey and I played together was on October 2, 1966. It was in Chicago and we were at the Bismarck Hotel. I had invited a friend—a friend of mine, a friend of Mickey's— to come over and speak to the ball club. His name was Billy Zeoli, president of Gospel Films. I remember standing in the back of the room that was set aside and most of the players where there in attendance. And looking over their shoulders at the fine, efficient, professional baseball players were there. And yet I knew that all of us had problems. Some financial, some marital—problems of various natures. And yet my friend, that day, gave the answer to each one of these problems in the person of Jesus Christ. He held his Bible up and he said, 'The Bible says three things: (1) One, the Bible says there's a problem and the problem is sin. (2) Two, the Bible gives the answer to the problem in the person of Jesus Christ. (3) Three, the Bible demands a decision.'

And then he turned around and he had a blackboard and a piece of chalk, and he wrote this question up on the blackboard: 'What have you done with Jesus Christ?' And then he went on to give three possible answers. Number one was to say 'yes', to accept Jesus Christ as Lord and savior. And I remember looking around that room at some of my teammates that I knew had said 'yes' to Christ. The second possibility was to say 'no'. And I knew there were some of us that were unwilling to give up perhaps what we had going at that time. And the third possibility was to say 'maybe', to put it off to a more convenient time with good intentions. But my friend made this statement. He said saying 'maybe', because of the X-factor of death, automatically puts you in the 'no' category.

I didn't really understand that then, but some years later—not too many years ago—we had a reunion of the 1961 New York Yankees in Atlantic City, New Jersey. The players were there in attendance. It was a wonderful time of thinking back and remembering. But in my room that night, I realized that three were not there. Roger Maris, who broke Babe Ruth's home run record and a battle with cancer; Elston Howard, that fine catcher on the ball club with a heart condition; and a young pitcher by the name of Duke Maas. And so I understood what he meant when he said, 'Because of the X-factor of death, it's really 'no.' So really only two choices, one to say 'yes', the other 'no'.

And then my big thrill in baseball when a young teammate of mine who played for the next seven or eight years came up and said, 'You know, I've never heard that before, a personal relationship with a living savior that gives to us in abundant life. I would like to receive Jesus Christ as my savior.' And that's the excitement, but there's more excitement. I came here to Dallas during the All-Star break this past month. Mickey Mantle and Whitey Ford and I serve on the BAT board, and I was here because of that. And I had gotten the number from Whitey, and I called Mickey and we had a great conversation together. And then the next morning—about six o'clock—he called my room and Betsy answered the phone and he said, 'Betsy, is Bobby there? I would like for him to pray for me.' And we had a wonderful time, on the telephone that morning, praying and I remember that I used the verse of scripture. I said, 'Mickey, there's a great verse in Philippians 4. It says, 'delight yourself in the Lord. Find your joy in him at all times. Never forget his nearness.' And then it says, 'tell God, in details, your problems, your anxieties. And the promises of peace of God which passeth all understanding shall keep our hearts and minds as we rest in Christ Jesus.'

We talked two or three more times and I went on back to South Carolina, and I received a call from Roy True, his friend and lawyer, and he said, 'Mickey's not doing very well and the family would like for you to consider the possibility of coming out and being in the service.' And I asked Merlyn if it would be all right if I could come on out, and she said 'yes'. Well, I came in on—I guess it was last Wednesday night. Friends picked me up at the airport and I spent the night with them, it was late. And the next morning, I drove over to Baylor Hospital. Whitey Ford was just walking out at the time, and Mickey had really perked up with Whitey's visit. And as I walked in and went over to his bed, he had that smile on his face. And he looked at me and the first thing he said was, 'Bobby, I've been wanting to tell you something. I want you to know that I've received Christ as my savior.' Well, I cried a little bit, I'm sure, and we had prayer together, and then in a very simple way I said, 'Mickey, I just want to make sure.' And I went over God's plan of salvation with him. That God loved us and had a plan, a purpose and a plan for all of us and sent his son, the Lord Jesus Christ, to shed his precious blood and promise in his word that if we repent of our sins and receive the Lord Jesus that we might not only have everlasting life, but the joy of letting him live his life in us. He said, 'That's what I've done.'

"Well, the big three came in that afternoon. That's Moose Skowron, Hank Bauer, and Johnny Blanchard. And they had a wonderful visit again with Mickey. My wife and I came back later that afternoon and I remember that Mickey was in bed, but he wanted to be in the reclining chair. And David and Danny and a couple of the others I think helped him over. He was laughing then. When David grabbed him, he said, 'Do you want to dance?' But he sat in the chair and my wife, Betsy, sat down by him and shared her testimony. And then she asked him a question. She said, 'Mickey, if God were here today and you were standing before him and he would ask the question, 'Why should I let you in my heaven?' what would you say?' And as quick as a flash, he said, 'For God so loved the world he gave his only begotten son and whosoever believeth in him shall not parish but have everlasting life.' Well, I guess it was a little bit later and I said, 'Mickey, you remember your day in New York? You had heard me use a little poem called "God's Hall of Fame". You talked about using it that day.' He said, 'Yeah, I should have.' I said, 'No. I'm not sure that was the right time Mickey. But you know I think it is the right time today. It says it all. It says:

'Your name may not appear down here
In this world's Hall of Fame.
In fact, you may be so unknown
That no one knows your name;
The headlines here may pass you by,
The neon lights of blue,
But if you love and serve the Lord,
Then I have news for you.

'This Hall of Fame is only good
As long as time shall be;
But keep in mind, God's Hall of Fame
Is for eternity.

'This crowd on earth they soon forget
The heroes of the past.
They cheer like mad until you fail
and that's how long you last.
But in God's Hall of Fame
By just believing in His Son
Inscribed you'll find your name.

> 'I tell you, friend, I wouldn't trade
> My name, however small,
> That's written there beyond the stars
> In that Celestial Hall,
> For any famous name on earth,
> Or glory that it shares;
> I'd rather be an unknown here
> And have my name up there.'

> Mickey's last press conference, he once again mentions his struggle with alcohol and a desire to be a dad to his boys. He also mentioned his real heroes—the organ donors. I hope you will all support the Mickey Mantle Foundation that addresses these issues and join his team.
>
> But, if Mick could hold a press conference from where he is today, I know that he would introduce you to his true hero. The one who died in his place to give him not just a longer physical life but everlasting life, his savior, Jesus Christ. And the greatest tribute that you could give Mickey today would be for you to receive his savior too.
>
> Let's bow for prayer.

Roy Clark followed by singing "Amazing Grace." Afterward, organ music played as the Mantle family and friends filed out of the sanctuary. The pallbearers (Berra, Ford, Bauer, Skowron, Blanchard, and Murcer) lifted the casket into the hearse. Inside the church, "The Lord's Prayer" was sung to conclude the ceremony. A private burial took place at Sparkman-Hillcrest Memorial Park.

On August 17, the Mantle family carried out Mickey's last wish and held a press conference to announce a new organ donor program. "My father made this a personal issue," said Danny Mantle. "We want to keep his commitment and dream alive. There are thousands of people waiting for organs." Approximately one million donor cards were printed with Mickey's liver transplant story and his plea for people to become organ donors. The cards were handed out to fans at major league baseball games across the country over Labor Day weekend. One report stated that requests for organ donor cards were up over 40 percent since Mickey's liver transplant.

Touching All the Bases

On August 25, 1996, the Yankees unveiled a 4,500-pound granite monument honoring Mickey in Monument Park at the stadium. He is the fourth Yankee to be immortalized in such a way. The first three were Miller Huggins, Lou Gehrig, and Babe Ruth. Mickey's monument reads: "Mickey Mantle 'A Great Teammate' (1931-1995). Winner of the Triple Crown: 1956. Most World Series Homers: 18. Selected to All-Star Game: 20 Times. Won MVP Award: 1956, 1957, 1962. Elected to Hall of Fame: 1974. A magnificent Yankee who left a legacy of unequaled courage.

Chapter Twenty-Eight

THOUGHTS ON A GREAT TEAMMATE

"He could run. He could throw. He outran balls playing the outfield. He was built like a brick wall. He was just a great helluva ballplayer. God gave him a lot of talent and he took advantage of it. He could do everything, and to me he was the greatest ballplayer I played with or against in my career. He was just a tremendous man, a gentleman and a great teammate."

Moose Skowron

***

"Once the game starts, no one on our ball club tries any harder than Mickey. Sometimes he tries too hard. I can see it killing him inside each time he comes back to the bench after he makes an out. You have no idea how badly he felt when his leg kept him from playing in all the World Series games against Brooklyn last year. When I say he really wanted to play no matter what, I'm not exaggerating one bit. He hates to sit on the bench. Like any good athlete, Mickey always wants to do better. He's never satisfied. But he isn't the kind of guy who plays all for himself. Even if he has a good day, he doesn't feel good about it if the club loses. In my book, that's the sign of a good ballplayer."

Billy Martin

★★★

"I don't know that Mickey was ever on the weights. He just got big and muscular without steroids, and he was pure power. I understand that he milked cows for a while in Commerce. I was born and raised on a farm in Iowa and I had to milk cows, and that'll build up that forearm I'll tell you."

Keith Speck

★★★

"Mickey has strong wrists, powerful forearms and a back that a heavyweight champion wouldn't be ashamed of."

Bill Dickey

★★★

"Of course, I haven't seen everyone who ever played baseball, but I think Mantle may have the best body for baseball that's ever been. It's by far the best I've seen."

Jerry Coleman

★★★

"The more clothes he takes off, the bigger he gets. You know he wears a 17 ½-inch collar."

Billy Martin

★★★

"At least three times I saw Mickey hit the ball on the fists or end of the bat and in disgust step out of the batter's box and whack the bat on the ground, breaking it. Then he would look up and start running down to first base just in time to see the ball going out of the park. He was so strong, occasionally he didn't even know when he'd hit a home run."

Tony Kubek

★★★

"The first time I played against the Yankees I snuck up near the cage to see him hit. The sound of the ball off the bat was enough to make me run back to the dugout. It was intimidating."

Jim Kaat

★★★

"Few people realize the terrific coordination he has. I've heard it said he gets all his hitting power from brute strength, but I disagree. I think the secret is in his timing, and Mick agrees with me. Take Bob Cerv. He's as strong, if not stronger than anyone on our club. But he doesn't have Mickey's timing. Who has? When Mantle hit them, so help me, they look off like golf balls disappearing over the horizon. He gets wrists, forearms, back, and everything into the ball at the moment of impact."

Billy Martin

★★★

"I've been with Mickey ever since he came up, and I never can quite bring myself to believe he hits those balls the way he does. You know, he hits them as though they don't count if they're under 400 feet."

Joe Collins

★★★

"His swing is so perfect and his power is so great that he hit that ball over 400 feet, right off the fists. A good hitter—and I mean a good hitter—considers himself to be going well to hit one 350 to 375 feet when he gets the fat part of his bat on it."

Joe Collins

★★★

"Nobody could drive a ball like Mickey. I'd hit one in the upper deck in batting practice and Mickey would follow me with a ball about 30 or 40 rows higher. Then he would just laugh like hell."

Hank Bauer

★★★

"The kid runs so fast he doesn't even bend the grass when he steps on it. He hits so hard when he swings now that no infielder who has any regard for his teeth can play in for a bunt. And if they play back, he'll be crossing first base just about the time they'll be picking up one of his bunts."

Casey Stengel

★★★

"I'd give him the bunt if he decided to bunt. We'd rather see Mantle bunt four times than swing away once and hit one out."

Al Weis

★★★

"There isn't any sense in stealing when you have fellas which can hit the ball out of the park. You don't have to steal with Mantle, because you've seen him go from first to third, and from first to home, too, as far as that's concerned, which he does faster than anybody playing ball today."

Casey Stengel

★★★

"Everybody used to talk about Tris Speaker, how when he was playing with Cleveland and being in so close and everything, how he could go back and get a fly ball. 'He actually outruns the ball,' they used to say. Which he did all right, but Speaker was outrunning the dead ball. This boy outruns the lively ball."

Casey Stengel

★★★

"Around 1960, during spring training, I was on a bus with Dr. Gaynor. He was the Yankee team physician. He was also the chief surgeon at Lenox Hills Hospital in New York where he gave an hour class once a week. He told me the story of how he once took X-rays of Mickey's knees, with no names on them, and put them up on a light box. He had all the doctors in the class evaluate them and then he said, 'Now I want you to tell me what kind of shape you think this guy is in with this knee.' The first physician said, 'Well, he's in a wheelchair.' The next doctor said, 'He might be on crutches or at least uses a walking cane.' Another doctor said, 'This guy can't walk, he shuffles.' They all had their versions from the wheelchair to the cane and everything in between. And then Dr. Gaynor stood up and said, 'Gentlemen, you are all wrong. Those are the knees of Mickey Mantle and he's playing center field for the Yankees tonight.' Needless to say, all of the doctors were amazed."

Johnny Blanchard

★★★

"I've seen him play when an ordinary guy would be home in bed. I've never seen anybody who drives himself the way Mantle does. When Mickey is out of the lineup because of an injury, you can be sure it's because it's actually impossible for him to play."

Tex Clevenger

★★★

"What I respected most about Mickey is that he played when he was hurt. He played hurt all the time. I dressed right next to Mickey. He would go get a massage first. The trainer, Gus Mauch, would rub his leg, put hot stuff on it, and then Mickey would go to his locker where he would wrap that foam rubber around from the ankle to the cheek of his fanny on both legs. It gave him a lot of support."

Moose Skowron

★★★

"He never played a game for me that he wasn't all taped up. I ask him how he feels and he says, 'O.K.' I ask him if he wants to play and he says, 'I want to play.' So I need him and I let him play. What should I do? Tie him to the bench?"

Casey Stengel

★★★

"I don't think there is a day that he isn't hurting somewhere. But you never hear him complain. His is a remarkable man. I don't know how he keeps going. Any other man would be on the bench when he is playing."

Casey Stengel

★★★

"By 1961, there seldom was a day when something wasn't bothering Mickey. It wasn't unusual for him to need help getting out of a cab because his legs were bothering him. He'd sort of brace himself and put out his hand. One of us would grab him by the wrist and literally pull him out of the cab. To fully appreciate Mickey, you would have had to see him after a ball game with his legs taped about from the thigh to the ankle. He wore these awkward rubber wraps, not the sophisticated braces of today. I'd look at the scars on his knees and wonder how he ever stood up, much less played. I once asked Mickey why he played on some days when he couldn't even get out of a cab. Mickey said, 'When I grew up, we didn't have any money, and I never saw a big-league game. I keep thinking that there might be a father out there who can afford to take his kid to only one game all year. And maybe that kid wanted to see me play. Tony, I just hated disappointing people, especially kids.'"

Tony Kubek

★★★

"The fact seems to be that baseball men who are physically and temperamentally closest to Mantle admire him in much the same way and for the same reasons as do fans who get no closer to the action than a bleacher seat. Not only has Mantle been a helluva ballplayer by any professional measure, but he has been a helluva ballplayer despite being crippled, hobbled, and flawed by injuries which, say other professionals, would have barred another man, not only from greatness, but even from playing. Players will tell you stories about Mantle playing in a World Series, his uniform dark with blood from an abscess; Mantle breaking up a game with one swing, a swing that twisted his face with pain; Mantle dragging a bunt and running all out on a knee that was precariously near total collapse. For his peers as well as the public, Mantle appears to fill the role of the wounded hero."

Bill Gilbert

★★★

"I see him swing sometimes and even from the outfield you can see the leg buckle under him and the way he winces in pain. I wince, too, when he does. It's like your own kid is in pain. You can feel the pain yourself. That's the way ballplayers feel about Mantle."

Carl Yastrzemski

★★★

"Nobody knows how much pain he endures but himself, and he'll never tell. About the only way I know how he feels is that he'll drop a casual remark. Like one day he'll say, 'My legs are feeling good.' Other times he'll tell me, 'Take everything you can get.' But he never says he's feeling bad."

Tom Tresh

★★★

"I didn't like the way Mantle was bunting on me. I figured he was taking advantage of my age. I was going to rack him up. But I watched him bandage his legs the last time I was in an All-Star game. I changed my mind. I figured any guy with legs like that is hurting himself more than me when he bunts."

Early Wynn

Thoughts on a Great Teammate

★★★

"Those legs of his. I had heard how they were all bandaged up. But I never realized how it was until I played with him in the 1962 All-Star game. Before the game, I happened to walk by the trainer's room and I saw him all taped up. I was amazed … all those bandages. They ran from his ankles all the way up. It took 15 minutes to get them all on."

Jack Kralick

★★★

"Sometimes you feel tired and low. You're not hitting and the doubleheaders have piled up and you feel like you just can't go out there anymore. Then you think about [Mickey] and what he must be going through and you say to yourself, 'If he can do it the way he must feel and the way he must be hurting, then I can do it, too.'"

Joe Pepitone

★★★

"Mickey would play in great pain. He sometimes played with pulled or strained muscles, a stiff neck and shoulder and with chronic problems with his knees and legs. When the other guys would see Mickey taping both his legs with that horrible thick bandage before every game, there was certainly no way they could jake out with a headache."

Whitey Ford

★★★

"Mickey never was one of those guys to hit a home run and then jump up and throw his arms up. No, he never hesitated at home plate. When he hit a ball, he lit out for first base with his head down. Even though he knew it was gone, he didn't la-di-da and he didn't want to show the pitcher up. He respected the pitchers."

Johnny Blanchard

★★★

"When he's in the lineup, he's a threat. I know he plays when he's hurt, but maybe the other pitcher doesn't know it. Just having him in there makes the rest of the lineup look stronger. It doesn't look the same without him."

Gil McDougald

★★★

"Mickey's a real holler guy on the bench. He does things to the rest of the bench. The other players sit there and hear Mantle pulling for a base hit. They just have to give their best."

Ralph Houk

★★★

"Mickey's in every game, even the ones he's not playing in. I remember Mickey with a pulled muscle, or a sore shoulder or a bad knee, on the top step of the dugout, yelling at me, cheering me on, rooting for a base hit. I don't know if it was his voice, or how loud he yelled, or just because it was Mantle, but he was the one you heard. He made you bear down. He made you concentrate. He makes that kind of contribution as long as he's around."

Tony Kubek

★★★

"Every once in a while I would have a bad game and I'd be sitting in my locker afterwards. I'd feel a hand on my shoulder and I'd turn around and it was Mickey. He'd say, 'You come with me tonight.' He'd take me to downtown New York, Manhattan, and we'd have a big steak and a couple of beers. We never talked about major league baseball. We'd talk about minor leagues, Joplin, Missouri, when Mick was there and stuff like that. Boy, you know, just that little steak with him and that trip downtown. I couldn't wait to get to the park the next day. I was really pumped up. The big guy No. 7 took you out to dinner! Holy cow, you know?"

Johnny Blanchard

★★★

"Last year, there were many times when I was down on myself, but Mickey would invite me to have dinner with him. I often visited his apartment, and he would sit and talk to me for hours. He told me how he had gone through the same things, and tried to help me raise my spirits. He was great."

Steve Whitaker

★★★

"One of the most moving moments of the 1961 season was at West Point, where we always played an exhibition game with Army's baseball team. We ate lunch at the West Point mess hall. When it came time for the 'Orders of the Day' the cadets began chanting, 'We want Mickey, we want Mickey!' Mickey was embarrassed, his head down. He didn't know what he was supposed to do. The cadets came to his table, picked him up, and carried him on their shoulders to the balcony of the mess hall. Mickey couldn't understand why the cadets wanted him, a civilian who was classified 4-F because of his leg problems during the Korean War. Only the most elite among the cadets were singled out for this honor. Others given it were Patton, Eisenhower, and MacArthur."

Tony Kubek

★★★

"You gotta appreciate the boy's reflexes. You see he don't wear a helmet when he bats. How often do you think he's been hit with a pitched ball? Now, that's because he's so quick up at the dish. It ain't that they don't throw at him. They do and at his feet, too, 'cause they'd like to pop him on that bum knee. But he's too quick."

Casey Stengel

★★★

"I came up from Jacksonville, and joined the Senators in 1962, and we were beating the Yankees, 4-2, when I came in to pitch in the eighth. I got them out in the eighth. In the ninth, Maris doubled, and up came Mantle. Mickey looked enormous. He looked huge. No hitter ever looked bigger. I was scared."

Steve Hamilton

★★★

"There was this game here at Yankee Stadium. We're ahead 1-0 in the bottom of the fourth when the wind and rain start blowing in from the outfield. I mean, it's a real gale. The Yankees get one man on base off me, but there are two out when Mantle comes up. I get the count to three-and-two against him, and now it's really blowing, the wind and rain smacking him right in the face. I can see he's having trouble seeing against the lights, so I figure I'll throw my best pitch, my fastball, and he'll never see it with all that water in his eyes. I put that ball exactly where I wanted it, low and outside, and I don't know how he ever touched it. But he drove it right into that gale, knocking it into the bullpen out there for a home run. The next inning, they call the game and we lose, 2-1."

Jim Grant

★★★

"It's hard to over-emphasize how completely Mantle is admired by other ball players, in a professional way. Few feel close to him; his teammates stick up for him but don't get too close, except for the few, who are his particular friends; but all ball players see in Mantle the superhuman gifts of physique and coordination they can only dream about for themselves. Like Ted Williams or DiMaggio or Stan Musial, Mantle is a ballplayer other ballplayers invariably watch take batting practice."

Leonard Koppett

★★★

"Nobody is half as good as Mickey Mantle."

Al Kaline

★★★

"As Mantle goes, so goes the Yankees."

Ralph Houk

★★★

"That boy, Mickey Mantle gives me more of a thrill than any player I've ever seen. He hits a lot of us the same way. I've been around a long time and I don't know of any player I ever got such a kick out of just watchin' him hit. Used to be I'd sit in the dugout in Kansas City or Detroit or wherever it might be an' all you could see when he began batting practice was empty stands with only the ushers watchin' the field. An' the only noise you'd hear would be the players kiddin' and the sound of the ball meetin' the bat. I'd get real lonesome waitin' for the writers to come into the dugout an' start me talkin'. But now you get to the parks long before the game an' you have to push through a crowd to get in. By the time we start hittin' the place is almost filled an' when Mantle belts one there's as much of a racket an' oohs and aahs as there is when he hits one durin' a game."

Casey Stengel

Thoughts on a Great Teammate

★★★

"Just as Jesse Owens was to track and field and Michael Jordan is to basketball, Mickey Mantle is to baseball; great athletes like Mickey Mantle and Joe DiMaggio transcend the game. They are heroes to every fan. Mickey Mantle certainly is one."

George Steinbrenner

★★★

"I know what a great price he's paid to be the best. There were a lot of times he played when the average guy would have sat it out. I guess it's because Mickey always has loved the game so much. Even when he's hurting real bad."

Billy Martin

★★★

"Very few people take your breath away, but that was the effect Mickey had. He was truly a great American hero. He was young and energetic, clean-cut and strong, seemingly invincible. He didn't stand at home plate and admire his home runs, and he wouldn't think of going on strike, and, to his detriment, he didn't take off enough time to care for his injuries properly. He just wanted to play ball, and play ball he did, but like all other classic heroes, there was a tragic side to him. … Whenever I am asked who influenced me most in my life, I might say Ernie Kovas and Woody Allen, or Charlie Chaplain and Laurel and Hardy; but whoever else I might say through the years, I will always say Mickey Mantle."

Billy Crystal

★★★

"I was a switch-hitter, so when I came up they compared me to Mickey. Nobody could be compared to Mickey. He was the best and the only one of his kind. I don't know if it hurt my career or not, but I did try to hit home runs like Mickey did. It just couldn't happen. It was just the greatest baseball experience of a lot of lives on the Yankees to play on the same team with Mickey Mantle. We not only respected him as the game's greatest player, we loved him as a man. How did we show it? We named children after him. I have a Mickey Tresh. I know about a dozen other Yankees who have kids named after him. As a Yankee fan, I idolized him. You'd think that when you get to meet someone you idolize, your opinion of him would have to go down—even just a little. With me, Mantle's gone up."

Tom Tresh

★★★

"Mantle was one of those players who was loved and admired by all teammates, and he loved and admired them. If you wore pinstripes, he would go to the wall for you."

Maury Allen

★★★

"Eddie Stanky was the manager of the Chicago White Sox, and Eddie hated the Yankees. He hated them with a passion. I don't know why, but he just hated the Yankees. So we had a meeting and he said, 'I don't want anybody talking to the New York Yankees players. I don't care who it is, nobody's going to talk to any Yankees players because it will cost you 50 dollars.' So I was playing first base, and Mickey got a base hit and Mickey says to me, 'Moose, how's the wife and kids doing?' I didn't say anything so Mickey says, 'Moose, I'm talking to you.' So I put the glove over my mouth and I said, 'I can't talk to you because it's going to cost me 50 dollars.' Mickey says, 'All that money I made you in all of those World Series, and I'm not worth 50 dollars?' So I start talking to him and that's when Eddie Stankey made a gesture like he was fining me 50 bucks, but he never fined me."

Moose Skowron

★★★

"Even the rookies. They come into the clubhouse awed, and quickly they're [Mickey's] friends. He puts them at ease."

Jerry Coleman

★★★

"Mickey always went out of his way to greet rookies. When a new player came into the clubhouse, Mickey was usually the first guy to shake his hand. In my first year with the Yankees, I was given No. 34 in spring training. Mickey took me into the clubhouse and said to Pete Sheehy, 'You better give Tony a lower number because he is going to be with us for a long time.' Mickey felt you gave number

34 to a ballplayer the way you gave 99 to a tackle—the higher the number, the lower the esteem. That's how I ended up with No. 10."

Tony Kubek

★★★

"This spring a group of us walked over to Mickey's locker to introduce ourselves. He told me he had read a lot about me and welcomed me to the Yankees. Later, during exhibition games, he'd pass me on the way to the dugout after an inning and tell me what a good play I'd made. Imagine Mickey Mantle taking time to tell me that. I remember one time I needed some extra tickets [to a Yankees game] for a date. I was standing at the batting cage when Mickey came onto the field. He called me over and said, 'If you need tickets, you can have all of mine.' It nearly floored me. I mean, here I was just a rookie and I hardly knew him. Also, he could have said it at the cage just as easily, where the other guys would have overheard. But that's the way Mantle does things."

Phil Linz

★★★

"The first time I started in the Stadium, I shut out the Senators. After the game, I went on the Red Barber TV show. It lasted about 15 minutes, and then I went to the clubhouse. I opened the door and there was a row of towels—a white carpet, you know—stretching from the door to my locker. Later I heard the idea was Mickey's. It really made me feel like part of the ball club."

Jim Bouton

★★★

"Gee, I idolized Mickey from the time I was seven. When I came up at the end of 1966, to become his teammate, I was in a terrible state. How would I talk to him? Should I call him Mr. Mantle? How could I play ball in the same outfield and keep my mind on the game? The day I reported, however, Mickey came over to me and said, 'What took you so long? I thought you'd be here a year or so ago. Anything you need, let me know.' Man, I didn't recover from that greeting for a long time."

Steve Whitaker

"I always remember the 1950 spring training. I was with Grand Forks and Mick was with Joplin. One day he came over and wanted me to walk to town to get some dry cleaning and we had a nice talk along the way. He had really changed over the winter; he looked strong and was more grown up. He told me about his training in Arizona that winter. That was when Casey and all the Yanks got their first look at Mick. I started a game against Joplin, and got Mick out on two ground balls to second. They beat me 3-0. But none of the players razzed me from the bench like most teams did. I always think that was because Mick didn't want to ride his old friend."

Bob Mallon

★★★

"We roomed together the first year. When he first got there I said, 'Mickey, you can't dress like that in New York.' He had hushpuppies and all that stuff on. He had a tie that looked to be about eight inches wide and it had a big peacock on it. I said, 'Tomorrow morning, I'm taking you to Eisenberg and Eisenberg and I'll buy you two suits.' Suits were about 25 to 35 bucks apiece in them days. He never got over that."

Hank Bauer

★★★

"I managed the Baltimore Orioles in 1966. I managed against Mickey. He hit his 500th home run off Stu Miller at Yankee Stadium. I was the manager of Baltimore, but I clapped for Mickey when he hit it. Most of the pitchers made Mickey do what we call 'jump rope'. They threw at his legs. He had the bad legs. I never asked my pitchers to do that."

Hank Bauer

★★★

"I was making about $10,000 a year at the time. We showed up at Yankee Stadium for the first game one season and Mickey opened his safe. We all had little safes with our uniform number on it. Mickey opened up his safe and found a $10,000 endorsement check that he had forgot about and had left in there. Mickey didn't miss the

$10,000 during the winter, but that was as much money as I made in a whole year!"

Bobby Richardson

★★★

"After Dad died, Mickey used to call me a lot. He would take me out to dinner once in a while. He realized how much I was hurting and it was his way of being there for me."

Billy Martin Jr.

★★★

"If it wasn't for Mickey getting exposure for me and Hank Bauer, we'd probably never gone to any card shows. He insisted that Hank and Moose were going to the card shows. He took me and Hank and Johnny Blanchard and Tommy Tresh to all of the shows. Certain guys needed money and he helped them out. Greer Johnson, Mickey's agent would set up the card shows and we made extra money. Then we'd help out Mickey because he couldn't finish all the items that he had so after the show, we'd go to his hospitality room, and he'd sit there and he'd keep signing baseballs and we'd put the balls back into the boxes for him."

Moose Skowron

★★★

"In '94 [Mickey] was here in St. Louis. They had '64 World Series get together between the Cardinals and the Yankees. He was signing autographs and I went down there and there was Skowron, Bauer and Blanchard and Bobby Richardson. I got to see them guys. And that's one thing. Mick took care of Skowron, Bauer, and Blanchard. When he signed autographs, it was a group thing. He said, 'If you want me, you've got these three men or I ain't coming.' A grateful Blanchard told Wiesler at the event, 'If it wasn't for Mickey, I don't know what I'd be doing.'"

Bob Wiesler

★★★

"The year I made the team as a rookie out of spring training, I didn't have a place to stay in New York, and Mickey liked to take in a young guy and get him squared away. When we checked in at the St. Moritz, the desk clerk said, 'That will be $125 a night.' I had about

40 bucks on me, so I knew this place wasn't for me. I picked up my suitcase and started out of the lobby. Mickey looked at me and I said, "Hey, Mick, I better ease down the street a ways because this place is kind of heavy for my blood. I can't afford anything around here.' Mickey responded with, 'Tell you what. I'll pay the $100 and you pay $25.' That's how I got to stay at the St. Moritz."

Tony Kubek

***

"Every once in a while, Mickey, Bob Cerv, and I would go out to eat after a game. Mickey was something else, because he would always say, 'Don't take your wallet out. I'll take care of it.' He was always good for that."

Bob Wiesler

***

"When I stayed with him, Mickey picked up so many checks that it got embarrassing. He wasn't in really great financial shape, either, but he wouldn't allow me to pay for anything."

Joe Pepitone

***

"We'd go to a bar and have a drink after we'd sign autographs. It would be me and Hank Bauer and [Mickey]. He'd give a girl a hundred dollars and we'd say, 'Mickey! That's too much money! Ya know? We had one drink apiece!' Mickey would reply, 'Well Moose, it's only two autographed balls.' People just don't know how much he's done for others. During one of Yogi's golf tournaments, Mickey alone raised $25,000 to donate to a boys' organization. He always looked out for a lot of us. That's just how he was."

Moose Skowron

***

"Mantle had a loyalty to his friends that grew out of his Northeast Oklahoma upbringing. He was an 'aw shucks, gee whiz' kind of guy. When the World Series concluded, Mantle went back to Commerce and convened all the ballplayers in that part of the Midwest and they had a charity game for the Crowder family at Miners Park in Joplin. The amount raised was nearly $2,000, which defrayed the cost of the funeral expenses, and other items that Mrs.

Crowder would need in order to raise her now-fatherless children."

John Hall

★★★

"It happened in Detroit, I think, and Yogi and Mickey always lockered side by side. Yogi would be the first one in the shower and he'd grab Mickey's deodorant. Mickey kinda got tired of that so he went to a drug store and he bought a bottle of Ban Roll-on and I don't know how he got it open. He emptied the stuff that was in there and he put pine tar in there! We all knew it and here comes Yogi out of the shower and he grabs Mickey's deodorant and rubbed it on and he couldn't raise his arms! The trainer had to come out and cut all of the hair from under his arms so that he could raise them!

"Mickey was always a prankster, doing something to keep the guys loose. At the fantasy camp, he'd always come late and he would run out to be an umpire and he'd have a bunch of toilet tissue hanging out of his pants! He did a lot of crazy things."

Hank Bauer

★★★

"Two friends and myself went to Ft. Lauderdale on spring break my senior year in high school. We went to the ballpark on a day when the Yankees were playing the Twins in a Grapefruit League Game. This was when Billy Martin was managing the Twins. Mickey was playing first base during the game. Martin would stand in the first-base coaching box and throw pebbles at Mickey every time there was a play at first. They joked back and forth with each other, and it was all very exciting for my friends and I, who were standing by the first-base line fence to be close to Mickey.

" When the game ended, my friends and I stayed along the first-base fence line in hopes of getting an autograph or two along with several other fans. To everyone's surprise, Joe DiMaggio, who was a spring training instructor, walked toward our location and said, 'Hi boys, what can I do for you?' Without hesitation, I said, 'Would you ask Mr. Mantle to come over?' Joe stopped and walked away without comment.

"I was afraid that I would not escape with my life, as several of the other fans began to turn on me. It was then that Mickey came out of the dugout walked up to us and said, 'Who sent DiMaggio to get me?' Everyone pointed at me. Mickey gave me an autographed ball. That was without a doubt the greatest moment of my life."

David Barrick—Mantle fan

APPENDIX

Mickey's Teammates

1947 Baxter Springs Whiz Kids

Barney Barnett	(Mgr)
Dick "Hog" Barnette	
Leroy Bennett	
Jim Bowers	
Bill Crow	
Guy Crow	
Nick Ferguson	
Charles "Frog" Heavin	
Bill Johnson	
Jim Kenaga	
Calvin Mishler	
Bocky Myers	
Wylie Pitts	
Bob Steele	
Jim Vaught	

1949 Independence Yankees

Harry Craft	(Mgr.)
Burleigh Grimes	(Mgr.)
Nick Ananias	(1B)
Jim Bello	(OF)
Jim Belotti	(1B/RF)
Ken Bennett	(P)
Bill Chambers	(LF)
John Cimino	(3B/CF)
James Cobb	(P)
Joe Crowder	(C)
Dick Duda	
Hal Groves	(1F)
Jack Hasten	(2B)
Bill Holderness	(P)
Arnold Joyce	(P)
Steve Kraly	(P)
Alvin Long	(P)
Robert Mallon	(P)

Burl Moffitt	(P)
Bob Newbill	(C)
Kenneth Rose	(2B)
Lou Skizas	(3B)
Keith Speck	(P)
Darrell Waska	
Charles Weber	(2B/RF)
Jack Whitaker	(C)
Bob Wiesler	(P)
Len Wiesner	(LF)

1950 Joplin Miners

Harry Craft	(Mgr.)
Dave Benedict	(P)
Al Billingsley	(2B)
Jerry Buchanan	(P)
Joe Crowder	(P)
Bill Drake	(P)
Emil Federow, Jr.	(P)
Dan Ferber	(P)
Dick Fiedler	(P)
Dick Gilman	(CF)
Tom Gott	(P)
Tom Hesketh	(P)
Dale Hittle	(P)
Steve Kraly	(P)
Carl Lombardi	(RF)
Cal Neeman	(C)
Carl Sellers	
Frank Simanovsky	(P)
Lou Skizas	(OF)
Lilburn Smith	(P)
Cromer Smotherman	(1B)
David Waters	(3B)
Lyle Westrum	(C)
Bob Wiesler	(P)
Len Wiesner	(LF)

1951 Kansas City Blues

George Selkirk	(Mgr.)
Johnny Blanchard	(OF)
Don Bollweg	(1B)
Andy Carey	(3B)

Dick Carr	(P)
Bob Cerv	(CF)
Clint Courtney	(C)
Rex Jones	(P)
Frank Logue	(P)
Gene Markland	(SS)
Zeke Melignano	(P)
Cliff Melton	(P)
Bob Muncrief	(P)
Ernie Nevel	(P)
Joe Page	(P)
Roy Partee	(C)
Bill Ramsey	(RF)
Bob Ross	(P)
Kal Segrist	(2B)
Keith Thomas	(RF)
Bob Thompson	(1F)
Bob Wiesler	(P)
Henry Wyse	(P)

During Mickey's 18-year career in the Major Leagues, he had 218 teammates. Below is a complete list in alphabetical order. The column titled "Years" represents the number of years that each player was on the Yankees with Mickey.

PLAYER	YEAR
Amaro, Ruben	3
Arroyo, Luis	4
Bahnsen, Stan	2
Barber, Steve	2
Barker, Ray	3
Bauer, Hank	9
Beck, Rich	1
Bella, Zeke	1
Berberet, Lou	2
Berra, Yogi	13
Blackwell, Ewell	2
Blanchard, Johnny	8
Blanco, Gil	1
Blaylock, Gary	1
Bollweg, Don	1
Bouton, Jim	7
Boyer, Clete	8
Branca, Ralph	1
Brenneman, Jim	1
Brickell, Fritz	2
Brideweser, Jim	3
Bridges, Marshall	2
Bright, Harry	2
Bronstad, Jim	1
Brown, Bobby	3
Brown, Hal	1
Bryan, Billy	2
Byrd, Harry	1
Byrne, Tommy	5
Carey, Andy	9
Carmel, Duke	1
Carroll, Tom	2
Cerv, Bob	9
Cicotte, Al	1

Clark, Horace	4
Clevenger, Tex	2
Clinton, Lou	1
Coates, Jim	5
Colavito, Rocky	1
Coleman, Jerry	7
Coleman, Rip	2
Collins, Joe	7
Courtney, Clint	1
Cox, Bobby	1
Cullen, Jack	3
Daley, Bud	4
Delgreco, Bobby	2
Demaestri, Joe	2
Dickson, Murry	1
DiMaggio, Joe	1
Ditmar, Art	5
Dixon, Sonny	1
Downing, Al	8
Duren, Ryne	4
Edwards, Doc	1
Fernandez, Frank	2
Ferraro, Mike	2
Ferrick, Tom	1
Ford, Whitey	15
Freeman, Mark	1
Friend, Bob	1
Gabler, Gabe	2
Gardner, Billy	2
Gibbs, Jake	7
Gonder, Jesse	2
Gonzalez, Pedro	3
Gorman, Tom	3
Gray, Ted	1
Grba, Eli	2
Grim, Bob	5
Hadley, Kent	1
Hale, Bob	1
Hamilton, Steve	6
Hegan, Mike	3
Held, Woodie	2
Henry, Bill	1
Hogue, Bobby	2
Hopp, Johnny	2
Houk, Ralph	4
Howard, Elston	13
Howser, Dick	2
Hunt, Ken	2
Hunter, Billy	2
James, Johnny	3
Jensen, Jackie	2
Jimenez, Elvio	1
John Cumberland	1
John Wyatt	1
Johnson, Billy	1
Johnson, Darrell	2
Johnson, Deron	2
Jurewicz, Mike	1
Keller, Charlie	1
Kennedy, John	1
Kenney, Jerry	1
Kipp, Fred	1
Konstanty, Jim	3
Kosco, Andy	1
Kraly, Steve	1
Kramer, Jack	1
Kubek, Tony	9
Kucks, Johnny	5
Kunkel, Bill	1
Kuzava, Bob	4
Larsen, Don	5
Leja, Frank	2
Lindy McDaniel	1
Linz, Phil	4
Long, Dale	3
Lopat, Ed	5
Lopez, Art	1
Lopez, Hector	8
Loren, Babe	2
Lumpe, Jerry	4
Maas, Duke	4
Maglie, Sal	2
Mapes, Cliff	1
Maris, Roger	7
Martin, Billy	6
McDermott, Mickey	1

Valo, Elmer	1
Verbanic, Joe	2
Verdi, Frank	1
Whitaker, Steve	3
White, Roy	4
Wiesler, Bob	3
Williams, Stan	2
Wilson, Archie	2
Wilson, George	1
Windhorn, Gordie	1
Womack, Dooley	3
Woodling, Gene	4

Length of Time with Mantle	**# Players**
1 Year	83
2 Years	52
3 Years	27
4 Years	15
5 Years	11
6 Years	6
7 Years	7
8 Years	7
9 Years	5
10 Years	1
11 Years	0
12 Years	1
13 Years	2
14 Years	0
15 Years	1
TOTAL	218

Dedication Speech by Tony Kubek

On April 16, 1998, Bricktown Ballpark in Oklahoma City, Oklahoma, dedicated a larger-than-life-size bronze statue of Mickey Mantle. The statue resides just outside the stadium. Present for the dedication were Tony Kubek, Whitey Ford, Yogi Berra, Johnny Blanchard, Hank Bauer, Moose Skowron, and Bobby Richardson. Below is the speech that Tony Kubek delivered on that day.

"A group of Mickey's teammates took a vote last night, and we decided that Yogi should make this speech. Unfortunately, he's got laryngitis. Yogi, it's too long. I'd read it like you wrote it, but we'd have to resurrect Casey Stengel to interpret.

"Merlyn and boys, and other friends and admirers of Mickey. David and Danny, you're grown men now, but I still picture you, along with Mickey Jr. and Billy, as that quartet of little rascals that your mom tried to keep up with while we were on those long road trips.

"Your dad would have loved this party. He would not have liked all the attention focusing on him. After Game 7 of the 1958 World Series, the news media rushed to Mickey's locker. He told them, 'You should be talking to Hank Bauer, Gil McDougald, Moose Skowron, and Bob Turley, they won the Series for us.' He directed the spotlight where it belonged. Mickey always deflected praise. He was too humble to accept the credit. Those were two pretty good World Series participants in 1957 and 1958. The Milwaukee Braves were led by Hank Aaron and Eddie Matthews; and the Yankees by Casey Stengel, Yogi, and Mickey. Two of the greatest left handers in the history of the game pitched in those series: Oklahoman Warren Spahn, and one of Mickey's closest friends, Whitey Ford.

"I don't know who the wealthiest person ever to come out of Oklahoma is, probably an oil man. Mickey, easily, would have been the richest if he hadn't picked up every restaurant check every time we went out. Heck, even Yogi couldn't pay, and we know how hard you tried. He'd have done the same here today—free tickets to tonight's home opener and all the hot dogs you can eat. Mickey was a generous man, and that was not only with his money. He did it with praise, his boyish smile, his gosh awful Okie humor, and the way he treated the wives and children of his teammates. If you were a first-year Yankee, Mickey was the first to greet you in the spring training camp. There was a reason that Clete Boyer and Tom Tresh, among many others, named their sons after Mickey. When Mickey was a rookie, Hank Bauer took him under his wing and Mickey never stopped trying to repay him. Elston Howard was the first African-American to wear a Yankee uniform. He developed into a Hall of Fame caliber player. The Yankees, like all of baseball, were slow to integrate their organization. Moose and Mickey's friendship helped Ellie to feel more at ease.

"In 1960, we lost the World Series in seven games to the Pittsburgh Pirates. Mickey was a hard loser and, also, a softy—he cried unashamedly. Several days after the defeat Mickey called to see how I was doing. He was still down from the loss, but especially sad for Bobby Richardson who was the MVP of that series. Mickey knew Bobby couldn't enjoy that award as much because we had lost. He always thought more about his teammates than himself.

"He was tough, an Oklahoma-bred leader which he proved again in the spring of 1961. Ralph Houk, our manager, made a difficult and—at the time—a very controversial move, asking Mickey to bat fourth so that Roger Maris could bat third for the good of the team. Mickey did it willingly, and had an April and May that set the tone for the rest of the season. His unselfishness lifted the entire team. The season of '61 proved to be special as we watched Roger and Mickey chase the Babe's home-run record. Roger's record has stood for over 36 years. During the pressure of that season no one helped Roger more or cheered harder than Mickey, especially after he was injured in September. He was a selfless ballplayer and person. Ask Moose, Hank, or John Blanchard, whom Mickey took along to make a few bucks whenever he went to a card-signing show. He was a loyal friend. If Mark McGwire; Ken Griffey Jr.; or any other player should challenge the season home-run record this year, Roger, with

Mickey alongside him will, in spirit, be standing along the parade route cheering him on.

"The Maris-Mantle, 3-4 combination in the lineup was the best of all time for a single season. I can't help thinking, though, how good the one prior to that was, Mickey third and Yogi fourth. Yogi was great with runners in scoring position. Picture this, if they pitched around Mickey, Yogi was up next. If they intentionally walked Mickey, Yogi would drive in the runners … and that was while he was still kneeling in the on-deck circle. Dr. Bobby Brown is a multifaceted man—a renowned cardiologist, also, American League president at one of the most critical times in baseball history. He did, however, have somewhat of a misspent youth rooming with Yogi and teaching him how to hit. Dr. Brown, you sent Yogi right to the Hall of Fame.

"Curt Gowdy and I worked together on the Game of the Week. We asked Mickey, shortly after he retired, if he would consider appearing with us. Curt figured he'd be a natural because of his knowledge of the game, but more so because of his charming personality. Curt convinced the brass to give Mickey a forum on a five-minute pregame show every Saturday. Mickey, as expected, was good. One show in Minneapolis, when Billy Martin was managing the Twins, we went to Billy's rec room to capture some memories on videotape about these two longtime friends … the day was unforgettable. It took us 12 hours to tape a three-minute segment. There was a lot that had to be edited. One live show Mickey came out with a large hand-printed sign across his chest with the word FILL on it. Mickey hadn't said a word for the first few minutes till Curt asked him what the sign was all about. Using that distinctive Oklahoma twang that he never lost, Mickey said, 'Cowboy, by the time you get done introducing everyone and you talk and Tony talks, there's no time left. All I do is fill this here space.'

"Another overlooked quality Mickey possessed was his sixth sense judging young, raw talent. One spring in the mid-'60s, a left-hand-hitting prospect who could run, throw, and had terrific baseball instincts came to camp. Mickey looked at him fielding ground balls and said, 'That young man is going to be a great outfielder some day.'

I said, 'They're grooming this guy to be the next Yankee shortstop.' Mickey was very discerning, he said, 'The Yankees will lose money if they play this young man at shortstop.' When I asked why, once again, he was astute, he said, 'I've watched him field a dozen ground balls and throw to first base. They're not going to be able to seat anyone behind the first baseman at Yankee Stadium when he's out there. What that arm he'll pick off five or six paying customers a game.' Mickey was right. Bobby Murcer went on to become an outstanding major leaguer … in the outfield.

"It's documented how far Mickey could hit a baseball, how fast he could run, his records, and how courageous he was playing through all the pain. He never bragged, unless it was about how far he could hit a golf ball. Another Oklahoman Hall of Famer Johnny Bench, is a topnotch striker of the golf ball. Ralph Terry, another Okie, won 20 games in the major leagues and competes on the Senior PGA Golf Tour. Bobby Murcer can attest to this. Even after Mickey turned 60, he was still driving them out.

"Mickey's presence is still felt by his family, friends, and Yankee teammates. Legends who cared about others leave an indelible legacy. Like each of us, Mickey was not always exemplary. He was far from perfect. Everyone credits him with being an American hero. There are those who say he was not a role model. In fact, Mickey said that himself. I think Mickey was wrong. In addition to his baseball talent, God blessed him with many admirable qualities. He admitted to having feet of clay. He never put himself on an unreachable pedestal. He was a humble man. He did not have a phony bone in his body. He showed compassion toward his friends and teammates when they were hurting. He always put winning before personal achievement. He was selfless in his approach to the game. He had an abiding love and respect for the game, its players and all for which it once stood. He was grateful to his dad for steering him to baseball and making it his life. He loved his family, but wished he had done better. Mickey always wanted to be there when needed. Humility, generosity, selflessness, loyalty, and compassion are virtues to be emulated. A lot is expected from a hero. The byname, role model, is subjective and ethereal, it's fragile.

Dedication Speech

"Those of us who played with Mickey loved him because he cared for us. He was the perfect teammate.

"Thank you, Tom Greenwade, for discovering Mickey for the Yankees.

"Thank you Oklahoma, for sharing one of the greatest with the baseball world."

MICKEY'S STATS

Hitting Stats

Yr	G	AB	R	H	2B	3B	HR	GS	RBI	BB	IBB	SO	SH	SF	HBP	GIDP	AVG	OBP	SLG
1951	96	341	61	91	11	5	13	0	65	43	-	74	2	-	0	3	.267	.349	.443
1952	142	549	94	171	37	7	23	2	87	75	-	111	2	-	0	5	.311	.394	.530
1953	127	461	105	136	24	3	21	1	92	79	-	90	0	-	0	2	.295	.398	.497
1954	146	543	129	163	17	12	27	0	102	102	-	107	2	4	0	3	.300	.408	.525
1955	147	517	121	158	R25	11	R37	1	99	113	6	97	2	3	3	4	.306	.431	.611
1956	150	533	132	188	22	5	52	1	130	112	6	99	1	4	2	4	.353	.464	.705
1957	144	474	121	173	28	6	34	0	94	146	23	75	0	3	0	5	.365	.512	.665
1958	150	519	127	158	21	1	42	0	97	129	13	120	2	2	2	11	.304	.443	.592
1959	144	541	104	154	23	4	31	0	75	93	6	126	1	2	2	7	.285	.390	.514

Yr	G	AB	R	H	2B	3B	HR	GS	RBI	BB	IBB	SO	SH	SF	HBP	GIDP	AVG	OBP	SLG
1960	153	527	119	145	17	6	40	0	94	111	6	125	0	5	1	11	.275	.399	.558
1961	153	514	132	163	16	6	54	1	128	126	9	112	1	5	0	2	.317	.448	.687
1962	123	377	96	121	15	1	30	1	89	122	9	78	0	2	1	4	.321	.486	.605
1963	65	172	40	54	8	0	15	0	35	40	4	32	0	1	0	5	.314	.441	.622
1964	143	465	92	141	25	2	35	0	111	99	18	102	0	3	0	9	.303	.423	.591
1965	122	361	44	92	12	1	19	1	46	73	7	76	0	1	0	11	.255	.379	.452
1966	108	333	40	96	12	1	23	1	56	57	5	76	0	3	0	9	.288	.389	.538
1967	144	440	63	108	17	0	22	0	55	107	7	113	0	5	1	9	.245	.391	.434
1968	144	435	57	103	14	1	18	0	54	106	7	97	1	4	1	9	.237	.385	.398
Career (18 years)																			
	2,401	**8,102**	**1,677**	**2,415**	**344**	**72**	**536**	**9**	**1,598**	**1,733**	**126**	**1,710**	**14**	**47**	**13**	**113**	**.298**	**.421**	**.557**

Fielding Stats

Year	POS	G	GS	OUTS	TC	TC/G	CH	PO	A	E	DP	PB	CASB	CACS	FLD%	RF	ZR
1951	OF	86	-	-	145	1.7	139	135	4	6	1	n/a	n/a	n/a	.959	0.00	-
1952	OF	141	-	-	374	2.7	362	347	15	12	5	n/a	n/a	n/a	.968	0.00	-
1952	3B	1	-	4	4.0	2	1	1	2	0	n/a	n/a	n/a	.500	0.00	-	
1953	OF	121	-	-	338	2.8	332	322	10	6	2	n/a	n/a	n/a	.982	0.00	-
1953	SS	1	-	-	0	0.0	0	0	0	0	0	n/a	n/a	n/a	.000	0.00	-
1954	OF	144	-	-	356	2.5	347	327	20	9	5	n/a	n/a	n/a	.975	0.00	-
1954	SS	4	-	-	10	2.5	10	5	5	0	1	n/a	n/a	n/a	1.000	0.00	-
1954	2B	1	-	-	2	2.0	2	2	0	0	0	n/a	n/a	n/a	1.000	0.00	-
1955	CF	145	-	-	385	2.7	383	372	11	2	2	n/a	n/a	n/a	.995	0.00	-
1955	SS	2	-	-	4	2.0	4	4	0	0	0	n/a	n/a	n/a	1.000	0.00	-
1956	CF	144	-	-	384	2.7	380	370	10	4	3	n/a	n/a	n/a	.990	0.00	-
1957	CF	139	-	-	337	2.4	330	324	6	7	1	n/a	n/a	n/a	.979	0.00	-

Year	POS	G	GS	OUTS	TC	TC/G	CH	PO	A	E	DP	PB	CASB	CACS	FLD%	RF	ZR
1958	CF	150	-	-	344	2.3	336	331	5	8	2	n/a	n/a	n/a	.977	0.00	-
1959	CF	143	-	-	375	2.6	373	366	7	2	3	n/a	n/a	n/a	.995	0.00	-
1960	CF	150	-	-	338	2.3	335	326	9	3	1	n/a	n/a	n/a	.991	0.00	-
1961	CF	150	-	-	363	2.4	357	351	6	6	0	n/a	n/a	n/a	983	0.00	-
1962	OF	117	-	-	223	1.9	218	214	4	5	1	n/a	n/a	n/a	.978	0.00	-
1963	CF	52	-	-	102	2.0	101	99	2	1	0	n/a	n/a	n/a	.990	0.00	-
1964	OF	132	-	-	225	1.7	220	217	3	5	1	n/a	n/a	n/a	.978	0.00	-
1965	LF	108	-	-	174	1.6	168	165	3	6	0	n/a	n/a	n/a	.966	0.00	-
1966	OF	97	-	-	174	1.8	174	172	2	0	0	n/a	n/a	n/a	1.000	0.00	-
1967	1B	131	-	-	1,188	9.1	1,180	1,089	91	8	82	n/a	n/a	n/a	.993	0.00	-
1968	1B	131	-	-	1,286	9.8	1,271	1,195	76	15	91	n/a	n/a	n/a	.988	0.00	-
Career (18 years)																	
	7	**2,290**	-	-	**7,131**	**3.1**	**7,024**	**6,734**	**290**	**107**	**201**	-	-	-	**.985**	**0.00**	-

Mickey's Stats

Baserunning Stats

Year	SB	CS
1951	8	7
1952	4	1
1953	8	4
1954	5	2
1955	8	1
1956	10	1
1957	16	3
1958	18	3
1959	21	3
1960	14	3
1961	12	1
1962	9	0
1963	2	1
1964	6	3
1965	4	1
1966	1	1
1967	1	1
1968	6	2
Career (18 years)	153	38

World Series Statistics

Year	POS	G	AB	H	2B	3B	HR	R	RBI	Avg	BB	SO	SB
1951	OF	2	5	1	0	0	0	1	0	.200	2	1	0
1952	OF	7	29	10	1	1	2	5	3	.345	3	4	0
1953	OF	6	24	5	0	0	2	3	7	.208	3	8	0
1955	OF	3	10	2	0	0	1	1	1	.200	0	2	0
1956	OF	7	24	6	1	0	3	6	4	.250	6	5	1
1957	OF	6	19	5	0	0	1	3	2	.263	3	1	0
1958	OF	7	24	6	0	1	2	4	3	.250	7	4	0
1960	OF	7	25	10	1	0	3	8	11	.400	8	9	0
1961	OF	2	6	1	0	0	0	0	0	.167	0	2	0
1962	OF	7	25	3	2	0	0	2	0	.120	4	5	2
1963	OF	4	15	2	0	0	1	1	1	.133	1	5	0
1964	OF	7	24	8	2	0	3	8	8	.333	6	8	0
Total	OF	63	230	59	6	2	18	42	40	.257	43	54	3

Index

Index

Index

Index

Index

Author's References

Personal Interviews:
Hank Bauer
Johnny Blanchard
Tony Kubek
Bob Mallon
Merlyn Mantle
Bobby Richardson
Bill "Moose" Skowron
Keith Speck
Bob Turley
Bob Wiesler

Books:
The Quality of Courage by Mickey Mantle
The Mickey Mantle Story by Ben Epstein
Mickey Mantle by Al Silverman
Memories of the Mick by Maury Allen
Mickey Mantle The Indispensable Yankee by Dick Schaap
The 50 Greatest Yankee Games by Cecilia Tan
Mickey Mantle's Greatest Hits by David S. Nuttall
Total Baseball by John Thorn and Pete Palmer with Michael Gershman
Baseball By The Numbers by Mark Stang and Linda Harkness
Sports Illustrated: The World Series by Ron Fimrite
Sixty-One by Tony Kubek and Terry Pluto
Season of Glory by Ralph Houk and Robert W. Creamer
Explosion! Mickey Mantle's Legendary Home Runs by Mark Gallagher
Slick by Whitey Ford and Phil Pepe
The Magnificent Yankees by Tom Meany
Wild High and Tight by Peter Golenbock
Whitey and Mickey by Whitey Ford, Mickey Mantle and Joseph Durso
The Mick by Mickey Mantle and Herb Gluck
All My Octobers by Mickey Mantle and Mickey Herskowitz
Our Mickey by Bill Liederman and Maury Allen
The Perfect Yankee by Don Larsen with Mark Shaw
October 1964 by David Halberstam
Sports In America by Pat Summerall
My Favorite Summer: 1956 by Mickey Mantle and Phil Pepe
Baseball Stars of 1957 by Bruce Jacobs
Ball Four by Jim Bouton
Guinness Book of World Records

Newspapers:
The New York Times
The Chicago Daily Tribune
The Los Angeles Times
The Washington Post
The Kansas City Star
The Kansas City Times
The Blade (Toledo, OH)
Star Tribune: Newspaper of the Twin Cities
The Terre Haute Tribune-Star

Author's References

Magazines:
Sport Magazine
Sports Illustrated
Baseball Digest
Look
The Saturday Evening Post
Sport
The Sporting News
Tuff Stuff
Guideposts
Beckett Baseball Monthly
Legend Sports Memorabilia
In Joplin
Spotlight
Maris and Mantle Magazine
Mickey Mantle Baseball's King
Who's Who in Baseball
Sports Stars
Baseball Digest
Power Baseball
Yankees Yearbook
Sport Scene
People
Official Baseball Annual
Baseball Yearbook
Business Progress
Complete Sports
Complete Sports Digest
Sports' Cavalcade

Web Sites:
www.retrosheet.org
www.sabr.org
www.baseballreference.com
www.baseballlibrary.com
www.baseball-almanac.com
www.ballparksofbaseball.com
www.mickey-mantle.com

Videos:
1953 World Series Highlight Tape
1961 World Series Highlight Tape
1964 World Series Highlight Tape
1968 A Day to Remember Ceremony Video Tape
Video of funeral on August 15, 1995

Audios:
Game Broadcast from October 8, 1956 (Perfect game)
Game Broadcast from September 3, 1961 (Two Mantle homers with sore arm)
Game Broadcast from April 9, 1965 (1st Astrodome homer)
Game Broadcast from September 19, 1968 (Gift of a Tiger)
Game Broadcast from September 27, 1968 (Mickey's last game)
Costas Coast to Coast Radio Broadcast from 1990
Yankee Stadium—The Sounds of a Half Century